Advanced Flash 5 ActionScript in Action

Dan Livingston

PH
PTR

Prentice Hall PTR
Upper Saddle River, NJ 07458
www.phptr.com

ISBN 0-13-093127-6

90000

9 780130 931276

Library of Congress Cataloging-in-Publication Data

Livingston, Dan
  Advanced Flash 5 ActionScript in Action / Dan Livingston.
      p. cm. -- (Advanced Topics for Web Professionals)
  Includes bibliographical references and index.
  ISBN 0-13-093127-6
    1. Computer animation. 2. Flash (Computer file) 3. Computer Graphics. 4. Web
sites--Design. I. Title. II. Series.

  TR897.7 .L58 2001
  006.6'96--dc21

                                                              2001021125

Editorial/Production Supervision: *Jan H. Schwartz*
Acquisitions Editor: *Karen McLean*
Cover Design Director: *Jerry Votta*
Cover Design: *Design Source*
Manufacturing Manager: *Alexis R. Heydt*
Buyer: *Maura Zaldivar*
Marketing Manager: *Bryan Gambrel*
Editorial Assistant: *Rick Winkler*
Art Director: *Gail Cocker-Bogusz*
Series Interior Design: *Meg VanArsdale*

 © 2001 Prentice Hall PTR
Prentice-Hall, Inc.
Upper Saddle River, NJ 07458

Prentice Hall books are widely used by corporations and government agencies for training, marketing, and resale.

The publisher offers discounts on this book when ordered in bulk quantities.
For more information, contact: Corporate Sales Department, Phone: 800-382-3419;
Fax: 201-236-7141; E-mail: corpsales@prenhall.com; or write: Prentice Hall PTR,
Corp. Sales Dept., One Lake Street, Upper Saddle River, NJ 07458.

Printed in the United States of America

10 9 8 7 6 5 4 3 2 1

ISBN 0-13-093127-6

Prentice-Hall International (UK) Limited, *London*
Prentice-Hall of Australia Pty. Limited, *Sydney*
Prentice-Hall Canada Inc., *Toronto*
Prentice-Hall Hispanoamericana, S.A., *Mexico*
Prentice-Hall of India Private Limited, *New Delhi*
Prentice-Hall of Japan, Inc., *Tokyo*
Prentice Hall Asia Pte., Ltd.
Editora Prentice-Hall do Brasil, Ltda., *Rio de Janeiro*

To Tanya Livingston, the Good Karma Queen

Contents

Foreword

I've written a few books on some pretty fun topics (PhotoShop, DHTML, and JavaScript), but I had a great time writing this book—Flash 5 is a hoot. Flash 5 can do some pretty amazing things, and I hope I've been able to show you some of these things well enough to get you excited too.

The Goal of This Book

When you're through with this book, you should have a thorough grasp of what Flash 5 and ActionScript can do, and know how to create a wide diversity of really engaging, fun, and useful interactive Flash movie. I'm talking fantastic navigation, awesome games, and efficient, robust applications.

Hopefully, given the foundation you'll get in this book, you'll be able to create new kinds of Flash movies that no one else has thought of.

The focus of this book is more technical than artistic, but I believe it provides a good springboard for programmers, animators, and artists alike.

Who This Book Is For

This book is for anyone who wants to include any level of complexity and interaction in their Flash movies. This can include navigation, games, and interaction with middleware and databases.

You can be a right-brained Flash designer who's making the reluctant leap into ActionScript or a seasoned, left-brained programmer who wants to create a custom interface to a back-end e-commerce system.

To get the most out of this book, you should already know some Flash basics:

- drawing
- tweening
- creating symbols
- creating buttons

That's it. If you know how to do these things at all, then you're ready for this book.

How This Book Teaches

Both my parents were teachers, and they shared the same philosophy. "There are three ways to teach," they said, "example, example, example." I think they're right on this one, and this book uses complete, fully functional examples for every aspect of interactivity and ActionScript in this book. All examples can be found on the accompanying CD and on Web sites at *www.phptr.com/advancedweb* and *www.wire-man.com/flash5/*.

I've tried to avoid using overly simple squares and circles to explain concepts (I mostly succeeded). Instead, I'll ask you to load small movies and manipulate them. You will see a number of examples using Jake the Fish, and I hope you'll forgive my small indulgence—it's the only way I can put my marine zoology degree to use.

Acknowledgments

First, thanks go to Karen McLean, my editor at Pearson PTR, for giving me the opportunity to write this book. It's been a treat to write this little tome. And, of course, thanks go to my wife Tanya, who let me stay home and write full-time for a few months (I recommend that everyone do this at least once).

I'd also like to thank Joshua Davis for graciously letting me use his open-source Flash movies that he's posted on *praystation.com* (I recommend visiting it at least once a week).

Extra thanks to James of *presstube.com* and to Branden of *figleaf.com* for the movie used in Chapter 7, "Complex Scripting."

And finally, to my reviewers, M.D. McDowell and Leon Atkinson, for slapping me into shape—the book is better for it.

Introduction to ActionScript

What Is ActionScript?

ActionScript is the scripting language Flash uses to control its movies and objects within the movies. If you want to do anything interactive in Flash, you'll need to use ActionScript. It allows you to execute different actions in a movie depending on what a user does or on what frame of the movie is being played.

ActionScript looks a lot like JavaScript, which Macromedia (the folks who wrote Flash) did on purpose. A specification called ECMA-262 was written to provide an international standard for the JavaScript language. ActionScript in Flash 5 is based on the ECMA-262 specification, so if you've used JavaScript before, a lot of ActionScript will look familiar to you. If you haven't used JavaScript before, don't worry—you'll get it.

Throughout this book, I'll be referring to *actions*. This is a general term, and an action roughly means "a chunk of Action-Script code that does something."

What Is ActionScript Good For?

Here's some of what you can do using ActionScript:
- Create multiplayer games
- Create engaging, user-aware navigation
- Send data to middleware like PHP and Cold Fusion
- Create and parse XML objects
- Communicate with JavaScript or ActiveX objects
- About a billion other things. You'll see.

What ActionScript Can't Do

- ActionScript can't talk directly to a database—you'll still need to use middleware like PHP, Cold Fusion, or ASP to do that.
- Unicode isn't supported, but ISO-8859 and Shift-JIS are.
- You can't use exception handling with `try`, `throw`, or `catch`.

Variables

If you're completely new to programming, it'll take a little while to master the fundamentals, depending on how linearly you can make your brain work. One of the most basic programming concepts is that of the variable. This is the same variable you saw in algebra class in junior high. Some simple examples:

```
// "x" is the variable
x = 3;

// "message" is a variable that holds a string,
// i.e., usually text
message = "Please press the next button."
```

You'll probably use variables mostly to keep track of what the user is doing and what state certain movie clips are in. If this isn't clear right now, keep reading—as you see more examples, it should become clearer.

Objects and Object-Oriented Scripting

Both ActionScript and JavaScript are called *object-oriented* scripting languages. Let's go over what this means, since it's an odd concept if you haven't been exposed to it before.

Scripting languages organize information into groups called *classes*. You can create multiple instances of these classes, which are called *objects*.

Classes and objects are just ways to group together chunks of information. To use a real-world analogy, you could create a "bicycle" class. That bicycle has lots of different properties to it, such as how many gears there are, how big the tires are, and what color it is. You can also perform some actions with the bike, such as pedal, brake, and turn (these are called *methods*).

In Flash 5, all movie clips are objects (also called *instances*) of the class MovieClip. Since all movie clips are objects of the same class, they all have the same properties and the same methods.

Buttons also act like objects. While there are some significant differences between buttons and movie clips, which we'll cover later, I consider it—as do many other Flash folk—useful to think of buttons as a kind of movie clip.

Flash has a number of predefined objects you can access: Array, Boolean, Color, Date, Key, Math, Mouse, Number, Object, Selection, Sound, String, XML, and XMLSocket. We'll be seeing many of these objects in the tutorial section of this book. These objects are treated with excruciating detail in Appendix B, "ActionScript Reference."

Creating a Class

You don't have to restrict yourself to using only classes that Flash 5 has provided, such as Movie Clips. You can create your own classes using constructor functions. This is pretty advanced stuff, and if you can't think of why you'd want to create a new class, don't worry about it—usually, only advanced programmers build their own classes. This section is for them. Say you want a to create a 1980s band:

```
function HairBand(p,s)
{
    this.hair = "big";
    this.hair_dye = true;
    this.number_members = p;
    this.number_synthesizers = s;
}

function Breakup()
{
    this.hair_dye = false;
    this.hair = "crew cut";
}

// Now, actually create two objects using
// the HairBand constructor function.
kajagoogoo = new HairBand(3,4);
softcell = new HairBand(2,1500);

// Create a method for a hairband
HairBand.kajagoogoo.partyover = Breakup;
```

Object and Frame Actions

Here's the basic structure of an action:

```
whenSomethingHappens(input variables)
{
    do stuff
}
```

We'll be elaborating on this basic structure significantly.

There are two kinds of actions: frame actions and object actions.

Object Actions—Movie Clips

Object actions are actions, or chunks of ActionScript code, that are attached to an object. Most of the time, an object is a symbol that's either a button or a movie clip. Graphic symbols can't have actions, nor can shapes you draw on that stage that aren't symbols. You can create your own objects, as we just saw.

An object action is associated with an instance of a symbol, not with the symbol itself. Here's an example (see Figure 1-1).

1. Load the movie *chapter1/fish_drag.fla*.
2. Control ➡ Test Movie.
3. Notice that by positioning the cursor over each of the fish and dragging your mouse, you can move the fish on the left, but not the one on the right. In fact, no matter where you click, you move the fish on the left and the right one stays put.

Both fish are instances of the same movie clip symbol, but only one of them has an action attached to it. Let's see what that action looks like. Exit from the movie test and return to the Flash editor (the main program). Option-click (Mac) or right-click (Windows) on the fish that's draggable (it's on the left). Choose **Actions**.

The Object Actions panel appears, as shown in Figure 1-2.

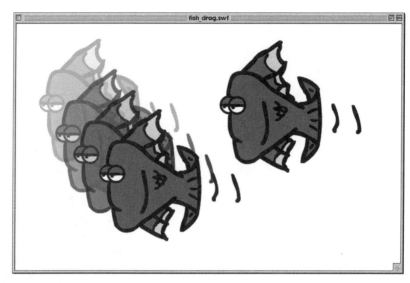

FIGURE 1–1 Dragging one of the fish

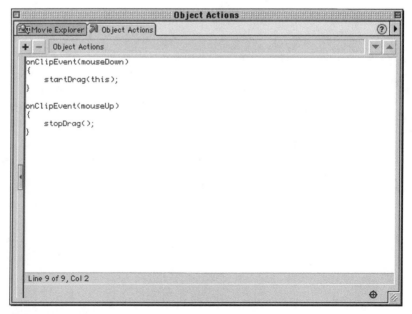

FIGURE 1–2 The Object Actions panel (Expert Mode)

The code that appears should be:

```
onClipEvent(mouseDown)
{
    startDrag(this);
}

onClipEvent(mouseUp)
{
    stopDrag();
}
```

These two functions never leave this object instance, no matter where this instance appears in the movie. The actions will happen to this object from the first frame of the movie all the way to the last frame of the movie. Object actions don't care what frame the movie is currently on (as long as the object actually exists in the movie at that frame).

The two functions you see are onClipEvents. All movie clip object actions have to live inside of an onClipEvent. onClipEvent is known as an *event handler.* An event is something that happens; for instance, the movie finished loading, the user pressed a mouse button, or the user hit the space bar. An event handler is a piece of Flash that is constantly looking for these events and lets ActionScript know when one of them occurs.

Since the fish symbol is a movie clip, each instance of that symbol gets an event handler called onClipEvent that will constantly look at the mouse and keyboard to see if the user is doing anything. If the user does do something, say, presses down the mouse button, the event handler looks at the Action-Script to see if that event exists anywhere in the code.

In this code, we're looking for two events, mouseDown and mouseUp. These refer to what the mouse button is doing. Is the mouse button currently being pressed down, or was it just released?

If the mouse button was pressed, then onClip-Event(mouseDown) is called, and everything inside the first set of curly braces is executed. As it happens, there's only one thing to do:

```
startDrag(this);
```

startDrag is what's called a *method*. Briefly put, a method does something (as opposed to a *property*, which just holds a specific bit of information). We'll examine this method briefly now and in more detail later (it's darn useful).

startDrag causes the object in question to mirror the motion of the mouse cursor. Notice that we didn't use start-Drag(), but rather used a startDrag(this). The start-Drag method requires a target; that is, it needs to know what it should start dragging. The easiest way to reference the current object is just to call it this. You'll see this being used again in this book.

The other way to refer to the object is

```
startDrag(_root.drag_fish)
```

where drag_fish is the name of the instance of the fish symbol. The _root part means "start looking from the top of the movie hierarchy." If this is confusing, don't worry. It is covered later in this chapter in the section "Dot Syntax."

Object actions that are on a movie clip have to be inside of an onClipEvent. The events are:

- load
- unload
- enterFrame
- mouseMove
- mouseDown
- mouseUp
- keyDown
- keyUp
- data

Object Actions—Buttons

The only real difference between actions that are attached to buttons instead of movie clips is that the event handler for buttons is on instead of onClipEvent. Otherwise, they're pretty much the same. The events for on are:

- press
- release
- releaseOutside

- rollOver
- rollOut
- dragOver
- dragOut
- keyPress

Here's an example that I doubt will find its way into one of your movies, but illustrates the on function nicely.

1. Load the movie *chapter1/face_button.fla*.
2. Control ➠ Test Movie.
3. Notice that when you press down on the mouse button, the fish appears.
4. Return to the Flash editor.
5. Click on the button symbol.
6. Window ➠ Actions to see the actions.

Frame Actions

Frame actions are like object actions, except that the actions are associated with a certain spot in the timeline instead of on an object. If a frame has some actions associated with it, those actions are carried when the playhead enters that frame.

A simple example would be stopping a movie at the last frame so that it doesn't loop, which Flash 5 movies do by default.

1. Open *chapter1/fish_cruise.fla*.
2. Notice the layer *Actions*. Creating this layer isn't necessary to place actions on, but I find it useful.
3. Double-click on the small *a* on the timeline on frame 60 on the actions layer.

The Frame Actions panel should appear, as shown in Figure 1-3 (notice it looks almost exactly like the Object Actions panel), with this code:

```
stop();
```

As you might predict, this command stops the movie in its tracks. It stays stopped unless some other action starts it up again.

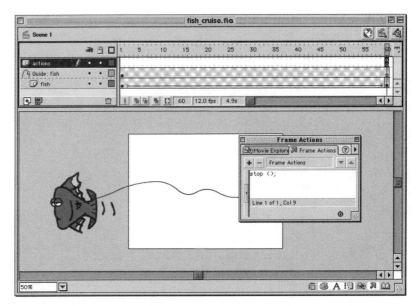

FIGURE 1-3 The timeline and the Frame Actions panel

Flash will place a frame action only on a keyframe. If you try to place a frame action on a regular frame, Flash will look backwards in the timeline until it finds a keyframe, and it'll place the frame action on that keyframe, not on the regular frame you clicked on. I recommend placing all of your frame actions on a separate layer—it makes organization much easier.

Dot Syntax

ActionScript uses what is called *dot syntax*. For example, if you have a movie clip called *red_shirt* inside of the movie clip called *santa_claus*, then one way to access that object is

```
_root.santa_claus.red_shirt
```

`_root` is the base of all Flash movies. If you want to find out where *red_shirt* is on the Stage, you could use

```
xPosition = _root.santa_claus.red_shirt._x;
```

`_x` is a property that returns the horizontal position of the object. We'll talk more about properties soon.

If you're familiar with JavaScript, dot syntax will look familiar to you; for example,

```
document.myForm.textBox.value = "Try again!";
document.image['nav'].src = 'images/clickme.gif';
```

If you're familiar with Flash 4, you're used to the *slash* syntax. Hopefully, you'll find dot syntax a little more intuitive and easier to use.

Properties

A *property* is a piece of an object. Most objects are simply collections of properties. Examples of some movie clip properties are:
- how wide it is (_width)
- where it is on the Stage (_x and _y)
- what frame is currently being played (_currentframe)
- how transparent it is (_alpha)
- its name (_name)
- whether it's visible or not (_visible)

Most properties can be read and altered. For example, let's see how wide a movie clip called *clue* is:

```
clueWidth = _root.clue._width;
```

If we don't like the value of clueWidth, we can change the width of *clue* like this:

```
_root.clue._width = 110;
```

or

```
_root.clue._width = _root.clue._width - 40;
```

All movie clip properties start with an underscore (_). That's just how Flash is. As we continue through the book, almost every example will have lots of properties in them, so if you're not clear on the concept yet, you will be soon.

Methods

A method is something an object can do, or something you can do to an object. For example, here are some things methods can do:

- stop a movie clip
- go to a certain frame and start playing there
- see if a movie clip is over another movie clip
- hide the mouse cursor
- calculate a cosine
- set the volume of a sound being played

Let's go to frame 10 of the *clue* movie clip and start playing from there:

```
clue.gotoAndPlay(10);
```

The method here is `gotoAndPlay`. All methods live inside objects—they don't exist on their own.

> **NOTE** Even when you see methods that look like they don't belong to an object, for example, a frame action whose only line of code is `stop()`, it's understood by Flash that the object in question is the movie clip the frame is in: it will always assume `this.stop()`. If the frame is in the main timeline, then the default timeline is `_root`, resulting in `_root.stop()`.

Remember we said that all movie clips you make are objects based on the master Movie Clip class? Well, that class has a whole bunch of properties and methods associated with it, and when you make a Movie Clip object, all those properties and methods become a part of your movie clip. This is a good thing—those properties and methods are vital to creating interactive Flash, and it would be a pain to have to create all those properties and methods yourself.

Functions

If you're getting fancy and writing some complicated Flash, you may find that the objects, methods, and properties that Flash provides don't quite meet your needs. Fortunately, Flash provides a way for you to create your own objects, properties, and methods using *constructor functions*.

If the predefined functions Flash provides don't quite meet your needs, you can create your own functions (if you've done work in JavaScript, the concept of functions will be quite familiar to you).

A function is a set of instructions that's executed only at certain times. We'll be using them in later chapters. We used an example of functions when we created HairBand earlier in this chapter. Functions can look (and act) a lot like methods. You'll see some of this overlap later as well.

Conclusion

If you're brand new to ActionScript, much of the preceding may have sounded like gobbledygook. If that's the case, don't worry—we'll go through a lot of examples that will make this theoretical talk more concrete. If you're a grizzled scripting veteran, you probably realize that you're already on familiar ground, and ActionScript will come easily for you.

Your First ActionScripts

I n this chapter, we'll go all the way from your first look at Action panels (where the ActionScript is typed in) to manipulating multiple timelines based on user input. After this chapter, you'll have all the basic tools you'll need to create a simple game in Flash 5.

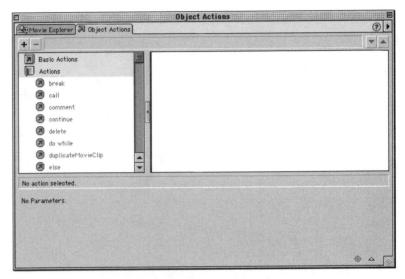

FIGURE 2–1 The Object Actions panel

Using the Actions Panels

The Actions panels are just a kind of panel, much like the other panels in Flash 5, such as Frame, Sound, or Align. You open and close Actions panels like you'd open and close any other panel on Flash 5. Flash 5 will recognize any code you place in an Actions panel immediately—you don't have to save the file to test it. The Actions panel toggles between the Object Actions (actions applied to movie clips and buttons) or Frame Actions, depending on what you've selected.

The Panels

Let's open one of the Actions panels up.

1. Open a new Flash file with File ⟹ New.
2. Window ⟹ Actions. The panel shown in Figure 2-1 should open.
3. Now click on **Frame 1** on the timeline. The panel's title changes to "Frame Actions," as shown in Figure 2-2.
4. Click anywhere on the Stage. The panel's title changes back to "Object Actions."

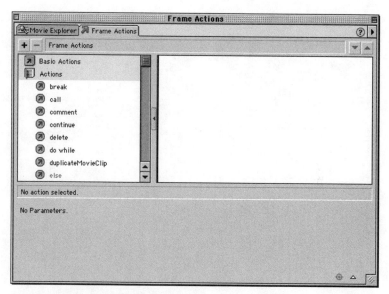

FIGURE 2-2 The Frame Actions panel

As you can see, the same panel serves for both frame actions and object actions. It's easy to make a mistake and enter your actions in the wrong panel, so make sure you check every time before you start entering code.

> **NOTE** If some of your actions suddenly disappear, check both Frame Actions and Object Actions panels. You may have entered your actions in the wrong panel. It happens to the best of us.

Let's look at all of the parts of an Actions panel. To see everything, let's look at an Actions panel that has something interesting in it.

1. Open the file *chapter2/drag_jake2.fla* from the CD.
2. Click on the small fish (the one without all the teeth).
3. Window ➠ Actions.
4. The panel should resemble Figure 2-3.

You'll note that there's another tab called Movie Explorer. We're ignoring that for now, but we'll get to it later.

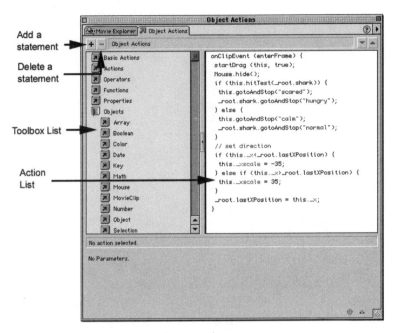

Add a statement

Delete a statement

Toolbox List

Action List

FIGURE 2–3 The parts of an Actions panel

Normal Mode Versus Expert Mode

Actions panels open up automatically in Normal Mode, unless you've changed your preferences. Normal Mode is Flash-assisted scripting—you drag commands from the Toolbox list to the Action list, and Flash prompts you for what parameters you should fill in. You aren't allowed to type commands directly into the scripting window while in Normal Mode.

Normal Mode can be helpful, since your actions are likely to be free of syntax errors. However, Normal Mode can act as something of a crutch because you don't have to remember all the parts of a command—Flash always tells you—so I strongly recommend that while you're learning ActionScript, you always switch to Expert Mode. Expert Mode allows you to type in everything: commands, parameters, and so on. You'll make more mistakes at first, but you'll learn ActionScript better, and that's our goal. So let's make Expert Mode the default mode of the Actions panels.

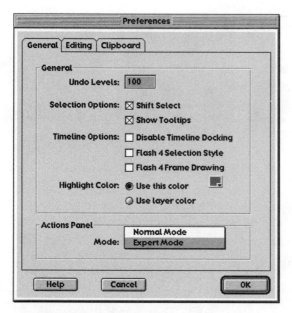

FIGURE 2–4 General Preferences

1. Edit ➠ Preferences.
2. Make sure the General tab is selected. See Figure 2-4.
3. Near the bottom, in the Action Panels section, change Mode from Normal Mode to Expert Mode.
4. Click OK.

Moving from Scene to Scene

Be careful with scenes: most animators, and even Macromedia, don't recommend using scenes except with long animations. We're discussing it here only because you should know how to do it.

Let's say our assignment is to create a Flash version of a PowerPoint presentation. It's for Buzzkill Industries, a young, edgy company that makes safety equipment. Someone else has created the slides for the presentation, and it's our job to make sure the presenter can move from slide to slide. For the purposes of this tutorial, we'll only deal with the first three slides of the presentation, shown in Figure 2-5.

1   **2**   **3**

FIGURE 2-5 All three slides of the Buzzkill presentation

1. Open the file *chapter2/buzzkill1.fla* on the CD.
2. Notice that there are three scenes—one for each slide. Each scene has one frame action on its last frame: stop().
3. Click on the last frame in the actions layer in each scene, and then choose Window ⮞ Actions to see the Action-Script. The only ActionScript you'll see is stop(). This stop method halts the playhead in its tracks. That is, it stops the Flash movie from playing further.
4. Go ahead and play with the movie, using Control ⮞ Test Movie.

> **NOTE** Always test your movies with Control ⮞ Test Movie, since that's the only way you can properly test your actions.

5. Notice that there's no way to go beyond the first scene/slide.
6. Close the window with the movie playing.
7. Go to the last frame in Scene 1 of the movie (frame 60) on the button layer.
8. Insert ⮞ Keyframe.
9. Window ⮞ Library.
10. Drag the Forward Button symbol onto the empty button layer. Make sure you're still on frame 60. Position the button wherever you want.
11. Click on the button.
12. Window ⮞ Actions.

13. Enter the following code:

```
on(release)
{
    gotoAndPlay("Scene 2","slide2");
}
```

14. Control ➧ Test Movie. Once the movie is playing, pressing the button should send you to the next scene.

Let's look at this code in detail. The first thing you see is the on(release); on is what's known as an *event handler*. If something happens, like the user presses down the mouse button or hits the keyboard, that's called an *event*. An event handler is some code that is executed when an event happens. For buttons in Flash, their event handler is the on(event) function. There are about a dozen events (for a complete list, see Appendix B, "ActionScript Reference"), but the only one we're dealing with is release, which is short for "when the user presses the mouse button and then releases it."

Once the user releases the mouse button, everything between the curly braces that follow the on(release) is executed. As it happens, there's only one line of code: gotoAndPlay("Scene 2", "slide2"). As you might have guessed, this command tells the playhead to jump to Scene 2 and start playing from the frame that has the label "slide2." In this case, frame 1 holds the "slide2" label.

Unfortunately, Flash isn't smart enough to look through all the scenes in your movie and find the right frame, if you've labeled it, so gotoAndPlay("slide2") wouldn't have worked. If you direct Flash to a frame label that doesn't exist, it'll start playing at frame 1.

Here's another way to do it:

```
on(release)
{
    gotoAndPlay("Scene 2", 1);
}
```

In this case, Flash goes to Scene 2 and starts playing at the first frame. I recommend using frame labels—it lets you move stuff around without having to keep track of frame numbers.

> **NOTE** Labels and actions do not have to go on their own layers. However, it's a good way to stay organized, especially as your movies get more and more complex. I recommend doing it, even if there's only one frame label or only one frame action. I also strongly recommend always using frame labels—never using frame numbers. Your ActionScript is less likely to have bugs down the road if you use frame labels.

Now let's add the two buttons on the second scene/slide.

1. Open up Scene 2.
2. Open up the Library if it isn't already open.
3. Go to the last frame in the movie (40) on the empty button layer.
4. Insert ⇒ Keyframe.
5. Drag the Backward Button and the Forward Button to the Stage and place them wherever you like.
6. Click on the Forward Button.
7. Open up the Actions panel if it isn't open.
8. Enter the following code:

```
on(release)
{
    gotoAndPlay("Scene 3","slide3");
}
```

9. Click on the Backward Button.
10. Enter the following code:

```
on(release)
{
    gotoAndPlay("Scene 1","slide1");
}
```

11. Save the file and Control ⇒ Test Movie.

For the final step, let's add the last button to the final slide.

1. Open up Scene 3.
2. Open up the Library (Window ⇒ Library) if it isn't already open.
3. Go to the last frame in Scene 3 on the button layer (frame 45).

4. Drag the Backward Button to the Stage and place it wherever you like.
5. Click on the Backward Button.
6. Open up the Actions panel if it isn't open.
7. Enter the following code:

```
on(release)
{
    gotoAndPlay("Scene 2","slide2");
}
```

8. Control ➡ Test Movie!

Now you can actually move from scene to scene inside your movie, and you learned something about buttons and event handlers along the way! Now let's make this a little more complex: it turns out that since the presenters are used to using PowerPoint, they forget that they have to press buttons on the screen to move from scene to scene. They want to be able to press the space bar and right arrow to move forward, and the left arrow to move back, just as in PowerPoint.

This isn't a problem at all. All we're doing here is adding events (user is pressing keys on the keyboard), so we can modify the buttons we already have to deal with those events.

1. Go back to the Forward Button on frame 60 of Scene 1.
2. Click on the button and open its Actions panel.
3. Add the following code:

```
on(release, keyPress "<space>")
{
    gotoAndPlay("Scene 2", "slide2");
}
```

4. Control ➡ Test Movie.

The new event we have here is `keyPress`, and part of using `keyPress` is to say immediately afterwards which key we're looking for. By using the `<>` brackets and spelling out *space*, we've made this code easier to read than if it were `keyPress " "`.

Now let's add the right arrow:

1. Enter the following code:

```
on(release, keyPress "<space>", keyPress "<right>")
{
    gotoAndPlay("Scene 2", "slide2");
}
```

2. Control ➡ Test Movie.

Whoops! You received an error. Flash doesn't like to have two of the same events in the same `on()` statement. Even though our two `keyPress` events are for different keys, they still count as the same kind of event. So we have to rewrite our code slightly:

```
on(release, keyPress "<space>")
{
    gotoAndPlay("Scene 2", "slide2");
}

on(keyPress "<right>")
{
    gotoAndPlay("Scene 2", "slide2");
}
```

Test the movie again to make sure it's working correctly.

Now that we have the first button working, getting the others to work won't take much extra effort. Here's the code for them:

Scene 2 Backward Button

```
// This button only needs one function, since only
// one key can be used to go backwards, as opposed to
// two keys to go forward.
on(release, keyPress "<left>")
{
    gotoAndPlay("Scene 1", "slide1");
}
```

Scene 2 Forward Button

```
on(release, keyPress "<space>")
{
    gotoAndPlay("Scene 3", "slide3");
}

on(keyPress "<right>")
{
    gotoAndPlay("Scene 3", "slide3");
}
```

Scene 3 Backward Button

```
on(release, keyPress "<left>")
{
    gotoAndPlay("Scene 2", "slide2");
}
```

To see the final movie, check out *buzzkill2.fla* on your CD.

Comments

Did you notice we introduced one new element? For the Scene 2 Backward Button, there are a few lines that start with two slashes. Those two slashes indicate that the rest of the line is a comment, which Flash completely ignores. Comments are only for programmers, not for the computer. Using comments appropriately is called *documenting your code.* Documenting your code is important, since at some point you'll have to fix your own old code when you don't remember how it works anymore, or someone else may have to work on your code. Programmers who document their code well are happy programmers.

on(event)

As a final note, here are all of the events that the on event handler can recognize:

- press
- release

- `releaseOutside`
- `rollOver`
- `rollOut`
- `dragOver`
- `dragOut`
- `keyPress`

These are discussed in greater detail later in the book and in Appendix B.

Messing with Movie Clips

Now that you know how to handle an event using a button (using the `on()` method we just talked about), let's look at handling events with movie clips. Movie clips have an event handler too, but it's called `onClipEvent`. Probably the biggest difference between `on` and `onClipEvent` is that, when it comes to mouse buttons, `on` can only see what happens directly on top of the button, while `onClipEvent` looks at the whole movie clip and the movie clip timeline. For example, if you click your mouse button down and up outside of a button, an on action will never see your mouse click. But a movie clip, which has to use `onClipEvent`, scans the entire movie and will see your mouse click, even if you clicked nowhere near the movie clip.

As you continue programming in ActionScript, you'll come across times when `on` will be most helpful and times when `onClipEvent` will be the best choice.

Let's see it in action. Open up the movie *chapter2/drag_jake1.fla*. It's a simple little movie (1 frame) with two symbols: Jake the Fish and a pea shark. The movie we're going to make will involve Jake swimming too close to the pea shark, and when the shark opens its mouth, Jake is scared until he swims away again. The user will determine Jake's position on the Stage.

The symbols on the Stage are both two-frame movie clips. One frame is the normal, non-close-contact pose, shown in Figure 2-6.

Figure 2-7 shows the two when they get too close.

FIGURE 2–6 Calm Jake and pea shark

FIGURE 2–7 Agitated Jake and pea shark

Let's get programming.

1. Open *chapter2/drag_jake1.fla.*
2. Click on Jake.
3. Open the Actions panel (it should say "Object Actions" at the top).
4. Enter this code:

```
onClipEvent(enterFrame)
{
    trace("mouse in movie");
}
```

5. Control ➡ Test Movie.

We've introduced two things here. The first is the onClipEvent(enterFrame). This event occurs whenever the movie's playhead starts a new frame. If your movie is set at 12 frames per second (the default), then the enterFrame event occurs 12 times every second, and the code inside onClip-Event(enterFrame) is run 12 times every second. Note that looping in movie clips is the default, so movies will always loop unless you set them not to.

So when the movie is running, the single line of code trace("mouse in movie") is called. trace is great tool—as you saw, it opens up a little output window and displays some text. It's my debugging tool of choice, and you'll be seeing more of it later.

Now let's do something more interesting than printing out some text.

1. Click on Jake.
2. Open the Actions panel.
3. Change the code to:

```
onClipEvent(enterFrame)
{
    startDrag(this, true);
}
```

4. Control ➠ Test Movie.

We briefly looked at startDrag earlier. It causes an object to follow a user's mouse anywhere in the movie. startDrag needs to be told which object on the movie should start following the user's mouse, and that's what this is for. It tells startDrag that the object to move is *this* one, that is, the object that the current action is attached to (in this case, the fish). The true signifies that the object to be dragged should have its center wherever the mouse cursor is.

As you might guess, startDrag is a useful component of many Flash games and adds a level of interactivity that would be hard to get otherwise.

if and hitTest

Continuing building the movie:

1. Get to Jake's Actions panel.
2. Enter this code:

```
onClipEvent(enterFrame)
{
    startDrag(this, true);
    if(this.hitTest(_root.shark))
    {
        this.gotoAndStop("scared");
    }
}
```

3. Control ➡ Test Movie

We just added our first bit of conditional logic (`if`) and another function (`hitTest`). Let's look at the `if` statement. Here's the basic structure of an `if` statement:

```
if(condition)
{
    statements;
}
```

It's pretty simple. If the condition is `true`, then the statements are executed. If the condition is `false`, then the statements are ignored. Here are some examples of conditions (note that conditions use two equal signs instead of one):

- `x == 5`
- `_root._xmouse < 94`
- `this.hitTest(_root.shark)`

All of these have to be either `true` or `false`—there's no in between. The last condition uses the `hitTest` function, and that always returns a `true` or `false` value, which is why we don't need an equals or greater than sign.

`hitTest` determines whether a certain movie clip is overlapping another movie clip. If the two are overlapping, it returns a `true` value. If not, it returns `false`. Here's how the function is structured:

```
movieClip1.hitTest(movieClip2)
```

If `movieClip1` is overlapping `movieClip2`, then this function returns a `true` value. For our code, determining `movieClip1` was easy—we're just referencing Jake the fish, so we use `this`. Referencing the shark takes a little extra work, since we need to tell the Flash where `movieClip2` is. If we just used

```
this.hitTest(shark)
```

Flash would assume that the `shark` object was a part of the `fish` object. However, both the shark and the fish are just objects on the main Stage. We tell Flash that an object is on the main Stage by prefacing it with `_root`, which means "start at the top level of the movie." So, if the user has dragged Jake over the shark, then `this.hitTest(_root.shark)` is `true`, and the statements inside the `if` statement are executed. The only statement there right now is

```
this.gotoAndStop("scared");
```

This is a little different than the `gotoAndStop` we saw earlier. Earlier, we were moving from scene to scene, but somehow, we're just moving to a different frame in a certain symbol. How'd we do that?

The key is using `this` before `gotoAndStop`. We're telling `gotoAndStop` exactly which movie clip we want to move forward in, and that movie clip is the fish movie clip. If we didn't use `this`, Flash would look for the frame labeled "scared" in the main timeline. But since we're using `this`, it knows to look at the fish's timeline, not the main one.

NOTE For those of you coming from Flash 4, this is a way to bypass the deprecated `tellTarget` function. You could also code

```
with(this)
{
    gotoAndStop("scared");
}
```

to get the same effect, with syntax a little closer to `tellTarget`.

Let's finish the movie now. Enter the following code into Jake's Actions panel:

```
onClipEvent(enterFrame)
{
    startDrag(this, true);
    if(this.hitTest(_root.shark))
    {
        this.gotoAndStop("scared");
        _root.shark.gotoAndStop("hungry");
    }
    else
    {
        this.gotoAndStop("calm");
        _root.shark.gotoAndStop("normal");
    }
}
```

Be sure to Control ➡ Test Movie.

We added an `else` statement that executes statements if the condition in the `if` statement isn't `true`. We're also moving the playhead in the shark symbol back and forth, depending on where the fish symbol is.

Now that you've manipulated multiple timelines based on user input (you did, honest), you're ready for the next step: changing actual properties of movie clips based on user input.

Changing Movie Clip Properties

Properties are bits of information about an object. They can be the object's position, how wide it is, what color it is, or how transparent it is. We're going to create a movie, piece by piece, that builds on what we've learned so far and allows the user to change a movie clip's properties. You'll learn several ways of altering a movie clip's properties and a cool way to use `startDrag` to make little sliders.

Figure 2-8 shows what your finished product will look like. Let's start.

1. Open *chapter2/drap_props1.fla*.
2. Click on the fish.
3. Open the Actions panel (make sure it's Object Actions).

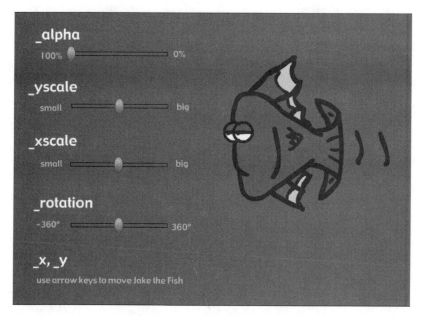

FIGURE 2–8 Finished movie

4. Enter the following code:

```
onClipEvent(keyDown)
{
    if(Key.getCode() == Key.LEFT)
    {
        this._x = this._x - 3;
    }
}
```

5. Control ➠ Test Movie. You can move the fish to the left by pressing the left arrow key. It works if you hold the key down as well.

Again, I'm throwing a few new things at you at once. Let's go over them one at a time.

onClipEvent(keyDown)

This is a movie clip's answer to `on(keyPress "[some key]")`. Notice that we don't spell out which key is being pressed in the first line, which `on(keyPress)` required us to do. If the user presses any key on the keyboard, this `keyDown` is called.

if (Key.getCode() == Key.LEFT)

Here's a new object called *Key.* It's an object that Flash comes with. It isn't an object like a movie clip—it's an object that ActionScript can see, but that doesn't appear in any movie. If you want to do anything with the keyboard and a movie clip, you'll probably be using the Key object in some way. If you're new to objects, the whole concept may seem a little weird to you, but keep plugging away and it'll sink in eventually (it takes everyone a while to get it the first time).

One of the methods associated with the Key object is `get-Code()`, which returns the character code of the last key pressed. Each key on your keyboard has a numeric character code. For example, the code of the left arrow is 37. If you press the left arrow, the `Key.getCode()` sees your left arrow press, and translates that to a 37.

Fortunately, this doesn't mean you have to know all the character codes in order to write ActionScript. The Key object also has some properties that provide us with some shortcuts. These shortcuts are in the form

```
Key.KEYNAME
```

For example, `Key.LEFT` returns the character code of the left arrow (37). `Key.SPACE` returns the character code for the space bar (32).

So `if(Key.getCode() == Key.LEFT)` sees if the character code of the last key pressed (`Key.getCode()`) is the same as the character code of the left arrow key (`Key.LEFT`). We could've written

```
if(Key.getCode() == 37)
```

and gotten the same result, but (1) no one wants to remember all those character codes, and (2) it's a lot easier to debug your actions when you use words instead of numbers.

See the double equals sign? That's how we signify equality in an `if` statement. We use a single equals sign when we want to assign a value to a variable.

_X

A movie clip's horizontal position is its _x property. It's measured from the left edge of the movie to the movie clip's center.
A movie clip's center is determined by wherever the little
crosshairs are when you're viewing that movie clip's symbol.
When you use _x, you have to be clear which _x you're talking
about. That's why we used this._x, because Flash needs to
know which movie clip's horizontal position you want.

Now let's add the rest of the arrows:

```
onClipEvent (keyDown)
{
    if(Key.getCode() == Key.LEFT)
    {
        this._x = this._x - 3;
    }
    else if(Key.getCode() == Key.RIGHT)
    {
        this._x = this._x + 3;
    }
    else if(Key.getCode() == Key.UP)
    {
        this._y = this._y - 3;
    }
    else if(Key.getCode() == Key.DOWN)
    {
        this._y = this._y + 3;
    }
}
```

There are two new things to notice here: the else if statement and the _y property. We use else if instead of this:

```
if(Key.getCode() == Key.LEFT)
{
    this._x = this._x - 3;
}
if(Key.getCode() == Key.RIGHT)
{
    this._x = this._x + 3;
}
if(Key.getCode() == Key.UP)
{
    this._y = this._y - 3;
}
```

```
if(Key.getCode() == Key.DOWN)
{
    this._y = this._y + 3;
}
```

because Flash can process else ifs faster than it can check all four if statements each time. It's not a huge speed difference, but it helps a little, and it's just good programming style—there's no reason to check if the *right* key was hit if we already know the *left* one was.

As you might have guessed, _y is the vertical position of the movie clip, measured from the top of the movie.

If you haven't already, test the movie and use all four arrow keys.

Good—we have a moving fish. Let's add a cool slider. The first slider will control the fish's _alpha property, which sets how transparent the object is. An _alpha of 100 means the object is completely opaque, and an _alpha of 0 means that the object is completely transparent. An object's default alpha setting is 100.

1. Open *chapter2/drag_props2.fla.*
2. Notice there are some new pieces on the stage: some extra text, a slider bar, and a slider, shown in Figure 2-9. Also, notice that each instance has a different name. This is a necessary thing—otherwise, Flash doesn't know which instance is what.
3. Go to the first frame of the actions layer, and got to Window ➡ Actions. Make sure you're entering a frame action.
4. Enter the following code:

```
// Get boundaries and position of the slider bar
alphaBounds = alphaBar.getBounds(_root);
_root.alphaBarXMin = alphaBounds.xMin;
_root.alphaBarXMax = alphaBounds.xMax;
_root.alphaBarYMid = alphaBar._y;

// Set slider position on slider bar
alphaSlider._x = _root.alphaBarXMin;
alphaSlider._y = _root.alphaBarYMid;
```

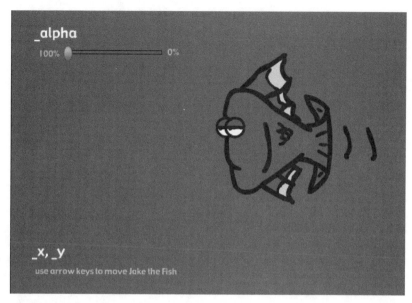

FIGURE 2–9 *drag_props2.fla* stage

Whoa!, I hear you say. What's all this? What we're doing here is positioning the little slider (called `alphaSlider`) exactly where we want it on the slider bar (called `alphaBar`). Why do this? Why not just place it where we want to on the stage and not worry about all this? Well, we could certainly do that, but since the slider is always going to be on the slider bar, this code lets us experiment with placing the slider bar and not have to spend a bunch of time repositioning the slider. This is especially helpful if you have a lot of movie clips that depend on the placement of another movie clip. It just takes out the guesswork.

Let's start dissecting this chunk of code.

alphaBounds = alphaBar.getBounds(_root);

If we're going to position the slider on the slider bar, we have to figure out where the slider bar is. The `getBounds` function returns four values: `xMin`, `xMax`, `yMin`, and `yMax`, which correspond to the left, right, top, and bottom edges of the movie clip in question. We're getting the edges of the movie clip alpha-Bar, which is the slider bar, in relation to the whole movie (_root). It may seem like odd syntax, but it works.

But if getBounds() returns four values, not just one, how do we get to those four values? We assign all four values to alphaBounds. This isn't a variable, though it looks like one. The line of code creates a small object called alphaBounds. The object alphaBounds we just created has four properties:

- alphabounds.xMin
- alphaBounds.xMax
- alphaBounds.yMin
- alphaBounds.yMax

So, we just created an object out of thin air! This isn't a movie clip object—it won't show up anywhere in the movie. It's a different beast, but still an object.

Global Variables

The next block of code creates some global variables.

```
_root.alphaBarXMin = alphaBounds.xMin;
_root.alphaBarXMax = alphaBounds.xMax;
_root.alphaBarYMid = alphaBar._y;
```

We've dealt with variables before, but those were all local variables (all variables are either local or global). That is, they worked as long as they were inside their little curly braces, { }. Outside of their braces, they have no meaning. For example,

```
onClipEvent(enterFrame)
{
    x = 5;
}

onClipEvent(keyDown)
{
    trace(x);
}
```

This wouldn't work. If you ran this movie, the `keyDown` function has no idea what `x` is, and the output window would be blank. To make `x` visible, change the code to

```
onClipEvent(enterFrame)
{
    _root.x = 5;
}

onClipEvent(keyDown)
{
    trace(_root.x);
}
```

Pressing a key would then result in a little output window with a 5 in it. Adding `_root` makes `x` a global variable, which means that it can be seen by every action in the movie, no matter where the action is.

We're creating `_root.alphaBarXMin`, `_root.alpha-BarXMax`, and `_root.alphaBarYMid` as global variables because we're going to be using them later. We're not using `yMin` or `yMax` because, as it ends up, we don't need them—vertical-wise, we only want to know where the vertical center of the slider bar is, not where vertical edges are. We get the vertical center by looking at `_y`, not `yMin` or `yMax`.

Positioning the Slider

Here's where we set the slider in its proper position.

```
// Set slider position on slider bar
alphaSlider._x = _root.alphaBarXMin;
alphaSlider._y = _root.alphaBarYMid;
```

There isn't anything terribly new here. We're setting the `_x` and `_y` positions of the `alphaSlider` object, and we're setting them according to a couple of global variables.

Making the Slider Slide

Let's add some movement to this little slider guy. We want the slider to move, but only in a certain way, under certain conditions:

- The slider only slides along the slider bar.
- The slider moves only if the user pressed down the mouse button while on top of the slider.
- When the user lifts the mouse button up, the slider stops moving.

Let's tackle these one at a time. First, let's make sure the slider only moves along the slider bar. Fortunately, the `start-Drag` function gives us an easy way to do that.

1. Click on the slider object.
2. Open the Object Actions panel.
3. Enter this code:

```
onClipEvent (mouseDown)
{
    startDrag(this, true, _root.alphaBarXMin,
      _root.alphaBarYMid, _root.alphaBarXMax,
      _root.alphaBarYMid);
}
```

4. Control ➡ Test Movie.

We've added some attributes to the `startDrag` function. Here's the syntax:

```
startDrag(movieClip, true/false, left edge, top edge,
right edge, bottom edge)
```

All those edges define a box that limits where the object can be dragged. Once the user's mouse moves outside that box, the object follows the mouse cursor as best it can, but stays within its box. To define the edges of the box, we used the global variables that were set by the first frame's actions. Notice that the top edge and bottom edge are the same variable. That's because we want the slider to move in a straight line back and forth—we don't want any vertical slider movement.

So the slider isn't going anywhere it shouldn't, but you can't stop the sliding. When the mouse button goes up, the slider's still moving. We can fix that with

```
onClipEvent (mouseUp)
{
    stopDrag();
}
```

You don't need to specify which object doesn't get dragged anymore. Since only one object can be dragged at a time, `stopDrag` disables whatever dragging is currently going on.

There's one more thing we need to do to make this slider move correctly. We only want it to slide when the user clicks on the slider itself, not anywhere in the movie. To accomplish this, we're going to bring back the `getBounds` function. Type the following code into the slider's object actions:

```
onClipEvent(mouseDown)
{
    // Get the boundaries for the slider
    bounds = this.getBounds(_root);

    // See if the user clicked inside the slider
    if((_root._xmouse <= bounds.xMax) &&
        (_root._xmouse >= bounds.xMin) &&
        (_root._ymouse <= bounds.yMax) &&
        (_root._ymouse >= bounds.yMin))
    {
        startDrag(this, true, _root.alphaBarXMin,
        _root.alphaBarYMid, _root.alphaBarXMax,
        _root.alphaBarYMid);
    }
}

onClipEvent(mouseUp)
{
    stopDrag();
}
```

Go ahead and test the movie.

With this latest modification, every time the user presses the mouse button, this code creates a little invisible object called `bounds` that holds the boundaries of the slider itself. Once that's done, the code looks at two new properties called `_xmouse` and `_ymouse`. These properties are the horizontal and vertical positions of the user's mouse. We added `_root`, so we get those coordinates in relation to the movie as a whole. We then check to see if the user's mouse coordinates are within the bounds of the slider. If they are, then dragging begins. If not, then nothing happens.

See the double &&? That's how we say AND in an if statement. For example, if we want to see "if A and B are true," the code looks like

```
if(A && B)
```

Both A and B must be true for the whole expression to be evaluated as true.

Still with me? If so, congrats—you're learning a lot quickly. Onward!

What we want the slider to do is actually change the _alpha property of the fish. As it turns out, we can't place this change of _alpha inside the onClipEvent(mouseDown), because that chunk of code is only executed the first time the user presses down on the mouse button. We want this _alpha property to be changed continually as long as the mouse cursor is in the movie.

Here's how we do it:

```
onClipEvent(enterFrame)
{
    xPos = _root._xmouse;
    percentage = 100 * ((_root.alphaBarXMax -
    xPos)/(_root.alphaBarXMax - _root.alphaBarXMin));
    _root.fish._alpha = percentage;
}
```

Add this code to the Actions panel with onClip-Event(mouseDown) and onClipEvent(mouseUp). Now test the movie (see Figure 2-10).

There's only one problem left. Did you notice it? Once you let go of the mouse button, the slider stays in place, but the _alpha property still changes if you keep moving the mouse! Somehow, we have to tell the code to stop changing _alpha when the user stops dragging. We can do this by creating yet another variable called _root.alphaDrag, which will be either true or false. If it's true, _alpha can change. If it's false, then _alpha won't change.

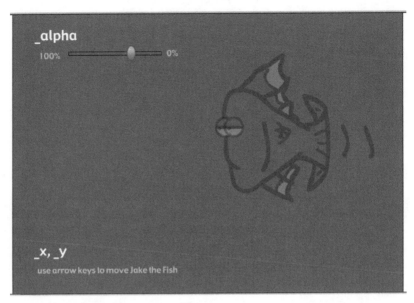

FIGURE 2–10 Making the fish disappear

Here's how to implement it.

1. Because we're thorough little coders, we create the variable in the frame action of the actions layer. Add this line to the existing variables:

```
_root.alphaDrag = false;
```

2. Now, go back to the slider's actions, and make the code look like this:

```
onClipEvent (mouseDown)
{
    // Get the boundaries for the slider
    bounds = this.getBounds(_root);

    // See if the user clicked inside the slider
    if((_root._xmouse <= bounds.xMax) &&
(_root._xmouse >= bounds.xMin) &&
        (_root._ymouse <= bounds.yMax) &&
(_root._ymouse >= bounds.yMin))
```

```
        {
                startDrag(this, true, _root.alphaBarXMin,
_root.alphaBarYMid, _root.alphaBarXMax,
_root.alphaBarYMid);
                _root.alphaDrag = true;
        }
}

onClipEvent(mouseUp) {
        stopDrag ();
        _root.alphaDrag = false;
}

onClipEvent(enterFrame)
{
        if(_root.alphaDrag)
        {
                xPos = _root._xmouse;
                percentage = 100 * ((_root.alphaBarXMax -
xPos)/(_root.alphaBarXMax - _root.alphaBarXMin));
                _root.fish._alpha = percentage;
        }
}
```

ABOUT THE CODE

Let's look at what we did. In the first function, we added _root.alphaDrag = true right after the startDrag. That's announcing to the rest of the movie, "The alpha slider is being dragged by the user!" In the mouseUp section, the user has released the mouse button, and _root.alphaDrag = false announces, "The user is not dragging the alpha slider!"

In the enterFrame section, we check if the user is dragging the alpha slider or not. If so, then _root.alphaDrag is true, and the statements changing the _alpha property are executed. If _root.alphaDrag is false, then the user isn't dragging the slider, and nothing changes.

Congrats! You made a working slider that not only moves like a slider should, but actually does something! If you understand what you've just done, that's an accomplishment, and you're well on your way to creating some fantastic Flash movies.

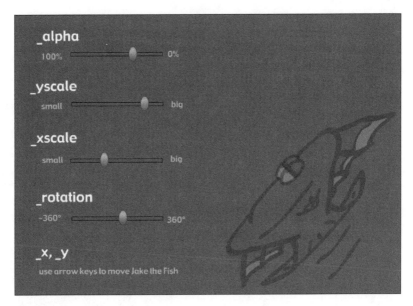

FIGURE 2–11 The final layout

Now let's make this little movie something a little bigger and more fun to use.

1. Open *chapter2/drag_props3.fla* (see Figure 2-11).
2. Don't panic. We've done all the hard work already. To make these sliders work, and do what we want them to, it's a matter of copying, pasting, and tweaking.
3. Click on the first frame in the actions layer, and open up the Frame Actions panel.
4. Enter the following code:

```
// Set variables
alphaBounds = _root.alphaBar.getBounds(_root);
_root.alphaBarXMin = alphaBounds.xMin;
_root.alphaBarXMax = alphaBounds.xMax;
_root.alphaBarYMid = _root.alphaBar._y;

heightBounds = _root.heightBar.getBounds(_root);
_root.heightBarXMin = heightBounds.xMin;
_root.heightBarXMax = heightBounds.xMax;
_root.heightBarYMid = _root.heightBar._y;
```

```
widthBounds = _root.widthBar.getBounds(_root);
_root.widthBarXMin = widthBounds.xMin;
_root.widthBarXMax = widthBounds.xMax;
_root.widthBarYMid = _root.widthBar._y;

rotateBounds = _root.rotateBar.getBounds(_root);
_root.rotateBarXMin = rotateBounds.xMin;
_root.rotateBarXMax = rotateBounds.xMax;
_root.rotateBarYMid = _root.rotateBar._y;


_root.alphaDrag = false;
_root.heightDrag = false;
_root.widthDrag = false;
_root.rotateDrag = false;


// set slider positions
_root.alphaSlider._x = _root.alphaBarXMin;
_root.alphaSlider._y = _root.alphaBarYMid;

_root.heightSlider._x = (_root.heightBarXMin +
_root.heightBarXMax)/2;
_root.heightSlider._y = _root.heightBarYMid;

_root.widthSlider._x = (_root.widthBarXMin +
_root.widthBarXMax)/2;
_root.widthSlider._y = _root.widthBarYMid;

_root.rotateSlider._x = (_root.rotateBarXMin +
_root.rotateBarXMax)/2;
_root.rotateSlider._y = _root.rotateBarYMid;
```

5. Remember, don't panic. All we're doing is copying the code from the alpha code and pasting it four times. Then, we're tweaking it some so that we have four separately named sliders and slider bars. There's only one small difference—the latest sliders are positioned in the middle of the bar instead of on the end.

6. Click on the slider under the `_yscale` heading. The slider's name is heightSlider.

7. Enter the following code (it should look familiar):

```
onClipEvent(mouseDown)
{
    // get the boundaries for the slider
    bounds = this.getBounds(_root);
```

```
        // see if the user clicked inside the slider
        if((_root._xmouse <= bounds.xMax) &&
            (_root._xmouse >= bounds.xMin) &&
            (_root._ymouse <= bounds.yMax) &&
            (_root._ymouse >= bounds.yMin))
        {
            startDrag(this, true, _root.heightBarXMin,
              _root.heightBarYMid, _root.heightBarXMax,
              _root.heightBarYMid);
            _root.heightDrag = true;
        }
    }

onClipEvent(mouseUp) {
    stopDrag();
    _root.heightDrag = false;
}

onClipEvent(enterFrame)
{
    if(_root.heightDrag)
    {
        xPos = _root._xmouse;
        percentage = 200 * (( xPos -
    _root.heightBarXMin)/(_root.heightBarXMax -
    _root.heightBarXMin));
        //trace(percentage);
        _root.fish._yscale = percentage;
    }
}
```

8. Control ➡ Test Movie.

The _yscale slider affects the height of the fish, and it's expressed as a percentage. So a yscale of 0 is a perfectly flat image, and a yscale of 200 stretches the image vertically to twice its original height.

Now let's do the same to the _xscale slider.

1. Click on the xscale slider. It's called widthSlider.
2. Open the Object Actions panel.
3. Enter the following code:

```
onClipEvent(mouseDown)
{
    // Get the boundaries for the slider
    bounds = this.getBounds(_root);

    // see if the user clicked inside the slider
    if((_root._xmouse <= bounds.xMax) &&
        (_root._xmouse >= bounds.xMin) &&
        (_root._ymouse <= bounds.yMax) &&
        (_root._ymouse >= bounds.yMin))
    {
        startDrag(this, true, _root.widthBarXMin,
          _root.widthBarYMid, _root.widthBarXMax,
          _root.widthBarYMid);
        _root.widthDrag = true;
    }
}

onClipEvent(mouseUp) {
    stopDrag();
    _root.widthDrag = false;
}

onClipEvent(enterFrame)
{
    if(_root.widthDrag)
    {
        xPos = _root._xmouse;
        percentage = 200 * (( xPos -
_root.widthBarXMin)/(_root.widthBarXMax -
_root.widthBarXMin));
        _root.fish._xscale = percentage;
    }
}
```

4. Test the movie

The _xscale slider affects the width of the fish, in much the same way _yscale affects the height. It's also expressed as a percentage. Now, let's finish the final slider.

1. Click on the slider under the _rotation heading.

2. Open up the Object Actions panel.

3. Enter the following code:

```
onClipEvent(mouseDown)
{
    // Get the boundaries for the slider
    bounds = this.getBounds(_root);

    // see if the user clicked inside the slider
    if((_root._xmouse <= bounds.xMax) &&
        (_root._xmouse >= bounds.xMin) &&
        (_root._ymouse <= bounds.yMax) &&
        (_root._ymouse >= bounds.yMin))
    {
        //trace("rotate on");
        startDrag(this, true, _root.rotateBarXMin,
_root.rotateBarYMid, _root.rotateBarXMax,
_root.rotateBarYMid);
        _root.rotateDrag = true;
    }
}

onClipEvent(mouseUp) {
    stopDrag ();
    _root.rotateDrag = false;
}

onClipEvent(enterFrame)
{
    if(_root.rotateDrag)
    {
        xPos = _root._xmouse;
        percentage = ( xPos -
_root.rotateBarXMin)/(_root.rotateBarXMax -
_root.rotateBarXMin);
        rotation = (percentage * 720) - 360
        _root.fish._rotation = rotation;
    }
}
```

4. Test that movie.

The _rotation property affects, well, the rotation of an image, and it's expressed in degrees. Positive degrees are in the clockwise direction, and negative degrees are in the counterclockwise direction. All images have a default _rotation of zero.

Check out *chapter2/drag_props_done.fla* to see the finished movie with all the code in place.

A Note About _xscale and _yscale

If you spin the fish part way, and then change the `_xscale` and `_yscale`, you'll notice that they don't quite affect the width and height of the viewing image—they change the height and width of the symbol in its original orientation. You have to try this to really understand it.

A Challenge

Create a single movie clip that contains the bar and the slider. Drag four of those instances to the stage and use those instead of the symbols that are there now.

Another Property-Changing Example

Don't worry—this example is simpler than the previous one. We're going to take the movie of Jake the fish swimming into the pea shark's mouth and getting scared, and we're going to add a little bit to it. We'll make Jake face in whatever direction the mouse is moving. If the mouse is moving left, Jake will face to the left. If the mouse is moving right, Jake will face to the right.

1. Open *chapter2/drag_jake2.fla.*
2. Click the frame in the actions layer and open up the Frame Actions panel.
3. Enter the following code:

```
// Set Jake's position
_root.lastXPosition = jake._x;
```

This sets a global variable called `_root.lastXPosi-tion`, and initializes it to Jake's current `_x`.

4. Click on Jake and open the Object Actions panel

5. Enter the following code:

```
onClipEvent(enterFrame)
{
     startDrag(this, true);
     if(this.hitTest(_root.shark))
     {
          this.gotoAndStop("scared");
          _root.shark.gotoAndStop("hungry");
     }
     else
     {
          this.gotoAndStop("calm");
          _root.shark.gotoAndStop("normal");
     }

     // set direction
     if(this._x < _root.lastXPosition)
     {
          this._xscale = -35;
     }
     else if(this._x > _root.lastXPosition)
     {
          this._xscale = 35;
     }
     _root.lastXPosition = this._x;
}
```

You'll notice we added a new chunk of code toward the end where we set Jake's direction based on his current _x and what his last x-position was. Take a look at how we're using _xscale here. If Jake is moving to the left (the first condition), then we change the _xscale to –35. The negative sign flips Jake around. If Jake is moving to the right (his _x is bigger than lastXPosition), then we set him to his original orientation. It's then necessary to update lastXPosition to keep up with Jake.

We're using 35 instead of 100 because this is a smaller version of Jake, and a 100% size would be too big for this movie. If you need convincing, change the values to 100 and –100. You'll see what I mean.

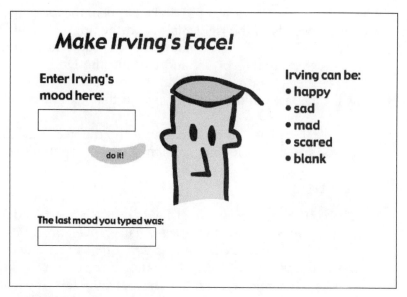

FIGURE 2–12 *Make Irving's Face*

Now let's add one line of code, just to make the movie a little easier to look at:

```
onClipEvent(enterFrame)
{
    startDrag(this, true);
    Mouse.hide();
    ...
```

Since Jake's so small, the mouse cursor overshadowed him. Fortunately, that's an easy thing to fix. `Mouse.hide()` simply hides the mouse cursor. It's still there, and responding to the user's movements, but it can't be seen. You can bring it back with `Mouse.show()`.

Text Fields, Arrays, and Loops

In this section, we'll work on a new movie and introduce dynamic and input text fields, along with arrays and looping. The movie we're creating is *Make Irving's Face*. See Figure 2-12.

Here's what we want to make happen: the user enters one of five words in the right place, and the appropriate frame of the Irving movie clip is shown. Each frame has a different expression. Typing in *sad* and clicking the Do it! button will cause the Irving movie clip to go to the sad frame. We also want the last thing the user typed in the box to appear in the lower text box.

We'll start with an overview of the different kinds of text fields, arrays, and looping, and then we'll jump into the code.

Text Fields

There are three kinds of text fields in Flash 5: static, dynamic, and input. Static text fields are what you've already used: it's just plain ol' text. Dynamic text is text that's associated with a variable and can be changed by ActionScript code. Input text is just like dynamic text, but the user can enter text into it as well. *Make Irving's Face* uses all three kinds of text fields.

Arrays

An array is like a variable that has some little variables in it. It's not too different from an object and its properties. Here's an example of an array:

```
arrayName[0] = 5
arrayName[1] = "hi there"
arrayName[2] = true
arrayName[3] = "this is the fourth element in this
array"
```

or

```
myFriends[0] = "Tanya"
myFriends[1] = "Jonathan"
myFriends[2] = "Sarah Jane"
myFriends[3] = "Mark & Spencer"
```

All arrays in ActionScript start with the first element as 0, not 1, as you might expect. Also, arrays in ActionScript are all instances of a grander Array object, but don't worry about that now. We'll deal with more arrays in later chapters.

Looping

You'll find that you'll often want to repeat a series of statements a certain number of times. This is where looping can be helpful. There are two common ways to create a loop: `for` statements and `do...while` statements.

`for` statements look like this:

```
for(initial condition; end condition; counter increment)
{
    statements;
}
```

An example:

```
for(loopCounter = 1, loopCounter < 10, loopCounter++)
{
    trace(loopCounter);
}
```

This would result in the numbers 1 through 9 being listed in an Output window.

`do...while` statements are very similar:

```
do {
    statements;
} while(condition)
```

Here's how we'd execute the same task as the `for` example using `do...while`.

```
loopCounter = 1;
do {
    trace(loopCounter);
    loopCounter = loopCounter + 1;
} while(loopCounter < 10)
```

When using simple counters like this, I usually find that using a `for` statement is easier. If you're testing for some condition other than a loop counter, `do...while` usually comes in handy. There are always exceptions, but that's the rule of thumb that's worked for me.

Creating the Movie

First, it's important to know that the Irv symbol has five frames, all of them labeled. The labels are "sad," "mad," "happy," "scared," and "blank."

1. Open the file *chapter2/irving1.fla.*
2. Click on the first frame of the actions layer.
3. Open the Frame Actions panel.
4. Enter the following code:

```
// Create face array
faceArray = new
Array("happy","sad","mad","scared","blank")
```

We just created an array called `faceArray`. Element by element, this array looks like this:

```
faceArray[0] = "happy";
faceArray[1] = "sad";
faceArray[2] = "mad";
faceArray[3] = "scared";
faceArray[4] = "blank";
```

1. Click on the Do it! button.
2. Open the Object Actions panel.
3. Enter the following code:

```
on(release)
{
    // loop through array and see
    // if irvMood matches anything in the
    // faceArray. If so, go to that label in the Irv
    for(i=0; i<5; i++)
    {
        if(_root.irvMood == faceArray[i])
        {
            _root.irv.gotoAndStop(faceArray[i]);
            break;
        }
    }

    _root.lastIrvMood = _root.irvMood;
}
```

4. Control ➠ Test Movie. Type in one of the five possible moods and click the Do it! button to see Irving's face change.

ABOUT THE CODE

Let's go over the code line by line (not counting the comments). We start with a `for` statement, using the simple variable i because it's shorter than `loopCounter`. We want to loop from 0 to 4, so we start i off at 0 and make sure it's always less than 5. We then increment it by 1 each time the loop is run (this is written as i++).

Once we're inside the loop, we run into an `if` statement that compares the value of the input text (`_root.irvMood`) and the value of the `faceArray` at element i. For example, if the user typed in *scared*, then the code starts looking through the array and stops when i=3, when _root.irvMood = faceArray[3].

Continuing with the example of the user typing *scared*, we tell the `irv` instance in our movie to go to the frame label "scared," that is, the value of `faceArray[3]`. It's vital that the frame labels in the Irv symbol exactly match the text in our `faceArray`. If those two don't match perfectly, then this code won't work.

Since we've found the right face to show, we don't need to keep looping—there's no reason to see if `irvMood = faceArray[4]`, since we know that it's equal to `faceArray[3]`. So, we jump out of the loop with the `break` statement. In this case, it's not a necessary statement, since the movie doesn't throw an error if we remove it. However, it's good programming style to not force any extra calculation if it can be avoided.

Finally, we set the value of the dynamic text variable `lastIrvMood`. It doesn't add to the movie, but it simply illustrates what a dynamic text field can do.

Associative Arrays

Flash also has what are called *associative arrays.* Here's an example:

```
assocArray = new Array();
assocArray["happy"] = "ice cream";
assocArray["sad"] = "worm in apple";
assocArray["excited"] = "you found a spellbook";
```

Associative arrays use strings instead of numbers as the array element. They can be a little harder to keep track of, but are extremely useful when you need them.

What You've Learned

- What the Actions panels are and what to use them for
- The real difference between object and frame actions
- `_x`
- `_y`
- `_xscale`
- `_yscale`
- `_xmouse`
- `_ymouse`
- `_alpha`
- `_rotate`
- Global variables
- `startDrag`
- `hitTest`
- `getBounds`
- `gotoAndPlay`
- `gotoAndStop`
- `trace`
- `if`
- `else`
- `else if`
- `Key.getCode, Key.KEYNAME`
- `onClipEvent(enterFrame, keyDown, mouseUp, mouseDown)`

- on(release, keyPress)
- Text fields and how to manipulate them
- Looping (for, break)
- Arrays

Not too shabby. This is a lot of material for your first foray into ActionScript. If you have a basic understanding of what we just went through, you're more than ready for the next chapter! We'll mostly be expanding on what was introduced here—more ways to use what you now know—instead of introducing another fleet of new properties and commands.

Adding Power to ActionScripts

N ow that you've been introduced to many of the basics of ActionScript, it's time to get a little fancy. First, we'll hone your skills by creating a simple space game. Then we'll move on to the more powerful features of ActionScript, show you some useful techniques for preloading a movie, make a screensaver that you can send your friends, and show you a way to code that will get a project finished quickly, but at a serious cost.

Honing Your Skills

In this section, we'll create a simple space game that uses only what was introduced in the last chapter. We'll take the sophistication level of your ActionScript up a few notches before I throw anything new at you.

Troubleshooting

One of the best ways to see if you're writing working code or not is to look at the colors in the Actions panel. Flashes uses syntax coloring, so pay attention—if your scripts don't turn green or blue or pink like they should, look more closely at your code.

Also, if you're creating something complex with Flash, check to see if you're coding something that can only be used with Flash 5. As of this writing, the Flash 5 plug-in isn't propagating as fast as Flash 4 did, and clients still want Flash 4 functionality.

Space Game

In this game, you're the ship at the bottom of the screen, fending off various enemy ships. They fire at you, and you can fire at them. Only one enemy appears at a time, and when you destroy it, the other enemy appears. There's no score, and there is an infinite number of both your ships and enemies, so you can play forever.

Figure 3-1 shows a screenshot.

THE PLAYERS

There are a total of three ships in this game. They are

1. Your ship (symbol name in the library is `mc_full-rocket`), shown in Figure 3-2.
2. The Manta (symbol name in the library is `mc_manta`), shown in Figure 3-3.
3. The Spike (symbol name is `mc_spikepod`), shown in Figure 3-4.

FIGURE 3–1 Screenshot of the space game in action

FIGURE 3–2 Full rocket symbol

FIGURE 3–3 Manta enemy ship

FIGURE 3–4 Spike enemy ship

Each ship's symbol is a movie clip, and there's a timeline for each one. The first frame is the ship at rest, looking normal. A short movie of each ship exploding begins on frame 2. The enemy ships have explosions that last for 10 frames, and your ship has an explosion that lasts for 34 (it's more interesting). The ships appear as normal until they're hit by another ship's shot. At the point when they're hit, their timelines are moved to the second frame and the explosion plays. The instance names have already been set for you in this movie. To see the instance names, select the object and look at the Instance panel.

The other three symbols in the movie are the three weapons, shown in Figure 3-5.

You can fire your shots whenever the mouse button is clicked, but you can only have one shot in the air at a time. The enemies fire constantly, but they also can only have one shot in the air at a time. Incidentally, this is not a particularly complex game. It will not sell a million units. But when you're done creating it, you'll have a more thorough understanding of all the bits of ActionScript that you were bombarded with in the last chapter.

FIGURE 3–5 The three weapons, from left to right, are your shot, the Manta shot, and the Spike shot

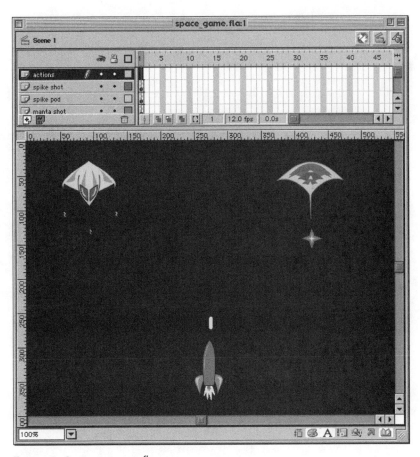

FIGURE 3–6 *space_game.fla*

Now that you know basically what we want the game to do, let's open up the movie and start working. We'll be building this game piece by piece, so if you get impatient, open up *chapter3/space_game_done.fla* to see the finished product.

1. Open *chapter3/space_game.fla* on the CD. It should look a lot like Figure 3-6.

2. Well, the first thing that has to happen is the rocket ship has to be draggable, but not all over the screen—we'll have to constrain the ship to a box on the bottom of the screen. Click on the rocket ship (the red one at the bottom).

3. Window ⮞ Actions.
4. Enter this code:

```
onClipEvent(enterFrame)
{
    startDrag( this, true, 50, 300, 500, 375 );
}
```

5. Control ⮞ Test Movie. So you can drag your ship, but you shouldn't always see all the shots and all the ships. Let's hide some of them.
6. Close the Flash Player.
7. Click on the first and only frame in the actions layer.
8. Open the Frame Actions panel.
9. Enter the following code:

```
// Set visibility properties
shot._visible = false;
mantaShot._visible = false;
spikeShot._visible = false;
spike._visible = false;
```

10. Test the movie. Everything except your ship and Manta should be invisible.

Wait a minute, I hear you say. What about the _root? That was important last time we made a movie. Why did it work without the _root? It works because since these actions are on a frame action in the main timeline, the _root is assumed. The frame is already on the root level, so it's already sitting at the top looking down. We can certainly add _root to the movie clip names, but in this case, we don't need to.

Well, the Manta is pretty boring just sitting there. Let's add some motion to it. We'll make the ship go back and forth. If we wanted, we could make a little movie clip that was the Manta moving back and forth across the screen. That would be an easy way to implement motion, but as it turns out, it makes it much harder if we want the Manta's shots to come from its guns. So we'll use the non-moving Manta, and use Action-Script to make it move.

The first thing we'll need is a way to keep track of which direction the Manta is moving in. We'll do that by setting up a global variable.

1. Open up the Frame Actions panel for the first frame in the actions layer.
2. Add this code to the property setting we just did:

```
// initialize enemy direction variable
enemyDirection = "right";
```

3. Wait a minute, I hear you say again. We're supposed to create a global variable, but enemyDirection doesn't have a _root before it. Is this a mistake? No, it isn't, and here's why. By creating this variable in a frame action on the main timeline, we automatically make it a global variable—it's the same reason that we didn't have to do it when we made the shots and the Spike ship invisible.
4. Click on the Manta.
5. Open the Object Actions panel.
6. Enter the following code:

```
// manta ship
onClipEvent(enterFrame)
{
    // move the manta
    if(_root.enemyDirection == "right")
    {
        if(this._x < 450)
        {
            this._x = this._x + 10;
        }
        else
        {
            _root.enemyDirection = "left";
            this._x = this._x - 10;
        }
    }
    else
    {
        if(this._x > 100)
        {
            this._x = this._x - 10;
        }
        else
        {
            _root.enemyDirection = "right";
```

```
                              this._x = this._x + 10;
                        }
                  }
            }
```

7. As always, test the movie.

ABOUT THE CODE

Let's look at this. We have two sections of code here—one that is executed if `_root.enemyDirection` is right, and one that's executed if it isn't (we're assuming that if the direction isn't right, then it must be left. If the direction is right, we see if the ship has gone too far to the right. If not, we increase its x-position by 10. If it has gone too far, we reverse the direction by changing `_root.enemyDirection` to left and decreasing the Manta ship's x-position by 10. The second chunk of code is the opposite: if the ship hasn't moved too far to the left, then it keeps moving left. If it has moved too far, then we reverse its direction.

Now that we have two ships moving, let's get them firing at each other. We'll start with the good guy ship. Since we're only allowing one shot to be in the air at one time, we'll create a global variable to keep track of whether there's a shot in the air or not.

1. Go to the frame in the actions layer.
2. Open up the Frame Actions panel.
3. Add the following code:

```
//set shot variables
ourHeroShotInAir = false;
```

4. Now click on the good guy ship.
5. Make sure the Object Actions panel is open.
6. Enter the following code:

```
onClipEvent(mouseUp)
{
    if(!_root.ourHeroShotInAir)
    {
        _root.shot._x = this._x;
        _root.shot._y = this._y - 50;
        _root.shot._visible = true;
```

```
          _root.ourHeroShotInAir = true;
      }
  }
```

7. Test the movie.

ABOUT THE CODE

Well, we're partway there. First of all, let's explain the exclamation point. It means *not*. In this instance, this means "if `_root.ourHeroShotInAir` is not `true`."

You noticed that pressing the button positioned the shot in the right place and made it visible, but the darn thing doesn't move. That's fine for now—we'll fix this next. Right now, look at the code. First, we're making sure that there isn't already a shot in the air. If there is, then clicking the mouse button should have no effect. If there isn't a shot in the air, we position the shot to match the ship's x-position, and we knock down the y-position some in order to make the shot emerge closer to the nose of our ship. Once the shot is positioned correctly, we then make it visible and switch the `ourHeroShotInAir` variable.

Well and good. Now let's make the shot move.

1. Click on the yellow shot and open the Object Actions panel.

2. Enter the following code:

```
onClipEvent(enterFrame)
{
    // see if ourHero shot is in the air
    if(_root.ourHeroShotInAir)
    {
        if(this._y > 0)
        {
            this._y = this._y - 20;
        }
        else
        {
            _root.ourHeroShotInAir = false;
            this._visible = false;
        }
    }
}
```

3. Test the movie.

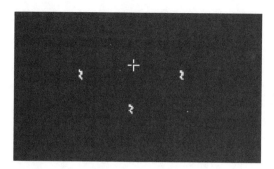

FIGURE 3–7 Manta shot

ABOUT THE CODE

Ah, that's better. The yellow pellet now cruises up the screen when you press the mouse button. And once it's off the screen, you can fire again. The first thing this action does is see if it should do anything. The `ourHeroShotInAir` has to be `true` for anything to happen. Remember that this variable is set to `true` by pressing the mouse button. If it is `true`, the code sees if the shot is still on the screen. If it is, then it's moved up the screen 20 pixels. If it's moved off the screen, it becomes invisible, `ourHeroShotInAir` becomes `false`, and we're ready to fire again.

We're making progress. It's time to add a deadly rain of fire from the Manta ship.

Since the Manta's shooting has the same limitation as the good guy, i.e., one shot at a time, we're going to use the same technique.

1. Go to the frame on the actions layer.
2. Open the Frame Actions panel.
3. Add the following code to the `//set shot variables` section:

```
mantaShotInAir = false;
```

4. Now, click on the Manta shot—not the Manta, but the object with the three little zigzags, shown in Figure 3-7.
5. Make sure the Object Actions panel is open.
6. Enter the following code:

```
// manta shot

onClipEvent(enterFrame)
{
    // see if appropriate for the manta to fire now
    if(!_root.mantaShotInAir)
    {
        this._x = _root.manta._x;
        this._y = _root.manta._y;
        this._visible = true;
        _root.mantaShotInAir = true;
    }
    else
    {
        // see if manta shot is off the screen
        if(this._y > 400)
        {
            this._visible = false;
            _root.mantaShotInAir = false;
        }
        else
        {
            this._y = this._y + 20;
        }
    }
}
```

7. Test the movie.

ABOUT THE CODE

What this code does is ensure that there's always a Manta shot in the air. If there isn't (and the first section of code is executed), the shot is positioned on top of the Manta and made visible. mantaShotInAir is flipped to true. If the Manta shot is in the air, the code then checks whether it's still on the screen or not. If it's not on the screen, then it becomes invisible and we note the shot is no longer in the air. If it is still on the screen, the Manta shot is brought down another 20 pixels.

Great—we have two moving ships viciously firing at each other, but there are no consequences to being hit. We can fix that, but there are two things to we should keep in mind. One, we don't want ships firing while they're exploding. If you get hit, you shouldn't be able to fire your weapon in the middle of an explosion. Second, we don't want ships to be hit by the same shot more than once. For example, say a shot hits a ship on the nose and the ship starts exploding. The code should then suspend checking to see if the ship's been hit or not, or it could notice that same shot is now near the hind end of the ship, and start the explosion all over.

The good news is that both of these dilemmas can be solved with two new variables.

1. Go to the frame in the actions layer.
2. Open the Frame Actions panel.
3. Add the following code:

```
// set hit variables
ourHeroDead = false;
mantaDead = false;
```

4. Don't bother testing the movie yet.
5. First, let's make sure that our hero can't fire while he's exploding. Click on the red rocket ship and open the Object Actions panel.
6. Alter the onClipEvent (mouseUp) code to this:

```
onClipEvent (mouseUp)
{
    if(!_root.ourHeroShotInAir && !_root.ourHeroDead)
    {
        _root.shot._x = this._x;
        _root.shot._y = this._y - 50;
        _root.shot._visible = true;
        _root.ourHeroShotInAir = true;
    }
}
```

ABOUT THE CODE

All we did was add another condition to the if statement: !_root.ourHeroDead. This means we can fire as long as we're not dead. Let's do the same thing to the Manta shot.

1. Click on the Manta shot.
2. Open the Object Actions panel.
3. Replace this line:

```
if(!_root.mantaShotInAir)
```

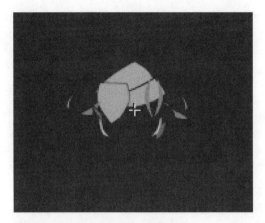

FIGURE 3–8 The Manta exploding

with this line:

```
if(!_root.mantaShotInAir && !_root.mantaDead)
```

Now the Manta won't fire if it's dead. We're all set to make things blow up now. Let's make the Manta blow up first.

1. Click on the Manta and open its Object Actions panel.
2. Add this code inside the `onClickEvent(enter-Frame)` section. Start typing right after the first curly brace ({):

```
// see if manta was hit
if(this.hitTest(_root.shot) && !_root.mantaDead)
{
    _root.shot._visible = false;
    _root.mantaDead = true;
    _root.manta.gotoAndPlay("pow");
}
```

3. Test the movie. The Manta should blow up now, as in Figure 3-8.

ABOUT THE CODE

We're using `this.hitTest` to see if the shot is overlapping the Manta and `!_root.mantaDead` to make sure that striking the Manta again with the shot isn't going to replay the explosion. If we've hit the Manta and it's not dead, then the shot is hidden (so the user can properly concentrate on the exploding Manta); we set the Manta's status to dead and play the explosion.

To make this something resembling a fair fight, let's allow the Manta to blow up our rocket ship.

1. Click on the rocket ship and open its Object Actions panel.
2. Add the following code inside the onClip-Event(enterFrame) section after the first curly brace:

```
// see if ourHero got nailed
if(this.hitTest(_root.mantaShot) && !_root.ourHeroDead)
{
    _root.ourHeroDead = true;
    this.gotoAndPlay("pow");
}
```

3. Test the movie and let the Manta hit you.

ABOUT THE CODE

This code is exactly like the code for the Manta, except that we're not hiding the Manta's shot after the explosion. The rocket's explosion is bright enough that I don't think the Manta's shot detracts from it. Decide which way you prefer, and make it so.

Take a break, if you haven't already. We've hit a milestone here, so get a drink of water, go for a little walk, chat with your significant other, and let this all sink in for a few minutes.

Okay. Ready?

Let's allow this game to go on further than one hit. Let's add some code to bring back the rocket ship after the explosion's over.

1. Click on the rocket ship and open its Object Actions panel.
2. Add this code to onClipEvent(enterFrame) section at the bottom of the section:

```
// reset ourHero's ship
if(this._currentframe == 35)
```

```
{
    _root.ourHeroDead = false;
    this.gotoAndPlay("start");
}
```

3. Test the movie.

ABOUT THE CODE

To see if the explosion's over, we have to see if the rocket ship's timeline has reached the end or not, and the end happens to be at frame 35. So, I'm introducing a new property, `_currentframe`, which simply returns which frame the current movie is on. If we have reached the end of the explosion, then we reset the rocket ship by bringing it back to life and starting its movie at the beginning.

Now we need the enemy ships to start alternating. Once the Manta is destroyed, the Spike should appear. When the Spike gets hit, once its explosion finishes, the Manta should reappear.

First, let's add some Spike-related variables.

1. Click on the frame in the actions layer and open up the Frame Actions panel.
2. Add a few variables into their correct sections:

```
spikeDead = true;
spikeShotInAir = false;

// set alternating enemy ships
lastEnemyAlive = "spike";
```

ABOUT THE CODE

We added three variables here; two of them should be familiar: `spikeDead` and `spikeShotInAir`, just like `mantaDead` and `mantaShotInAir`. However, now that we're alternating between the two enemy ships, we'll need to know which one to bring to the forefront, and we'll do that with `lastEnemyAlive`. You'll see how it works soon.

1. Click on the Manta.

2. Update the `hit` code by adding the `lastEnemyAlive`
    line:

```
// see if manta was hit
if(this.hitTest(_root.shot) && !_root.mantaDead)
{
    _root.shot._visible = false;
    _root.lastEnemyAlive = "manta";
    _root.mantaDead = true;
    _root.manta.gotoAndPlay("pow");
}
```

3. Continue typing in code with the following:

```
// see if the manta just finished playing explosion
if(this._currentframe == 11 && _root.lastEnemyAlive ==
"manta")
{
    // bring spike to life
    _root.spikeDead = false;
    _root.spike._visible = true;
    _root.spike.gotoAndStop("start");
}
```

4. Test the movie. When you hit the Manta, it should blow
    apart, and the Spike ship should appear.

ABOUT THE CODE

The first chunk of code includes the new line `_root.last-`
`EnemyAlive = "manta"`, which sets the stage for the Spike
ship to appear. The second chunk of code is completely new, so
let's look at it one line at a time.

The goal of this latest bunch of code is to bring the Spike
ship forth when the Manta ship has finished blowing up. Let's
dissect the two conditions in the `if` statement.

```
this._currentframe == 11
```

The Manta explosion lasts until frame 11, so we want to be
sure the explosion has played itself out fully. Here's the problem:
when the Manta finishes exploding, it stays at frame 11 until the
Spike gets blown up and brings the Manta ship back to the
movie by making it visible and moving the Manta's timeline to
frame 1. If this was our only condition, it would always be `true`,
and the Spike ship's playhead would constantly be set to

"start", no matter what else was happening in the movie. So, if we ever tried to play the explosion of the Spike ship, it wouldn't get very far before it would be reset to "start". Thus, this one condition isn't enough, and we need some others.

```
_root.lastEnemyAlive == "manta"
```

By adding this condition, we ensure that it's time for the Spike to make its appearance: the Manta was the last living enemy ship on the scene, so it's time for the Spike to appear. Otherwise, the first condition would be true while the Spike was alive and firing at the rocket ship, and the explosion for the Spike ship would never happen.

Once you get past the reasoning for these conditions, the rest of the code is a little easier to follow. We mark the Spike ship as alive, make it visible, and go to the beginning of its timeline.

Let's review where we are so far (we're almost done). The rocket ship works exactly like it should, so we don't need any more code there. The Manta ship and its shot work like they should, so we're done there. The only thing that needs work is the Spike ship and its shot. The code for those two are almost exactly like the Manta ship and its shot, so let's just enter for the Spike elements without further ado. HINT: copy and paste—it's much easier than typing it from scratch.

1. Click on the Spike ship and open its Object Actions panel.
2. Enter the following code:

```
//spike
onClipEvent(enterFrame)
{
    // see if spike was hit
    if(this.hitTest(_root.shot) && !_root.spikeDead)
    {
        _root.shot._visible = false;
        _root.spikeDead = true;
        _root.lastEnemyAlive = "spike";
        _root.spike.gotoAndPlay("pow");
    }

    // see if the spike just finished playing explosion
    if(this._currentframe > 10 &&
_root.lastEnemyAlive == "spike")
```

```
    {
        // bring manta to life
        _root.mantaDead = false;
        _root.manta._visible = true;
        _root.manta.gotoAndStop("start");
    }

    // move the spike
    if(_root.enemyDirection == "right")
    {
        if(this._x<450)
        {
            this._x = this._x+10;
        } else {
            _root.enemyDirection = "left";
        }
    }
    else
    {
        if(this._x>100)
        {
            this._x = this._x-10;
        } else {
            _root.enemyDirection = "right";
        }
    }
}
```

3. Test the movie. You should get a moving but nonfiring Spike ship that explodes when hit, and is replaced by the Manta ship.

4. Let's move straight on to the Spike shot. Click on the Spike shot and open its Object Actions panel.

5. Enter the following code:

```
// spikeShot
onClipEvent(enterFrame)
{
    // see if it's appropriate for the spike to fire now
    if(!_root.spikeShotInAir && !_root.spikeDead)
    {
        this._x = _root.spike._x;
        this._y = _root.spike._y;
        this._visible = true;
        _root.spikeShotInAir = true;
    }
```

```
    else
    {
        // see if spike shot is off the screen
        if(this._y > 400)
        {
            this._visible = false;
            _root.spikeShotInAir = false;
        }
        else
        {
            this._y = this._y + 40;
        }
    }
}
```

6. One last thing: we need to modify the code for the red rocket ship so that it's looking to see if it was hit by the Spike shot as well as the Manta shot. Click on the rocket ship.

7. Open the ship's Object Actions panel.

8. Replace this code

```
if(this.hitTest(_root.mantaShot) && !_root.ourHeroDead)
```

with this code

```
if((this.hitTest(_root.mantaShot) ||
this.hitTest(_root.spikeShot)) && !_root.ourHeroDead)
```

9. Test the movie (you're done!).

ABOUT THE CODE

All we did was modify the `if` statement to look for both the `mantaShot` and the `spikeShot`—we added an extra condition for the Spike shot and introduced the or symbol, which is the two vertical lines (||).

Congrats! That took some time and some conceptual brain twisting (especially if you're new to programming). Since we've gone through several versions of the code in different places, I'll list all of the final code below. There's code in seven places: the frame action, the three ships, and the three shots.

The Frame Action

```
//set variables
ourHeroShotInAir = false;
ourHeroDead = false;

// set enemy ship variables
mantaDead = false;
mantaShotInAir = false;
spikeDead = true;
spikeShotInAir = false;
enemyDirection = "right";
lastEnemyAlive = "spike";

// set properties
shot._visible = false;
mantaShot._visible = false;
spikeShot._visible = false;
spike._visible = false;
```

The Our Hero Rocket Ship

```
onClipEvent(enterFrame)
{
    startDrag( this, true, 50, 300, 500, 375 );

    // see if ourHero got nailed
    if(this.hitTest(_root.mantaShot) &&
!_root.ourHeroDead)
    {
        _root.ourHeroDead = true;
        this.gotoAndPlay("pow");
    }

    // reset ourHero's ship
    if(this._currentframe == 35)
    {
        _root.ourHeroDead = false;
        this.gotoAndPlay("start");
    }
}

onClipEvent(mouseUp)
{
    if(!_root.ourHeroShotInAir)
    {
        _root.shot._x = this._x;
        _root.shot._y = this._y - 50;
```

```
            _root.shot._visible = true;
            _root.ourHeroShotInAir = true;
        }
}
```

The Yellow Pellet Shot

```
onClipEvent(enterFrame)
{
    // see if ourHero's shot is in the air
    if(_root.ourHeroShotInAir)
    {
        if(this._y > 0)
        {
            this._y = this._y - 20;
        }
        else
        {
            _root.ourHeroShotInAir = false;
            this._visible = false;
        }
    }
}
```

The Manta Ship

```
// manta ship
onClipEvent(enterFrame)
{
    // see if manta was hit
    if(this.hitTest(_root.shot) && !_root.mantaDead)
    {
        _root.shot._visible = false;
        _root.lastEnemyAlive = "manta";
        _root.mantaDead = true;
        _root.manta.gotoAndPlay("pow");
    }

    // see if the manta just finished playing explosion
    if(this._currentframe == 11 && _root.lastEnemyAlive
== "manta")
    {
        // bring spike to life
        _root.spikeDead = false;
        _root.spike._visible = true;
        _root.spike.gotoAndStop("start");
    }
```

```
// move the manta
if(_root.enemyDirection == "right")
{
    if(this._x < 450)
    {
        this._x = this._x + 10;
    }
    else
    {
        _root.enemyDirection = "left";
        this._x = this._x - 10;
    }
}
else
{
    if(this._x>100)
    {
        this._x = this._x - 10;
    }
    else
    {
        _root.enemyDirection = "right";
        this._x = this._x + 10;
    }
}
}
```

The Manta Ship Shot

```
// manta shot
onClipEvent(enterFrame)
{
    // see if it's appropriate for the manta to fire now
    if(!_root.mantaShotInAir && !_root.mantaDead)
    {
        this._x = _root.manta._x;
        this._y = _root.manta._y;
        this._visible = true;
        _root.mantaShotInAir = true;
    }
    else
    {
        // see if shot is off the screen
        if(this._y > 400)
        {
            this._visible = false;
            _root.mantaShotInAir = false;
```

```
        }
        else
        {
            this._y = this._y + 20;
        }
    }
}
```

The Spike Ship

```
// spike ship
onClipEvent(enterFrame)
{
    // see if spike was hit
    if(this.hitTest(_root.shot) && !_root.spikeDead)
    {
        _root.shot._visible = false;
        _root.spikeDead = true;
        _root.lastEnemyAlive = "spike";
        _root.spike.gotoAndPlay("pow");
    }

    // see if the spike just finished playing explosion
    if(this._currentframe > 10 && _root.lastEnemyAlive
== "spike")
    {
        // bring manta to life
        _root.mantaDead = false;
        _root.manta._visible = true;
        _root.manta.gotoAndStop("start");
    }

    // move the spike
    if(_root.spikeDirection == "right")
    {
        if(this._x<450)
        {
            this._x = this._x+10;
        } else {
            _root.spikeDirection = "left";
        }
    }
    else
    {
        if(this._x>100)
        {
            this._x = this._x-10;
```

```
        } else {
            _root.spikeDirection = "right";
        }
    }
}
```

The Spike Ship Shot

```
// spikeShot
onClipEvent(enterFrame)
{
    // see if it's appropriate for the spike to fire now
    if(!_root.spikeShotInAir && !_root.spikeDead)
    {
        this._x = _root.spike._x;
        this._y = _root.spike._y;
        this._visible = true;
        _root.spikeShotInAir = true;
    }
    else
    {
        // see if shot is off the screen
        if(this._y > 400)
        {
            this._visible = false;
            _root.spikeShotInAir = false;
        }
        else
        {
            this._y = this._y + 40;
        }
    }
}
```

Power Handling Movie Clips

By *power handling,* I mean

1. Making copies of movie clips (duplicateMovieClip)
2. Removing copies of movie clips (removeMovieClip)
3. Loading whole movies from another URL into your page (loadMovie)
4. Unloading them again (unloadMovie)

5. Attaching movies from the Library onto your playing movie clip, even if that attached movie wasn't originally in your movie (`attachMovie`)

This treatment of movies and movie clips can be useful for both artistic and functional reasons. Duplicating a movie clip can result in some fantastic patterns and designs, and being able to load a movie from another URL can increase the scope of what your Flash movie can do.

Background: Levels

The Flash Player (both as standalone and as something embedded in a Web page) organizes Flash movies into virtual layers called *levels*. The movie that opens the Flash player is automatically placed on level 0. Any other SWF movies that are loaded into that Flash player can be specified to load in level 0, replacing the original movie, or can be put into any other level above the original movie (level 1, 2, 198, etc.). Any movie that is loaded above the level 0 movie has a transparent stage, allowing you to see the movie below in any area that is not filled. Any time you load a movie on a level that is currently occupied by another movie, it is replaced by the newly loaded movie.

Duplicating Movie Clips

We'll start by duplicating a single movie clip when the user clicks the mouse, and we'll place it on another level.

1. Open *chapter3/duplicate1.fla* from the CD. The movie should look like Figure 3-9.
2. Just a circle with a blue-to-black radial gradient. If you look in edit symbol mode at the `mc_ball` animation by double-clicking the instance on the stage, the size of the ball also changes, along with the placement of the gradient, over 30 frames.
3. Click on the ball and open its Object Actions panel.
4. Enter this code:

```
onClipEvent(mouseUp)
{
    this.duplicateMovieClip("ball1", 1);
```

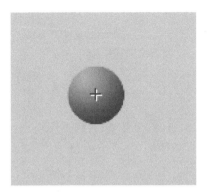

FIGURE 3–9 The blue ball

```
        _root.ball1._x = Math.random() * 500;
        _root.ball1._y = Math.random() * 400;
}
```

5. Test the movie.

ABOUT THE CODE

We're creating a duplicate of this movie clip instance; that is, the ball. It's just like copying and pasting the ball, only it happens while the movie is playing. The new movie clip must have a new name, which is *ball1*. We're also placing this `ball1` on level 1, just above level 0.

Then, we're randomly setting the x- and y-positions of the new ball. We're using `Math.random` to accomplish this. `Math.random` returns a value between 0 and 1, so to create a random number from 0 to 500, use the code above.

Note that the new movie clip starts playing at frame 1, not at whatever frame the original ball is playing in. All duplicated movie clips start playing at frame 1.

Notice also that if you press your mouse button twice, the ball1 movie clip disappears and then reappears in a new place. This will happen every time you try to place a movie clip on a level that already has a movie clip on it. That is, the new movie clip will replace the old one.

Now, let's say that we want to add a new ball every time the user clicks the mouse, so clicking three times will result in three new balls on the screen. To do this, we'll have to place each new ball on its own level. To keep track of which level to use, we'll create a new variable called `counter` and place it on the root level.

1. With *chapter3/duplicate1.fla* still open, go to the frame in the actions layer.
2. Open the Frame Actions panel.
3. Enter this code:

```
// initialize counter variable
counter = 1;
```

4. Click on the ball and make sure its Object Actions panel is open.
5. Enter this code:

```
onClipEvent (mouseUp)
{
    this.duplicateMovieClip("ball" + _root.counter,
_root.counter);
    setProperty("_root.ball" + _root.counter, _x,
Math.random() * 500);
    setProperty("_root.ball" + _root.counter, _y,
Math.random() * 400);
    _root.counter = _root.counter + 1;
}
```

6. Test the movie

ABOUT THE CODE

We're doing exactly what we did before, except that now we're using `_root.counter` both to name the instance of the ball and to place the new instance on its own level. Did you try it? You probably noticed something odd. The first time you clicked, one ball appeared. The second time you clicked, two new balls appeared. Click again, and four new balls arrive. Keep clicking, and the result is similar to Figure 3-10—each time you click, the number of balls doubles instead of appearing one at a time. What's going on?

When you duplicate a movie clip, you not only duplicate the image, you duplicate its object actions as well. The first time you clicked the mouse button, you created ball1, which

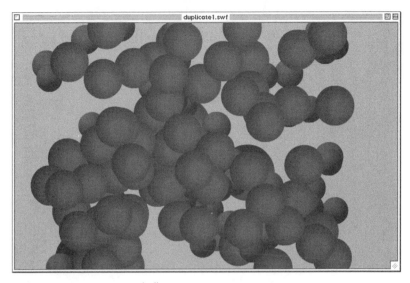

FɪGURE 3–10 Many, many balls

has the same code attached to it as ball does, so now there are two movie clips that are looking for the `mouseUp` event. Click the mouse, and both ball and ball1 run their code, and each creates a new ball of its own, so two balls appear: ball2 and ball3. Click the mouse again, and all four balls run their code and create four new balls.

You may have also noticed that we started using `set-Property` instead of simply setting the property as we did in the previous example. This is because we're dynamically creating the name of the object: `"ball"` + `_root.counter`. When you use a variable in the object's name, you have to use `setProperty`.

The lesson here is that an object's actions are duplicated along with the actual object when you use `duplicateMovieClip`. That's interesting, but how do we get our movie to produce only one ball at a time instead of the constant doubling?

1. Click on the ball and make sure the Object Actions panel is open.
2. Add this `if` statement:

```
onClipEvent(mouseUp)
{
    if(this._name == "ball")
    {
        this.duplicateMovieClip("ball" +
_root.counter, _root.counter);
        setProperty("_root.ball" + _root.counter,
_x, Math.random() * 500);
        setProperty("_root.ball" + _root.counter,
_y, Math.random() * 400);
        _root.counter = _root.counter + 1;
    }
}
```

3. Test the movie.

ABOUT THE CODE

We introduced a new property here, _name. This property is whatever you name a movie clip in your movie. Since there's only one movie clip with the name *ball* (all the others have a number at the end), no matter how many balls there are, only the code in one of them will ever get executed. Thus, only one ball will appear for every mouse click.

Removing Movie Clips

Flash also allows you to remove movie clips that have been brought into existence by duplicateMovieClip. All you need to know to remove a movie clip is its name. Here's some code that will start removing movie clips, so there are only 10 new movie clips in the movie at any one time.

1. Click on the ball and make sure the Object Actions panel is open.

2. Change the code to include this new if statement:

```
onClipEvent(mouseUp)
{
if(this._name == "ball")
    {
        this.duplicateMovieClip("ball" +
_root.counter, _root.counter);
        setProperty("_root.ball" + _root.counter,
_x, Math.random() * 500);
```

```
        setProperty("_root.ball" + _root.counter,
_y, Math.random() * 400);
        if(_root.counter > 10)
        {
            removeMovieClip("_root.ball" +
(_root.counter-10));
        }
        _root.counter = _root.counter + 1;
    }
}
```

3. Test the movie.

ABOUT THE CODE

We added a few lines that see if the value of `_root.counter` is greater than 10. If it is, then we remove the movie clip that has ball and whatever (`_root.counter – 10`) is. So, if `_root.counter` is 11, we remove ball1. If `_root.counter` is 27, we remove ball17.

The upshot of all this is that there will always be a maximum of 11 balls on the screen: the first one (ball) and 10 others.

Duplicating with Purpose

While the ball example demonstrates how to create a duplicate of a movie clip, it's not the most useful thing in the world. There are both artistic and functional reasons to use `duplicate-MovieClip`. Let's look at some artistic ones first, because you can create some beautiful images with some very simple code. We'll examine more functional reasons in Chapter 7, "Complex Scripting," when we cover inertia and elasticity.

1. Open *chapter2/spinner1.fla*.
2. We start with a single instance called `circle` on the stage. See Figure 3-11.
3. By creating a single frame action:

```
counter = 1
```

4. And then adding this code to the `circle` object:

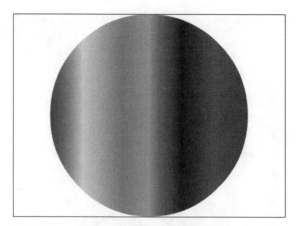

FIGURE 3–11 Initial symbol for *spinner1.fla*

```
onClipEvent(enterFrame)
{
    if(this._name == "circle" && _root.counter < 50)
    {
        this.duplicateMovieClip("circle"+
_root.counter, _root.counter);
        setProperty("_root.circle"+ _root.counter,
_rotation, _root.counter*2);
        setProperty("_root.circle" + _root.counter,
_xscale, 100-(2*_root.counter));
        setProperty("_root.circle" + _root.counter,
_yscale, 100-(2*_root.counter));

        _root.counter = _root.counter + 1;
    }
}
```

5. You get the result shown in Figure 3-12.

ABOUT THE CODE

We're creating a little loop, using `enterFrame` and an incrementing `_root.counter`, and each time the loop executes, another copy of `circle` is created, each one a little smaller and a little more rotated than the previous one.

Now, using even simpler code, let's create the image in Figure 3-13.

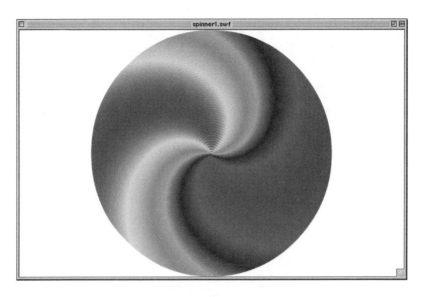

FIGURE 3–12 Final image once *spinner1.fla* has played

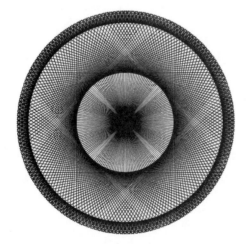

FIGURE 3–13 *spinner2.fla*, once movie has played

1. Open *chapter3/spinner2.fla*. This also has a single frame action of `counter = 1`.
2. Click on the square and enter this code into its Object Actions panel:

FIGURE 3–14 Pulsing thing

```
onClipEvent(enterFrame)
{
    if(this._name == "square" && _root.counter < 180)
    {
        this.duplicateMovieClip("square"+
_root.counter, _root.counter);
        setProperty("_root.square"+ _root.counter,
_rotation, _root.counter*2);

        _root.counter = _root.counter + 1;
    }
}
```

3. Test the movie. It runs slowly, but it's worth it.

There's nothing new in this code, so we won't bother dissecting it.

Now, let's create an animation that would be almost impossible to make without `duplicateMovieClip`. It's a little creepy, but pretty interesting. The final product looks like Figure 3-14.

1. Open *chapter3/whatisthatthing.fla*.
2. Open up the sphere symbol from the symbol list.
3. Notice that this movie clip is a simple circle with a gradient. There are two aspects that change during its shape tweens: its size shrinks and the tint changes. That's it.
4. Go back to the main scene.
5. Notice the ever-present frame action `counter = 1;`.

6. Click on the sphere (note its instance name is "sphere0", not "sphere") and enter the following code:

```
onClipEvent(enterFrame)
{
    if(this._name == "sphere0" && _root.counter <50)
    {

        this.duplicateMovieClip("sphere"+
_root.counter, _root.counter);

        // determine x-direction movement
        xOrig = getProperty("_root.sphere" +
(_root.counter-1), _x);
        xDiam = getProperty("_root.sphere" +
(_root.counter-1), _xscale);
        xRandom = Math.random()*(xDiam/5);
        xDirection = Math.random();
        if(xDirection < .5)
        {
            xRandom = xRandom * -1;
        }
        // determine y-direction movement
        yOrig = getProperty("_root.sphere" +
(_root.counter-1), _y);
        yDiam = getProperty("_root.sphere" +
(_root.counter-1), _yscale);
        yRandom = Math.random()*(yDiam/5);
        yDirection = Math.random();
        if(yDirection < .5)
        {
            yRandom = yRandom * -1;
        }

        // alter properties
        setProperty("_root.sphere" + _root.counter,
_x, xOrig + xRandom);
        setProperty("_root.sphere" + _root.counter,
_y, yOrig + yRandom);
        setProperty("_root.sphere" + _root.counter,
_xscale, 100-(_root.counter*2));
        setProperty("_root.sphere" + _root.counter,
_yscale, 100-(_root.counter*2));
```

```
        _root.counter = _root.counter + 1;
    }
}
```

7. Test the movie.

ABOUT THE CODE

What we're doing here is creating a duplicate of the first sphere and then moving it in a random direction, as well as shrinking it somewhat. Most of this code is concerned with determining the x- and y-positions of the newly duplicated clip, so let's go over that.

Our goal is to determine placement based on the size of the sphere—big spheres are moved further than little spheres. The final movie looks more organic that way. So first, we get the size and placement of the previous sphere by using the `get-Property` function, and place those values into the variables `xOrig` (for position) and `xDiam` (for size).

Second, we determine how far over the new sphere is going to move, by creating a number between 0 and the diameter divided by 5. That is, `Math.random` creates a random number between 0 and 1, which gives us a result between 0 and `xDiam/5`. Why 5? I liked how it looked. Feel free to try other numbers, and see what you think.

To add more randomness to where we place the just-duplicated sphere, we also decide which direction the sphere will move: positive or negative. We set `xDirection` to a random number between 0 and 1 (using `Math.random`). If `xRandom` is less than .5, we reverse the direction by –1. Otherwise, the pulsating thing would always trail down to the lower right, since the x and y positions would constantly increase.

Once we set how far the new sphere will move in the x and y directions, we start setting properties. First we set the position of the new sphere, which is just the position of the previous sphere modified somewhat. Second, we shrink the sphere by a factor based on `_root.counter`.

I encourage you to play with the numbers and the math on this example—you can come up with some pretty bizarre animations, and it'll help you learn the material more thoroughly as well.

Loading Movies

You can also load a movie from a completely different SWF file. If your movie is being played on the Web, the SWF file can be anywhere on your Web site, but it can't be outside your domain. This is so no one can steal your Flash movie and use it as their own (and it keeps you honest, too).

You can load a movie anywhere in your currently playing movie, and either have it replace your current movie, or just be there in addition to your current movie. We'll examine both ways (you can also load a movie into another movie clip, but we don't examine that method here).

1. Open *chapter3/duplicate2.fla*.
2. Click on the ball and open its Object Actions panel.
3. Enter the following code:

```
onClipEvent (mouseUp)
{
    if (this._name == "ball")
    {

        this.duplicateMovieClip("ball" +
_root.counter, _root.counter);
        setProperty("_root.ball" + _root.counter, _x,
Math.random() * 500);
        setProperty("_root.ball" + _root.counter, _y,
Math.random() * 400);
        if (_root.counter > 10)
        {
            removeMovieClip("_root.ball" +
(_root.counter-10));
        }

        if (_root.counter == 20)
        {
            loadMovie("whatisthatthing_done.swf",
1);
        }

        _root.counter = _root.counter + 1;
    }
}
```

4. Test the movie and click about 25 times. See Figure 3-15.

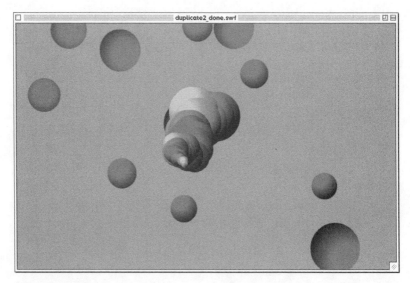

FIGURE 3–15 The pulsating thing in the middle of your movie

ABOUT THE CODE

We added the `if` statement that looks to see if the `_root.counter` is 20, and if so, that *pulsating thing* movie is loaded into level 1. The whole movie is loaded, along with all of its code, so it all executes at the same time *duplicate2.fla* movie is executing.

In order to replace our original movie with the loaded one, load the new movie into level 0 and replace

```
loadMovie("whatisthatthing_done.swf", 1);
```

with

```
loadMovie("whatisthatthing_done.swf", 0);
```

and see what happens after about 20 clicks. Notice all the balls from `duplicate2` disappear, and no amount of clicking will bring them back. Once that movie is replaced, it's gone.

Now let's look at unloading a movie.

1. Change

```
loadMovie("whatisthatthing_done.swf", 0);
```

   back to

```
loadMovie("whatisthatthing_done.swf", 1);
```

2. Add another `if` statement, like so:

```
onClipEvent(mouseUp)
{
    if(this._name == "ball")
    {

        this.duplicateMovieClip("ball" +
_root.counter, _root.counter);
        setProperty("_root.ball" + _root.counter,
_x,  Math.random() * 500);
        setProperty("_root.ball" + _root.counter,
_y,  Math.random() * 400);
        if(_root.counter > 10)
        {
            removeMovieClip("_root.ball" +
(_root.counter-10));
        }

        if(_root.counter == 20)
        {
            loadMovie("whatisthatthing_done.swf",
1);
        }
        else if(_root.counter == 25)
        {
            unloadMovie(_level1);
        }

        _root.counter = _root.counter + 1;
    }
}
```

3. Test the movie, and click until the gray thing disappears.

ABOUT THE CODE

We added the `else if` section of code. If `_root.counter` gets to 25, we then remove whatever movie clip or movie that happens to be at level 1. Notice we used a different way to reference a level this time: `_level N`, where `N` is the level. We could have used plain ol' 1, but both ways work.

If, for some crazy reason, you want to completely blow away all movies playing, change:

```
unloadMovie(_level1);
```

to

```
unloadMovie(_root);
```

and watch everything go away.

That's about it for unloading movies. Next, we'll look at attaching movies.

Attaching Movie Clips

Flash allows you to attach movie clips to other movie clips, which establishes something of a parent/child relationship between the two clips. For example, if you attach movie clip B to movie clip A, A is the parent movie clip. Whatever you do to A, the same action automatically happens to B. If you move A, B comes along for the ride. If you rotate A, B rotates as well.

This linking of properties from parent to child is known as *inheritance*. When objects (movie clips, in this case) are children of other objects, the children inherit the properties of their parents—properties like position, rotation, and scaling.

You can even attach another movie clip C to B. In this case, what you do to C only happens to C. What you do to B, happens to B and C. What you do to A, happens to both B and C.

To illustrate this, we'll build ourselves a monster. We'll start with the basic body, shown in Figure 3-16.

Then, we'll add legs, a head, some bolts, a hand, and an arm, shown in Figure 3-17. Each is its own movie clip, but they will all be children to the parent that is the body.

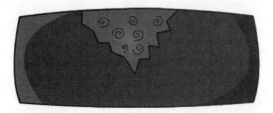

FIGURE 3–16 The body we'll start with is our parent movie clip

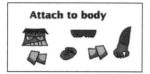

FIGURE 3–17 The movie clips we'll add to the body

FIGURE 3–18 The movie clips we'll add to the legs

Then, we'll attach some feet to the legs, shown in Figure 3-18. These will both be children to the parent movie clip of the legs, which in turn is a child to the body movie clip.

We'll make the body, and only the body, draggable. As we add movie clips to the body, those will be draggable along with the body.

The function we'll use is called `attachMovie`. Its syntax is

```
someMovieClip.attachMovie( nameOfInstance, newName, depth)
```

1. Open *chapter3/frank1.fla*. It should look like Figure 3-19.
2. Note that this movie uses a mask layer over the body layer. That doesn't affect our actions, but we haven't used one yet, so you should be aware of it.
3. Click on the large `body` object (named *body* in the Instance panel).
4. Enter the following code:

```
onClipEvent (mouseDown)
{
    if((_root._xmouse > 20) &&
(_root._xmouse < 588) &&
        (_root._ymouse > 200) &&
(_root._ymouse < 592))
    {
        startDrag(this, false, 20, 200, 588, 592);
    }
}
```

FIGURE 3-19 Opening shot of *Frank* movie

```
onClipEvent (mouseUp)
{
    stopDrag();
}
```

5. Test the movie.

ABOUT THE CODE

The chunk of code allows dragging of the body object when the user presses the mouse button down while they're in the main box of the movie. When the mouse button is released, dragging is turned off.

Now let's start adding some movies.

1. In order for a movie clip to be attached to another, it has to be linked and named in a special way. We'll link the "head" symbol, and then enter some code.
2. Open the Library.
3. Click on the "head" symbol.
4. Under the Options menu, go to Linkage….
5. Click Export this symbol.
6. In the Identifier text field, enter "head".
7. Click OK.
8. Back in the Flash movie, click on the tiny head.
9. Enter this code:

```
onClipEvent(mouseDown)
{
    // see if user clicked on this image
    bounds = this.getBounds(_root);

    // see if the user clicked inside the head
    if((_root._xmouse <= bounds.xMax) &&
(_root._xmouse >= bounds.xMin) &&
        (_root._ymouse <= bounds.yMax) &&
(_root._ymouse >= bounds.yMin))
    {
        //attach the head
        _root.body.attachMovie("head","head", 15);
    }
}
```

10. Test the movie. Click on the head, and then drag the body around (see Figure 3-20).

ABOUT THE CODE

If the user clicks on the screen within the bounds of the small head, then the "head" symbol in the library is called and attached to the body object. The attached movie clip is also called *head*, and it's placed on level 15. The center of the head is placed directly on top of the center of the body. However, this isn't exactly the look we were after. We need to change the position of the head relative to the body. Fortunately, this isn't difficult.

FIGURE 3–20 The head on top of the body

1. Below the line of code with `attachMovie`, enter:

```
//position the head
_root.body.head._y = -160;
```

2. Test the movie.

ABOUT THE CODE

Notice that we can't access `head` directly from `_root`, since head is a child of `body`, just like `body` is a child of `_root`. So, we have to tell Flash to start looking in `_root`, then to look in `body`, and then to look at `head`. Also, the y-position of the head (-160) is not relative to `_root`. Otherwise, the head would've been positioned off the screen. The positioning of the head is relative to the center of the `body` object. As far as the head is concerned, the `body` object is its whole universe. The head object doesn't know where on the main stage it is, because, as far as the `head` object is concerned, the `body` object *is* the main stage. So, in order to position a child of a movie clip, you have to position it in relation to its parent.

We're also placing the head on level 15, which is pretty far up. We don't need to put it this far, but we will just to make the

FIGURE 3–21 The big nasty hand

example more obvious. We'll be placing the bolts below the head, so they'll both be on layers underneath the head.

ATTACHING THE HAND

Let's attach the monster's hand, shown in Figure 3-21.

Remember that we first have to link the hand symbol. Then we can attach it.

1. Open the Library, if it isn't already open.
2. Click on the "hand" symbol.
3. Choose Linkage... from the Options menu.
4. Choose Export this symbol.
5. Enter "hand" for Identifier.
6. Click OK.
7. Back in your Flash movie, click on the hand and open its Object Actions panel.
8. Enter the following code:

```
onClipEvent(mouseDown)
{
    // see if user clicked on this image
    bounds = this.getBounds(_root);


    // see if the user clicked inside the hand
    if((_root._xmouse <= bounds.xMax) &&
(_root._xmouse >= bounds.xMin) &&
        (_root._ymouse <= bounds.yMax) &&
(_root._ymouse >= bounds.yMin))
    {
        //attach the hand
        _root.body.attachMovie("hand","hand", 3);
```

```
        //position the hand
        _root.body.hand._y = -96;
        _root.body.hand._x = 207;
        _root.body.hand._rotation = -22;
    }
}
```

9. Test the movie. Click on the head and the hand, and drag everything around.

ABOUT THE CODE

This hunk of code is almost identical to the code for the head. The only differences are (1) we're placing the child movie clip on level 3 instead of 15, (2) the x- and y-positions are different, and (3) we added a change in rotation. For the rotation, notice that only the hand gets rotated, not the whole body.

Let's do all the other pieces that attach to the body now, which are the arm, the two bolts, and the pants. We'll do the feet and the fading later.

Remember to link all the symbols! Here are the identifiers you should use:

_ right bolt ➡ "rightBolt"
_ left bolt ➡ "leftBolt"
_ left arm ➡ "arm"
_ pants ➡ "legs"

Once that's done, go ahead and enter the chunks of code. Figures 3-22, 3-23, 3-24, and 3-25 illustrate the right bolt, left bolt, left arm, and pants, respectively.

Right Bolt

```
onClipEvent(mouseDown)
{
    // see if user clicked on this image
    bounds = this.getBounds(_root);
```

FIGURE 3–22 The right bolt

```
    // see if the user clicked inside the rightBolt
    if((_root._xmouse <= bounds.xMax) &&
(_root._xmouse >= bounds.xMin) &&
        (_root._ymouse <= bounds.yMax) &&
(_root._ymouse >= bounds.yMin))
    {
        //attach the rightBolt
        _root.body.attachMovie("rightBolt","rightBolt",
14);

        //position the rightBolt
        _root.body.rightBolt._x = 100;
        _root.body.rightBolt._y = -128;
    }
}
```

Left Bolt

```
onClipEvent(mouseDown)
{
    // see if user clicked on this image
    bounds = this.getBounds(_root);

    // see if the user clicked inside the leftBolt
    if((_root._xmouse <= bounds.xMax) &&
(_root._xmouse >= bounds.xMin) &&
        (_root._ymouse <= bounds.yMax) &&
(_root._ymouse >= bounds.yMin))
    {
        //attach the leftBolt
        _root.body.attachMovie("leftBolt","leftBolt",
13);

        //position the leftBolt
        _root.body.leftBolt._x = -94;
        _root.body.leftBolt._y = -121;
    }
}
```

FIGURE 3–23 The left bolt

Left Arm

```
onClipEvent(mouseDown)
{
    // see if user clicked on this image
    bounds = this.getBounds(_root);

    // see if the user clicked inside the arm
    if((_root._xmouse <= bounds.xMax) &&
(_root._xmouse >= bounds.xMin) &&
        (_root._ymouse <= bounds.yMax) &&
(_root._ymouse >= bounds.yMin))
    {
        //attach the arm
        _root.body.attachMovie("arm","arm", 6);

        //position the arm
        _root.body.arm._y = -17;
        _root.body.arm._x = -191;
    }
}
```

FIGURE 3–24 The left arm

Pants

```
onClipEvent(mouseDown)
{
    // see if user clicked on this image
    bounds = this.getBounds(_root);

    // see if the user clicked inside the legs
    if((_root._xmouse <= bounds.xMax) &&
(_root._xmouse >= bounds.xMin) &&
        (_root._ymouse <= bounds.yMax) &&
(_root._ymouse >= bounds.yMin))
```

FIGURE 3–25 The pants

```
        {
                //attach the legs
                _root.body.attachMovie("legs","legs", 10);

                //position the legs
                _root.body.legs._y = 87;
        }
}
```

Did you test the movie and try to attach all the body parts?

ATTACHING THE FEET

When we attach feet to our monster, they'll attach to the legs object, not to the body. This means several things will be true: (1) the feet will appear above the legs, no matter what we set the levels to, and (2) whatever we do to the legs object will also happen to the feet object.

So, when we do something to the body object, it will happen to the legs, since the legs are attached to the body. And if anything happens to the legs, it will happen to the feet, since the feet will be attached to the legs. If we set the alpha value of the body to be 50, both the legs and the feet will immediately have an alpha value of 50 as well.

Let's attach the left foot.

1. Open the Library, if it isn't already open.
2. Click on the mc_foot_left symbol.
3. Choose Linkage… from the Options menu.
4. Choose Export this symbol.
5. Enter "leftFoot" as the Identifier.
6. Click OK.
7. Back in your Flash movie, click on the small left foot and open its Object Actions panel. See Figure 3-26.

FIGURE 3–26 The left foot

8. Enter the following code:

```
onClipEvent(mouseDown)
{
        // see if user clicked on this image
        bounds = this.getBounds(_root);

        // see if the user clicked inside the leftFoot
        if((_root._xmouse <= bounds.xMax) &&
(_root._xmouse >= bounds.xMin) &&
            (_root._ymouse <= bounds.yMax) &&
(_root._ymouse >= bounds.yMin))
        {
            //attach the leftFoot
        _root.body.legs.attachMovie("leftFoot","leftFoot",
          3);

            //position the leftFoot
            _root.body.legs.leftFoot._x = -68;
            _root.body.legs.leftFoot._y = 83;
        }
}
```

9. Test the movie. Note that you have to add the legs before you add the left foot. Until you add the legs, the foot has nothing to attach to, so nothing happens. It's a little surprising no error message appears, but that's how Flash 5 works.

ABOUT THE CODE

The only thing that's different here is how we access this movie clip. That is, instead of _root.body.leftFoot, it's _root.body.legs.leftFoot. It's not a huge coding difference, but it's a significant one. When we're positioning the left

FIGURE 3–27 The right foot

foot, we're positioning it relative to the legs object, not to the body object. To the left foot, the legs object is the end of the universe, so all positioning occurs relative to that object.

Adding the right foot is a nearly identical process.

1. Open the Library, if it isn't already open.
2. Click on the `mc_foot_right` symbol.
3. Choose Linkage… from the Options menu.
4. Choose Export this symbol.
5. Enter `"rightFoot"` as the Identifier.
6. Click OK.
7. Back in your Flash movie, click on the small right foot and open its Object Actions panel. See Figure 3-27.
8. Enter the following code:

```
onClipEvent(mouseDown)
{
    // see if user clicked on this image
    bounds = this.getBounds(_root);

    // see if the user clicked inside the rightFoot
    if((_root._xmouse <= bounds.xMax) &&
(_root._xmouse >= bounds.xMin) &&
        (_root._ymouse <= bounds.yMax) &&
(_root._ymouse >= bounds.yMin))
    {
        //attach the rightFoot
    _root.body.legs.attachMovie("rightFoot","rightFoot",
      4);

        //position the rightFoot
        _root.body.legs.rightFoot._x = 102;
        _root.body.legs.rightFoot._y = 86;
    }
}
```

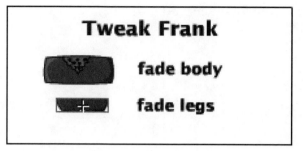

FIGURE 3–28 The Tweak Frank box

9. Test the movie.

ABOUT THE CODE

There's nothing new here that you didn't see with the left foot.

Congrats! We've attached all the movies we're planning on attaching for this example. We're not done, though. We're going to add some code that alters the alpha settings for both the pants and the legs, and check out what happens. This will give you a more intuitive feel for what happens when movies (or, more precisely, children of other movie clip objects) are attached to each other.

First, we'll make the small body image in the "Tweak Frank" box (see Figure 3-28) act like a button that toggles the alpha setting of the main body object between 30 and 100. Then, we'll make the pants image in the same box do the same thing, but just to the `legs` object.

We'll start by creating a few global variables to keep track of what state the fading is in.

1. Click on the frame in the actions layer, and open the Frame Actions panel.

2. Enter the following code:

```
bodyFade = false;
legsFade = false;
```

3. Click on the small body image and open its Object Actions panel.

4. Enter the following code:

```
onClipEvent(mouseDown)
{
    // see if user clicked on this image
    bounds = this.getBounds(_root);

    // see if the user clicked inside the body
    if((_root._xmouse <= bounds.xMax) &&
        (_root._xmouse >= bounds.xMin) &&
        (_root._ymouse <= bounds.yMax) &&
        (_root._ymouse >= bounds.yMin))
    {
        // tweak body
        if(_root.bodyFade)
        {
            _root.body._alpha = 100;
            _root.bodyFade = false;
        }
        else
        {
            _root.body._alpha = 30;
            _root.bodyFade = true;
        }
    }
}
```

5. Test the movie.

ABOUT THE CODE

This code doesn't introduce any new concepts. Clicking on the little body causes the code to check the value of _root.body-Fade. If it's true, then the body object is set to full opacity, and _root.bodyFade becomes false. If _root.bodyFade is already false (its default state), the body object is made semi-transparent, and _root.bodyFade becomes true.

The thing to notice is that if you make the body semi-transparent and then attach all of its pieces, those pieces are automatically semitransparent. The attached movie clips immediately inherit all of the parent's properties, no matter when those properties are set.

Now let's do a similar job on the pants in the Tweak Frank box.

1. Click on the pants in the Tweak Frank box and open its Object Actions panel.
2. Enter the following code:

```
onClipEvent(mouseDown)
{
    // see if user clicked on this image
    bounds = this.getBounds(_root);

    // see if the user clicked inside the body
    if((_root._xmouse <= bounds.xMax) &&
        (_root._xmouse >= bounds.xMin) &&
        (_root._ymouse <= bounds.yMax) &&
        (_root._ymouse >= bounds.yMin))
    {
        // tweak legs
        if(_root.legsFade)
        {
            _root.body.legs._alpha = 100;
            _root.legsFade = false;
        }
        else
        {
            _root.body.legs._alpha = 30;
            _root.legsFade = true;
        }
    }
}
```

3. Test the movie. Experiment with fading the legs, then the body, and attaching pieces.

ABOUT THE CODE

As before, this chunk of code doesn't do anything ground-breaking, but experimenting while you're testing the movie should prove fruitful. Notice especially what happens when both the legs and the body are faded: The legs are closer to transparency than the rest of the body. How is this possible when the body object is set to have an alpha of 30? Why do the legs seem to have a lower setting?

Its because the alpha setting is a percentage: 100 percent is fully opaque, 0 percent is completely transparent. Thus, the legs are set to an alpha setting of 30 percent by clicking on the little legs icon, so both the feet and the legs are at 30 percent opacity. Then fade the body. Since the legs are a part of the body, their opacity becomes 30 percent of what it already is, resulting in an opacity of 9 percent.

This may seem a little confusing, but keep pressing buttons, and examining it. Seeing it in action is always helpful.

ALL THE CODE

Here's the code for every object and frame in this movie. Remember, you have to export the symbols that are getting attached via the Linkage…item in the Library's Options menu.

Frame Action

```
bodyFade = false;
legsFade = false;
```

Big Body Object

```
onClipEvent (mouseDown)
{
    if((_root._xmouse > 20) &&
        (_root._xmouse < 588) &&
        (_root._ymouse > 200) &&
        (_root._ymouse < 592))
    {
        startDrag(this, false, 20, 200, 588, 592);
    }
}

onClipEvent (mouseUp)
{
    stopDrag();
}
```

Head

```
onClipEvent (mouseDown)
{
    // see if user clicked on this image
    bounds = this.getBounds(_root);

    // see if the user clicked inside the head
    if((_root._xmouse <= bounds.xMax) &&
        (_root._xmouse >= bounds.xMin) &&
        (_root._ymouse <= bounds.yMax) &&
        (_root._ymouse >= bounds.yMin))
```

```
    {
        //attach the head
        _root.body.attachMovie("head","head", 15);

        //position the head
        _root.body.head._y = -160;
    }
}
```

Right Bolt

```
onClipEvent(mouseDown)
{
    // see if user clicked on this image
    bounds = this.getBounds(_root);

    // see if the user clicked inside the rightBolt
    if((_root._xmouse <= bounds.xMax) &&
        (_root._xmouse >= bounds.xMin) &&
        (_root._ymouse <= bounds.yMax) &&
        (_root._ymouse >= bounds.yMin))
    {
        //attach the rightBolt
      _root.body.attachMovie("rightBolt","rightBolt",
        14);

        //position the rightBolt
        _root.body.rightBolt._x = 100;
        _root.body.rightBolt._y = -128;
    }
}
```

Left Bolt

```
onClipEvent(mouseDown)
{
    // see if user clicked on this image
    bounds = this.getBounds(_root);

    // see if the user clicked inside the leftBolt
    if((_root._xmouse <= bounds.xMax) &&
        (_root._xmouse >= bounds.xMin) &&
        (_root._ymouse <= bounds.yMax) &&
        (_root._ymouse >= bounds.yMin))
    {
        //attach the leftBolt
        _root.body.attachMovie("leftBolt","leftBolt",
         13);
```

```
            //position the leftBolt
            _root.body.leftBolt._x = -94;
            _root.body.leftBolt._y = -121;
        }
    }
```

Left Arm

```
onClipEvent(mouseDown)
{
    // see if user clicked on this image
    bounds = this.getBounds(_root);

    // see if the user clicked inside the arm
    if((_root._xmouse <= bounds.xMax) &&
        (_root._xmouse >= bounds.xMin) &&
        (_root._ymouse <= bounds.yMax) &&
        (_root._ymouse >= bounds.yMin))
    {
        //attach the arm
        _root.body.attachMovie("arm","arm", 6);

        //position the arm
        _root.body.arm._y = -17;
        _root.body.arm._x = -191;
    }
}
```

Pants

```
onClipEvent(mouseDown)
{
    // see if user clicked on this image
    bounds = this.getBounds(_root);

    // see if the user clicked inside the legs
    if((_root._xmouse <= bounds.xMax) &&
        (_root._xmouse >= bounds.xMin) &&
        (_root._ymouse <= bounds.yMax) &&
        (_root._ymouse >= bounds.yMin))
    {
        //attach the legs
        _root.body.attachMovie("legs","legs", 10);

        //position the legs
        _root.body.legs._y = 87;
    }
}
```

Left Foot

```
onClipEvent(mouseDown)
{
    // see if user clicked on this image
    bounds = this.getBounds(_root);

    // see if the user clicked inside the leftFoot
    if((_root._xmouse <= bounds.xMax) &&
        (_root._xmouse >= bounds.xMin) &&
        (_root._ymouse <= bounds.yMax) &&
        (_root._ymouse >= bounds.yMin))
    {
        //attach the leftFoot
_root.body.legs.attachMovie("leftFoot","leftFoot", 3);

        //position the leftFoot
        _root.body.legs.leftFoot._x = -68;
        _root.body.legs.leftFoot._y = 83;
    }
}
```

Right Foot

```
onClipEvent(mouseDown)
{
    // see if user clicked on this image
    bounds = this.getBounds(_root);

    // see if the user clicked inside the rightFoot
    if((_root._xmouse <= bounds.xMax) &&
        (_root._xmouse >= bounds.xMin) &&
        (_root._ymouse <= bounds.yMax) &&
        (_root._ymouse >= bounds.yMin))
    {
        //attach the rightFoot
_root.body.legs.attachMovie("rightFoot","rightFoot",
  4);

        //position the rightFoot
        _root.body.legs.rightFoot._x = 102;
        _root.body.legs.rightFoot._y = 86;
    }
}
```

Body—Tweak Box

```
onClipEvent(mouseDown)
{
    // see if user clicked on this image
    bounds = this.getBounds(_root);

    // see if the user clicked inside the body
    if((_root._xmouse <= bounds.xMax) &&
        (_root._xmouse >= bounds.xMin) &&
        (_root._ymouse <= bounds.yMax) &&
        (_root._ymouse >= bounds.yMin))
    {
        // tweak body
        if(_root.bodyFade)
        {
            _root.body._alpha = 100;
            _root.bodyFade = false;
        }
        else
        {
            _root.body._alpha = 30;
            _root.bodyFade = true;
        }
    }
}
```

Pants—Tweak Box

```
onClipEvent(mouseDown)
{
    // see if user clicked on this image
    bounds = this.getBounds(_root);

    // see if the user clicked inside the legs
    if((_root._xmouse <= bounds.xMax) &&
        (_root._xmouse >= bounds.xMin) &&
        (_root._ymouse <= bounds.yMax) &&
        (_root._ymouse >= bounds.yMin))
    {
        // tweak legs
        if(_root.legsFade)
        {
            _root.body.legs._alpha = 100;
            _root.legsFade = false;
        }
        else
        {
            _root.body.legs._alpha = 30;
```

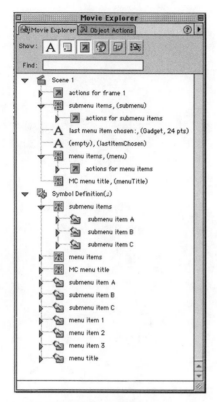

FIGURE 3-29 The Movie Explorer

```
                    _root.legsFade = true;
            }
        }
}
```

Movie Explorer

You may have noticed an extra tab whenever you opened the Actions panels: Movie Explorer. This is a great feature of Flash, even though for newbies, it may take a little getting used to.

1. Open *chapter3/menu_done.fla*. It'll look something (but not exactly) like Figure 3-29.

The Movie Explorer dissects your movie into all of its different parts: frames, scenes, layers, sounds, actions, symbols,

FIGURE 3–30 Movie Explorer filtering buttons

text, and so on, and it places all of these parts in a hierarchy, with Scenes and the Library (or Symbol Definition[s]) reigning supreme. Fortunately, you don't have to wade through all of those parts each time you look at Movie Explorer—you can filter out different aspects of your movie using the Filtering buttons, shown in Figure 3-30.

Selecting and deselecting these buttons determines what Movie Explorer shows you. The five buttons we'll be looking at are:

_ Show Text (see Figure 3-31)
_ Show Buttons, Movie Clips and Graphics (see Figure 3-32)
_ Show ActionScripts (see Figure 3-33)
_ Show Video, Sounds and Bitmaps (see Figure 3-34)
_ Show Frames and Layers (see Figure 3-35)

FIGURE 3–31 Show Text button

FIGURE 3–32 Show Buttons, Movie Clips and Graphics button

FIGURE 3–33 Show ActionScripts button

FIGURE 3–34 Show Video, Sounds, and Bitmaps button

FIGURE 3-35 Show Frames and Layers button

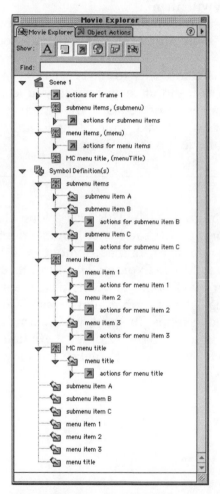

FIGURE 3-36 Movie Explorer with Show buttons, Movie Clips and Buttons button, and Show ActionScripts button selected

Select the Show buttons, Movie Clips and Buttons button, and the Show ActionScripts button. Deselect all others. Your Movie Explorer should now look like Figure 3-36.

Notice the structure of this movie. There are seven buttons, and each button is also found inside a movie clip. The button instances inside those movie clips (you can tell they're instances because they have a little orange dot on them) all have actions associated with them.

Scene 1 has all of those movie clips in it (there are only three of them), and each of those instances has actions associated with it.

This movie has some complexity to it, yet see how easy we were able to dissect it? If it didn't seem easy to you, consider how long it would've taken to understand the structure without Movie Explorer. It would take much longer, and you'd never be sure you actually found everything.

Conclusion

Stand up and take a biiiiiig stretch. This was a long chapter, and we covered a lot of ground. You honed your ActionScript skills, learned to duplicate, load, unload, remove, and attach movie clips, and explored Movie Explorer. Heady stuff.

In the next chapter, we'll look at a whole new series of ActionScript commands—the ones that allow Flash 5 to communicate with back-end systems. In short, we'll learn how to drive Flash movies from a database. It's pretty exciting stuff. Oh, and Smart Clips, too—a cool way to make your movie and ActionScripts more modular.

Serious Interactivity

Using ActionScript to affect what's going on inside the Flash player gives you an impressive number of ways your movies can respond to user interaction. However, almost every Web site these days of any size or usefulness has a database backend, and the site's Web pages are generated dynamically.

FIGURE 4–1 The arrow button

If Flash is to have any future as a Web interface, it has to be able to send and receive data from such backend systems. Fortunately, the folks at Macromedia realized this and built that functionality into Flash. In this chapter, we'll cover this functionality, which allows Flash to act as middleware in some ways, like PHP and Cold Fusion, but it still can't connect directly to a database. We'll cover Flash's use of XML in the next chapter.

Linking to the Outside World

In your career as a Flash wizard, you'll probably want to link to other Web pages at some point. This is pretty easy to do.

1. Open *chapter4/linking1.fla*.
2. Click on the arrow-in-a-circle button, shown in Figure 4-1, and open its Object Actions panel.
3. Enter this code:

```
on(release)
{
    getURL("linking_page1.html")
}
```

4. File ➡ Publish.
5. Copy *chapter4/linking_page1.html* from the CD to wherever your exported Flash file is.
6. Open the resulting HTML file, *linking1.html,* in your browser of choice and click on the button.

ABOUT THE CODE

As you may have guessed, the `getURL` action acts like the HREF of an anchor tag. Pressing the button will take the browser to whatever URL you specify.

You can also open a new browser window using `getURL`. You can add a target to the `getURL` action.

1. Change the code to:

```
on(release)
{
    getURL("linking_page1.html", "_blank");
}
```

2. Save the file, publish it, and test the page in a browser. When you click on the button, a new browser window appears, and the page loads in that window.

ABOUT THE CODE

If you add a second attribute to the `getURL` action, Flash sees that as the same as the `target` attribute of an anchor tag. That is,

```
getURL("linking_page1.html", "_blank")
```

is the same as

```
<a href="linking_page1.html" target="_blank">
```

The `target` can be the name of a window, or one of several reserved words:

- `_blank` opens a new window.
- `_self` opens the new page in the current window.
- `_top` opens the page in the top-level frame in the current window. In other words, it removes all the frames and fills the browser with the new page.
- `_parent` opens the page in next higher-level frame in the current window.

You can also use `getURL` to send variables that exist in your Flash file. This can be useful if you're trying to update a database with data that the user just entered, or with what they're doing (like adding items to their shopping cart). You can send them via `post` or `get` methods. Let's try it.

1. Open *chapter4/linking1.fla*, if it isn't already open.
2. Click on the frame in the actions layer, and open the Frame Actions panel.
3. Enter the following code:

```
shirt = "red";
```

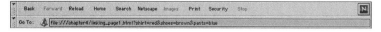

FIGURE 4-2 Screenshot of browser location bar

4. Click on the button and open its Object Actions panel.
5. Change the code to:

```
on(release)
{
    pants = "blue";
    getURL("linking_page1.html", "_blank", "get");
}
```

6. Save and publish the file. Open the page in a browser, click on the button, and notice the URL. As shown in Figure 4-2, the URL should end with:

```
linking_page1.html?shirt=red&pants=blue
```

ABOUT THE CODE

The third attribute in the `getURL` action determines whether any existing variables are sent via the `get` method (in the URL) or the `post` method (in a separate HTTP header). Notice that the variables are those attached to the object (the button) and global variables. Variables attached to other movie clips are not sent. For example, if we had another movie clip in the movie that contained a variable called `"shoes"`, that variable would not be sent by the button's `getURL` action.

Flash will always view the second attribute as a target assignment. That is, if your code is

```
getURL("linking_page1.html", "get")
```

Flash will look for a browser window called `"get"`. If Flash doesn't find one, it will open a new browser window. And since Flash thought `"get"` was the name of a browser window, it won't try to send any variables.

If you want to send variables and stay in the same browser window, use this code:

```
getURL("linking_page1.html", "_self", "get")
```

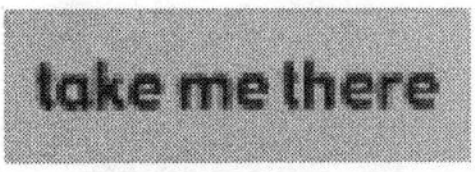

lake me there

FIGURE 4–3 Box with button

As an alternative, you can also replace _self with just two quotation marks:

```
getURL("linking_page1.html", "", "get")
```

I recommend using _self, because when you read the code later, it's easier to tell what what's going on. Doing what you can to use the code itself to indicate what it's doing is known as *self-documenting code*. It's a good thing. Not a replacement for real documentation, but it's still a good thing.

Instead of linking to an HMTL page, you can send variables to a PHP or Cold Fusion page:

```
getURL("validate_form.php", "_self", "post")
```

or

```
getURL("update_resume.cfm", "_self", "post")
```

Transparent Buttons

In the Flash file *linking1.fla,* did you notice the text with the grey box over it? It's shown in Figure 4-3 (if you open the actual file on your computer, the box is turquoise).

The text is plain ol' text—nothing new there. The turquoise box may be new to you, though. It's a transparent button, and it can be a handy tool. Let's look more closely at this button.

1. Open the file *linking1.fla,* if it isn't open.
2. Open the Library and double-click the transparent symbol.
3. Notice there's nothing there. There are no keyframes anywhere except in the hit frame, as you can see in Figure 4-4.

This button is invisible in the movie the user sees, but it works exactly like its more visible brethren. Fortunately, Flash colors these buttons turquoise automatically. Otherwise, they'd be a mite hard to find once you've placed them on your stage.

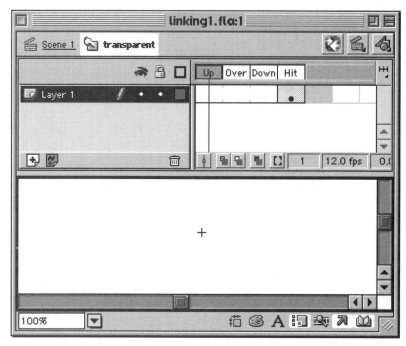

FIGURE 4-4 The frames and symbol of a transparent button

But make sure you don't have simple buttons enabled in the control menu, or you won't be able to see the button at all!

WHY A TRANSPARENT BUTTON?

A transparent button can be placed over anything: text, parts of a movie clip, and so on. It can make some functionality much easier to implement. An example would be to place a few buttons over selected words in a paragraph of text. Those buttons could then act as links. That way, you can change the text as much as you want and not have to create separate text buttons for the words that are links. You can also have a single, invisible button symbol that can be used over and over simply by changing the scale and size once it's on the stage.

We'll be seeing some more examples in Chapter 7, "Complex Scripting."

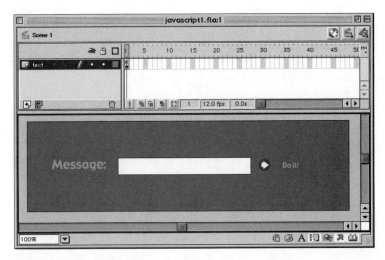

FIGURE 4–5 *javascript1.fla*

Calling JavaScript Using getURL

One of the fortunate uses of `getURL` is that it can call Java-Script functions that are on the same page that contains the Flash movie. Again, the syntax is similar to HTML's HREF attribute in the anchor tag.

1. Open the file *chapter4/javascript1.fla* (see Figure 4-5).
2. Note the name of the input text is `"userMessage"`. Remember that text can be static text, dynamic text, or input text.
3. Click on the arrow button and open its Object Actions panel.
4. Enter the following code:

```
on(release)
{
    url = "javascript:showAlert('" +
_root.userMessage + "')";
    getURL(url);
}
```

5. Export the movie to create an SWF file.
6. Open a text editor, and load *chapter4/javascript1.html*.

7. Notice the JavaScript in this file:

```
function showAlert(message)
{
    alert(message);
}
```

8. Open a browser and load *chapter4/javascript1.swf*.
9. Enter some text and press the arrow button.
10. Voilà! The text you type in a Flash movie appears in a JavaScript alert box.

ABOUT THE CODE

If you've written some JavaScript before, this technique will look familiar to you—it's a common way for links to call Java-Script functions instead of other Web pages. If you're not familiar with JavaScript, see the note for the world's shortest JavaScript tutorial.

> **NOTE** JavaScript is a computer language that is placed inside an HMTL document. Despite the name, it has absolutely nothing to do with Java. When you place some JavaScript inside an HTML document, that script is run when the Web page loads in the user's browser. JavaScript can do things like image rollovers, form validation, and fancy DHTML. Like ActionScript, it can respond to user events. There are about a million books available on JavaScript (including one or two by yours truly), so if you're interested, opportunities to learn abound.

Something you should know: calling non-user-defined functions this way is not recommended. For example, the code below would presumably have the same effect of the user pressing the Back button on the browser.

```
getURL("javascript:history.go(-1)");
```

However, in practice, this doesn't always work—some-times you'll have to click a button twice to make getURL do what you want it to do. It'll work more reliably if you create a function in your HTML page and place the command there. For example, placing this in your Flash file:

```
getURL("javascript:back()");
```

and this in your HTML page:

```
function back()
{
    history.go(-1);
}
```

will give you the result you want every time. Hint: sometimes, try setting the load order to "top down" in File ➡ Publish Settings. It's a solution that shouldn't make a difference, but sometimes it does.

Receiving Data

Flash 5 also has the ability to pull data from other pages. This data can be dynamic or static. Your Flash movie can pull data from these pages at any point in your movie, and any object in the movie can pull the data. You can access data using the `loadVariables` function.

The good news (great news, if you're a backend programmer) is that the `loadVariables` function can also send variables to a page. That is, the Flash movie can send data to a script, which can access a database, interact with a Java servlet (or anything), and then send back any relevant data to the Flash movie, which can then update its display to show the user the new, updated information. This is absolutely huge in importance, and we'll go over the details of how it works in this section.

First, let's start off with a simple example of pulling data from a text file. Say we have a Web site whose home page contains a new quote every day. The quote lives on a separate text file, and it's up to us to get it.

1. Open the text file *chapter4/quotes.txt*. Note that it has only one line:

```
quote=hi+there!
```

2. Open the file *chapter4/quotes1.fla.*
3. Note that there are two elements in this movie: some static text and some dynamic text. The static text is the blue Quote of the Day, shown in Figure 4-6.

FIGURE 4–6 Quote of the Day

The dynamic text is a large, multiline block of text named `"quote"`, shown in Figure 4-7.

4. Click in the frame in the actions layer and open its Frame Actions panel.

5. Enter the following code:

```
loadVariables("quotes.txt", _root)
```

6. Test the movie. "hi there!" should appear almost as soon as the movie starts playing.

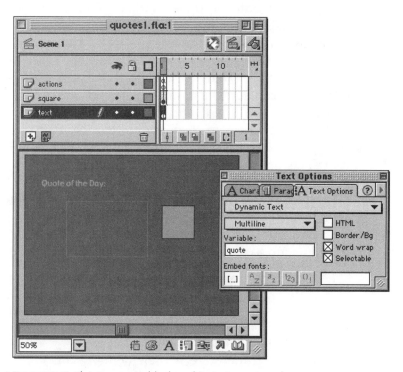

FIGURE 4–7 The "quote" block and its Instance panel

ABOUT THE CODE

The frame action looks for the file called *quotes.txt* and places its URL-encoded variables at the movie's root level. Since there's only one variable, `"quote"`, this action creates a single global variable. And since that variable shares a name with the text field, the text fields displays the variable's value.

> **NOTE** It's important that you name all of your variables, objects, and text fields and that they have different names, no matter where they are in the movie or what level they're on. Besides being good programming practice, Macromedia has noticed some irregularities when some items have the same name. So keep 'em all different. The two `quotes` variables above are the same here because we want them to be the same thing—the value of the big quote box.

The first attribute of `loadVariables` determines which file Flash should load the variables from. This file can live anywhere in the same subdomain as the Flash movie. For example,

DOMAIN	SUBDOMAIN
www.wire-man.com	wire-man.com
camel.llama.wire-man.com	llama.wire-man.com
wire-man.com	wire-man.com

Here's the rule: if the domain has only two components, the subdomain is the same as the domain. If the domain has more than two components, then remove the last level to find the subdomain.

The second attribute of `loadVariables` tells Flash where to place the variable(s) that are in the file. You can place variables in the root level, in a specific movie clip, or on a level. Let's try placing the variable in some different places and see what happens.

1. Open the file *chapter4/quotes1.fla* if it isn't already open.
2. Open the Library.
3. Drag the square symbol to the square layer (see Figure 4-8).

FIGURE 4–8 The square

4. Click on the frame in the actions layer and open its Frame Actions panel.
5. Change the code to:

```
loadVariables("quotes.txt", square)
```

6. Test the movie. No dynamic text should appear.

ABOUT THE CODE

Since we're placing the "quote" variable into the `square` object, it's a different variable from the text field's "quote" variable. Instead of `_root.quote`, the loaded variable is now `_root.square.quote`.

Now let's place that variable into a level.

1. Change the code to:

```
loadVariables("quotes.txt", _level0);
```

2. Test the movie. It works!
3. Now, change the code to:

```
loadVariables("quotes.txt", _level1);
```

4. Test the movie. No good! Placing the variable into level 1 removes it from the root level's view. To access the variable now, we'd have to use `_level1.quote`.
5. Code-tweaking time again! Let's call the level just by using the level number:

```
loadVariables("quotes.txt", 0);
```

6. Test the movie. Nothing happens.
7. Okay, let's change the code one more time:

```
loadVariablesNum("quotes.txt", 0);
```

8. Test the movie. It works!

ABOUT THE CODE

We introduced a semi-new function called `loadVariables-Num`. If you're going to place variables in a level and call that level by its number only, you have to use `loadVariables-Num`. You won't find much documentation about it, but if you're working in Normal Mode, Flash will insert it for you.

Sending Variables with loadVariables

Sending variables and receiving variables as separate steps is useful, but to build seriously useful applications, you have to be able to send data to a script or database and receive information based on what you originally sent. We haven't seen a way to do that yet, but here it comes, and it's pretty simple.

```
loadVariables(filename, target, "get"/"post")
```

That's it—just the `"get"`/`"post"` part. That'll send all available variables to the indicated file. If that file has some scripting in it, it can accept the variables Flash sends to it, do whatever it needs to do, and then output its own variables, which Flash will then read and place in the `target`. As with `getURL`, not all variables in the Flash movie are sent. Only global variables and those within the object that contains the `loadVariables` function are sent (like the `getURL` example in the section "Linking to the Outside World").

Formatting the Variables so Flash Can Read Them

When Flash looks at a file with the intent of reading some variables, those variables need to be in a specific format. They need to be in URL-encoded format, like this:

```
variable1=value1&variable2=value2&variable3=value3
```

If there are spaces in one of the values, replace the space with a plus sign, like this:

```
quote1=Whever+you+go,+there+you+are.&addressNum=180&suite=2
```

Also, there can't be any carriage returns in the file before the list of variables. The variables have to be on the first line of the file, or Flash won't recognize the list.

> **NOTE** If you're using Cold Fusion as your middleware, be sure to use `<CFSETTING ENABLECFOUTPUTONLY="yes">` in order to eliminate the white space that Cold Fusion automatically inserts into the resulting code.

The other way to both send and receive variables in one shot is to use `XML.sendAndLoad`, which we'll cover in detail in the next chapter.

FSCommand

The `fscommand` in Flash 5 is an interesting thing. It can be used to access a specific JavaScript function, or it can be used to control the standalone Flash Player. Note that `fscommand` doesn't work in Netscape 6.

Let's look at the way to access JavaScript via `fscommand`. It's not the way I recommend accessing JavaScript from Flash— `getURL` is easier. We'll go over it just so you know.

Let's say you wanted to mimic the JavaScript function `showAlert`.

1. Open *chapter4/javascrip1.fla,* if it isn't still open.
2. Click on the arrow button and open its Object Actions panel.
3. Enter this code:

```
on(release)
{
    fscommand("alert",_root.userMessage);
}
```

4. Save the file. Don't test it yet.
5. Open your Publication Settings by going to File ➥ Publish Settings.
6. Click the HTML tab, shown in Figure 4-9.

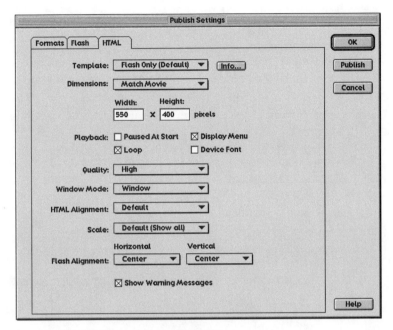

FIGURE 4–9 HTML tab of the Publish Settings

7. From the Template pull-down menu, choose Flash with FSCommand.
8. Click the Publish button.
9. Fire up your text editor of choice.
10. Open up the *javascript1.html* file you just created.
11. See what got published:

```
<SCRIPT LANGUAGE=JavaScript>
<!--
var InternetExplorer =
navigator.appName.indexOf("Microsoft") != -1;
// Handle all the FSCommand messages in a Flash movie
function javascript1_DoFSCommand(command, args) {
  var javascript1Obj = InternetExplorer ? javascript1
: document.javascript1;
  //
  // Place your code here...
  //
}
// Hook for Internet Explorer
```

```
if(navigator.appName &&
navigator.appName.indexOf("Microsoft") != -1 &&
    navigator.userAgent.indexOf("Windows") != -1 &&
navigator.userAgent.indexOf("Windows 3.1") == -1) {
    document.write('<SCRIPT LANGUAGE=VBScript\> \n');
    document.write('on error resume next \n');
    document.write('Sub javascript1_FSCommand(ByVal
command, ByVal args)\n');
    document.write(' call
javascript1_DoFSCommand(command, args)\n');
    document.write('end sub\n');
    document.write('</SCRIPT\> \n');
}
//-->
</SCRIPT>
```

12. Good heavens. This is a lot for a little alert box. Replace the

```
// Place your code here...
```

with

```
alert(args)
```

13. Save the HTML file.

14. Fire up your browser and open *javascript1.html*. Type in some text and click the button.

ABOUT THE CODE

The `fscommand` has a few limitations and, as you can see, some bells and whistles you may not always want. `fscommand` can only call a JavaScript function that has a specific name, that is, `movieName_DoFSCommand`. The movie name is determined by the Flash movie's filename. Also, this function has to have two arguments, `command` and `args`.

CONTROLLING STANDALONE FLASH PLAYER

Fortunately, `fscommand` has uses other than calling JavaScript. You can also use it to control the standalone Flash player. For example,

FIGURE 4-10 The resized movie

FIGURE 4-11 The unresizable movie

1. Open *chapter4/javascript1.fla*.
2. Click on the frame in the actions layer and open its Frame actions layer.
3. Enter the following code:

```
fscommand("allowscale", "true");
```

4. Test the movie. Notice that as you resize the window, the movie resizes as well, as in Figure 4-10.
5. Go back to the Flash movie.
6. Change the code to:

```
fscommand("allowscale", "false");
```

7. Test the movie. Notice, as shown in Figure 4-11, that as you resize the window, the movie doesn't resize.

ABOUT THE CODE

This is a simple example of fscommand working with the Flash Player. We're simply setting whether the user's altering of the window size affects the proportions of our movie.

fscommand can work with other aspects of the Flash player (with varying degrees of success, in my experience); for example, you can use it to quit the player or to dim some of the contextual menu items. You can also use fscommand to call other applications, but we won't go into that functionality in this book.

We'll, we've covered some of the most useful aspects of Flash in a few pages. To fully work with these functions, I strongly recommend that you connect with someone who knows a middleware language and can give you a way to create dynamic Web pages. Unfortunately, there's only so much we can put on the CD.

Now we'll look at a different aspect of Flash—Smart Clips.

Smart Clips

Smart Clips are just plain ol' movie clips, like all the others we've seen in this book. Any movie clip we've made so far could be a Smart Clip.

The only difference between a Smart Clip and a regular movie clip is that Smart Clips allow certain variables within the movie clip to be changed via a new panel called Clip Parameters. That's it. You could change those variables by editing the ActionScript yourself, but if the movie clip is a Smart Clip, you can change the values of some of those variables through the Clip Parameters panel.

What Good Are Smart Clips?

The whole idea behind Smart Clips is to allow a programmer to create a movie clip and all its actions, and then provide a little window for nonprogrammers to change certain aspects of the movie clip, without changing or breaking the programmer's code. It's a great idea, and very useful for larger Web sites that have tons of people (or even just several) working on them.

An Example: Dexter Dean Clothes

The example we'll use to illustrate Smart Clips is the sales page of Dexter Dean's Web site. Dexter Dean is a fictional clothing store catering to semi-hip Internet-type people. They have a sales page that

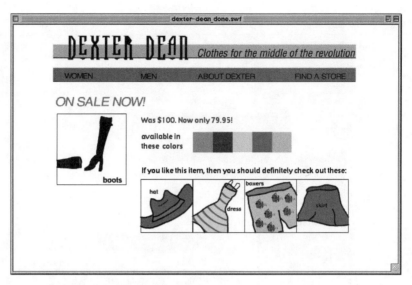

FIGURE 4-12 Dexter Dean's sales page

1. Highlights a certain sales item
2. Has a place for the price
3. Says which colors the item is available in
4. Shows four related items to further entice the user

Figure 4-12 shows what the finished page could look like.

Now, say the marketing folk at Dexter Dean want to be able to change sales items all the time—they want to be able to change the items that are on sale, the sale prices, the available colors, and the related items. Smart Clips give us a way to create the Flash file and hand it over to the marketing folk, who can then change certain aspects of the file to their heart's content, as long as they only change the Smart Clip.

To make the Smart Clip useful, we have to create some variables that the movie clip takes into account and reacts to. Based on what the marketing folk want, this leaves us with:

- which item is on sale
- the item's price
- the colors the item comes in (up to five)
- the four related items

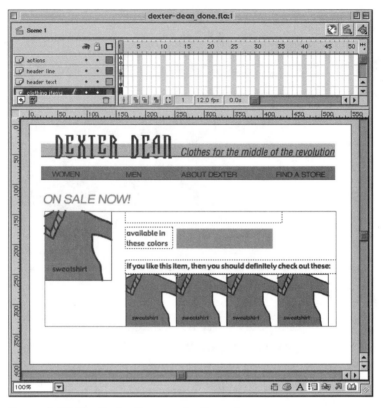

FIGURE 4–13 The Dexter Dean movie–Scene 1

Let's start!

1. Open *chapter4/dexter-dean1.fla,* shown in Figure 4-13.
2. Note that the page is divided into two basic sections: the header and the sales section. The whole sales section is a movie clip called *all clothes.*
3. Open the Library.
4. Double-click the all clothes symbol to modify that symbol.
5. Click the top text box—the empty one.
6. Open the Text Options panel. Note that this text field's variable is price.
7. Go back to Scene 1.
8. Click on the all clothes symbol in the Library.

FIGURE 4–14 Define Clip Parameters dialog box

9. Go to the Options menu in the Library and choose
    Define Clip Parameters.... You'll see a dialog box that
    looks like Figure 4-14.

A *clip parameter* is a variable that the Smart Clip uses and that
appears in the Clip Parameters panel. Thus, a clip parameter is
a variable that someone can change without touching any
ActionScript in your movie.

We're going to make the value of the price box a clip
parameter.

1. Click on the plus sign at the top of the dialog box.
2. Double-click varName under the Name column.
3. Replace varName with price.
4. Double-click defaultValue in the Value column.
5. Replace defaultValue with an empty string.

FIGURE 4–15 The Smart Clip icon

6. Ignore Type for now. We'll get to it soon.
7. Click OK.
8. Look at the Library. The icon for all clothes has changed, as shown in Figure 4-15. You just created a Smart Clip!

Now, let's make that Smart Clip do something. Since we just added a clip parameter, we have to delete the current instance of `mc_clothes_all` on the Stage and drag in a new mc_clothes_all symbol. Unfortunately, changing a symbol's clip parameters doesn't carry over to any instances of the symbol on the stage before the parameters were applied.

1. Delete the instance of all clothes on the Stage.
2. Drag a new instance of mc_clothes_all to the Stage from the Library.
3. Click on the new instance.
4. Open the Clip Parameters panel by going to Window ➧ Panels ➧ Clip Parameters, shown in Figure 4-16.
5. Double-click the blank space under Value.
6. Enter in some text. Any text will do.
7. Test the movie. Your new text should appear in red next to the large orange sweatshirt.

ABOUT OUR ACTIONS

We started with an ordinary, everyday movie clip with a text field called `price`. We then created a clip parameter for that movie clip, and we called it `price` as well. At the point that we created a clip parameter, our movie clip became a Smart Clip. We then updated our movie clip on the stage with the Smart Clip from the Library. We then highlighted the instance and opened up that instance's Clip Parameters. We said that the value of `price` should be whatever you typed in. Then, once the movie started playing, Flash saw that the value of `price` should be your text, and caused the variable `price` in the clip

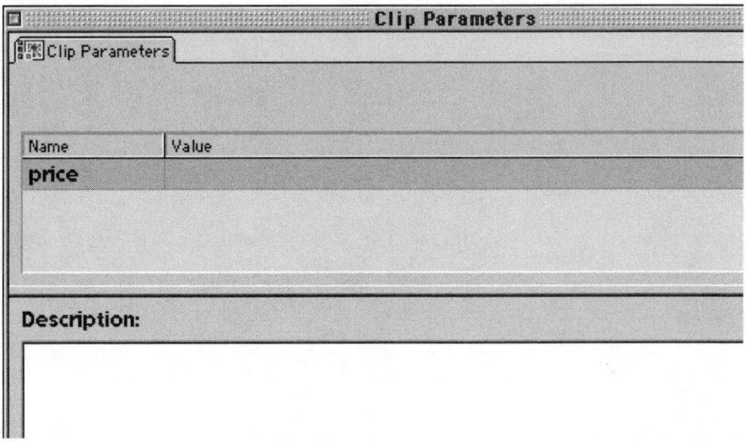

FIGURE 4–16 The Clip Parameters panel

to have the value of what you typed. All clip parameters are placed inside the clip object.

For example, if we called our Smart Clip instance `sale`, you would access the price variable from anywhere by calling `_root.sale.price`.

Now, let's create a clip parameter to allow someone to choose the item that'll be on sale. First, let's look at the movie clip that holds all of the clothes.

1. Open the Library, if it isn't already open.
2. Double-click on the clothes symbol. It should look like Figure 4-17.
3. Notice that we have nine sections in this movie clip, each marked with its own frame label. The labels are: sweatshirt, t-shirt, shorts, boxers, socks, boots, hat, dress, and skirt. When the user chooses a sales item, we want this movie clip to go to the appropriate frame and stay there. Figure 4-18 shows what all of the clothes look like.
4. Open up the all clothes symbol.
5. Notice that we have five instances of the clothes symbol in this clip. For now, we'll just concentrate on the big one to the left—the actual sales item.
6. In the Library, click on the all clothes symbol.

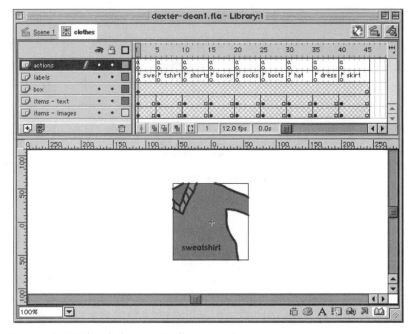

FIGURE 4–17 The *clothes* movie clip

FIGURE 4–18 All the clothes

FIGURE 4-19 The Values dialog box

7. Choose Define Clip Parameters... from the Options menu.

8. Click the big plus sign to add a parameter.

9. Double-click `varName` and enter *saleItemName*.

10. Double-click Default in the Type column.

11. Choose List and press <enter>.

12. Note that `defaultValue` just turned into `List[]`. What we've just done is create a clip parameter called `salesItemName` that will become a drop-down list instead of a field we type text into.

13. Now, in order to populate this pull-down list, double-click on the (`List[]`). A new dialog box entitled Values should appear, as shown in Figure 4-19.

14. We'll be entering all nine clothing options in this dialog box. Click the big plus sign.

15. Double-click the `"defaultValue"` text.

16. Enter `sweatshirt` and press <enter>.

17. Keep pressing the plus sign until there are eight more entries, i.e., eight more `defaultValues`.

18. In no particular order, change those default values to be `t-shirt`, `shorts`, `boxers`, `socks`, `boots`, `hat`, `dress` and `skirt`.

19. You can change the order of these values by selecting one of them and clicking the up and down arrows in the dialog box. Give it a try.

20. When you have all nine entries, press OK.

Great! We've created a new clip parameter. Now, let's set that parameter and see if it works.

1. Go back to Scene 1 on the Stage.
2. Click on the all clothes instance.
3. Window ➡ Panels ➡ Clip Parameters.
4. Wait a minute. Where's our `salesItemName`? Ah, we changed the clip parameters, which means we have to replace the instance on the Stage.
5. Go back to Scene 1 on the Stage.
6. Delete the instance of all clothes.
7. Drag a new instance from the Library.
8. Window ➡ Panels ➡ Clip Parameters.
9. Ah. There it is. Double-click on `sweatshirt` (or whatever clothes item you had as first in the list), and choose `boots` from the list.
10. Test the movie.

Hey! Nothing happened! What's up?

Well, while we constructed our Smart clip exactly right, we forgot one thing: we need some code that actually takes that Smart Clip variable and does something with it. Let's do that quickly.

1. Double-click on the all clothes symbol in the Library to enter Editing Mode.
2. Click on the sales item instance and open its Object Actions panel.
3. Enter this code:

```
onClipEvent(load)
{
    this.gotoAndStop(_parent.saleItemName);
}
```

4. Now test the movie.

ABOUT THE CODE

When this instance loads, the code moves the playhead to the value of _parent.salesItemName. Why _parent? When we set the clip parameter, we set it for the instance of the mc_clothes_all clip. Since this mc_clothes instance is a part of the mc_clothes_all instance, it's a child of mc_clothes_all. The clip parameter is part of mc_clothes_all, so that's where that variable lives. In order for the clothes instance to access the variable, it has to look up one level. We could also access the variable using _root.sale.saleItemName, but using _parent makes the code more modular and less dependent on the structure of the movie as a whole.

DETERMINE THE RELATED ITEMS

Since we're building a decent retail site, we certainly want to do some cross-selling. We also want to be able to determine which four clothing items will be displayed in addition to the main sale item. We'll do this by creating four more lists: xSale1Name, xSale2Name, xSale3Name, and xSale4Name. The values of these lists will be exactly the same as saleItem-Name. It's a little tedious, but it'll give you some needed practice to become comfortable creating clip parameters.

We'll go over all the steps to create xSale1Name, and then leave you to create the other three on your own.

1. Click on the mc_clothes_all symbol in the Library.
2. Choose Define Clip Parameters... from the Options menu.
3. Click the big plus sign.
4. Double-click varName in the Name column and replace it with "xSale1Name".
5. Double-click Default in the Type column and choose List from the pull-down menu.
6. Double-click (List[]) in the Value menu. The Values dialog box should appear.
7. Add these values: boots, boxers, dress, hat, shorts, skirt, socks, sweatshirt, and t-shirt.
8. Click OK.

You've created the necessary clip parameter for xSale1Name. Now, repeat these steps to create xSale2Name, xSale3Name, and xSale4Name.

Now that those are entered, let's add the necessary actions to the four related item instances in the all clothes Smart Clip.

1. In the Library, double-click on the mc_clothes_all symbol to open its editing mode.

2. Looking at the four smaller instances of the mc_clothes_all symbol, click on the one to the far left. Its instance name is crossSale1.

3. Open that object's Object Actions panel.

4. Enter the following code:

```
onClipEvent (load)
{
    this.gotoAndStop(_parent.xSale1Name);
}
```

5. Now, click on the next instance to the right. Its name is crossSale2.

6. Open its Object Actions panel and enter this code:

```
onClipEvent (load)
{
    this.gotoAndStop(_parent.xSale2Name);
}
```

7. Moving on, click on the next instance to the right. Its name is crossSale3.

8. Open its Object Actions panel and enter this code:

```
onClipEvent (load)
{
    this.gotoAndStop(_parent.xSale3Name);
}
```

9. Again, click on the next instance to the right. Its name is crossSale4.

10. Open its Object Actions panel and enter this code:

```
onClipEvent(load)
{
    this.gotoAndStop(_parent.xSale4Name);
}
```

11. All we need to do now is replace the `clothes_all` instance on the Stage, since we've changed the clip parameters. Go back to Scene 1.

12. Delete the instance of `mc_clothes_all`.

13. Drag a new instance of `mc_clothes_all` from the Library onto the Stage.

14. Great! We've put all the pieces in place.

15. Window ⟹ Panels ⟹ Clip Parameters.

16. The panel should look like Figure 4-20.

17. Change the values of the related items to whatever you want.

18. Test the movie!

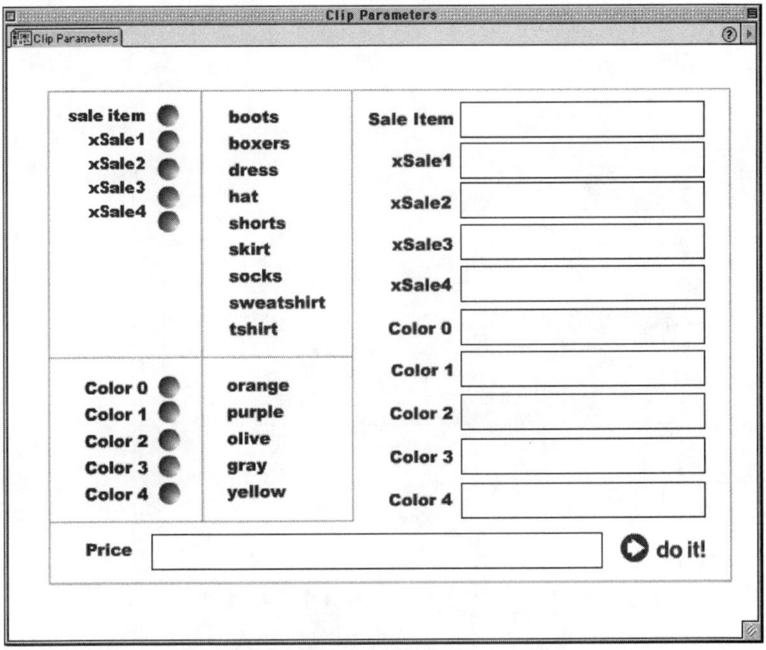

FIGURE 4-20 The Clip Parameters panel

ABOUT THE CODE

We're doing the same thing for the related items as we did for the main sale item. Based on the value of xSale[*something*]Name, we're moving the playhead of each of the clothes instances. And we're using _parent, because the variable is in the instance of all clothes, the parent object of the clothes instances.

Congratulations! We've done a big job here and learned a lot about Smart Clips. We're not quite done, though. We still need to determine which colors are available for each sales item.

DETERMINING COLORS

Every clothing item is available in a number of predetermined colors, from 0 to 5. To allow this, we have another symbol to use, called colorSquare. It looks like Figure 4-21.

We have five colors to choose from: orange, purple, olive, yellow, and gray.

What makes this different from the clothing items is that the number of colors is variable. Here's how we'll deal with this:

1. In the Library, click on the all clothes symbol.

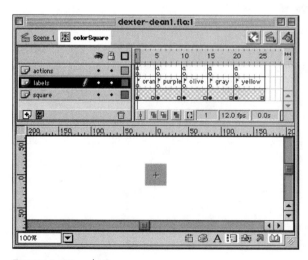

FIGURE 4–21 colorSquare

2. In the Options menu; choose Define Clip Parameters....
3. Click the big plus sign.
4. Double-click "varName" in the Name column and replace it with "availColors".
5. Double-click Default in the Type column and choose Array from the drop-down menu.
6. Click OK.

ABOUT OUR ACTIONS

The Array choice when defining clip parameters allows us to input a variable number of entries into the array. This will become more clear in a bit.

Now, let's add some actions to our little colored squares.

1. In the Library, double-click the all clothes symbol.
2. Click on the color square furthest to the left. Its name is colorSquare0.
3. Open its Object Actions panel and enter this code:

```
// colorSquare0
onClipEvent(load)
{
    if(_parent.availColors.length >= 1)
    {
        this.gotoAndStop(_parent.availColors[0])
    }
    else
    {
        this._visible = false;
    }
}
```

4. Now, click on the colored square just to the right. Its name is colorSquare1.
5. Open its Object Actions panel and enter this code:

```
// colorSquare1
onClipEvent(load)
{
    if(_parent.availColors.length >= 2)
    {
        this.gotoAndStop(_parent.availColors[1])
```

```
    }
    else
    {
        this._visible = false;
    }
}
```

6. Now, click on the colored square just to the right. Its name is colorSquare2.

7. Open its Object Actions panel and enter this code:

```
// colorSquare2
onClipEvent(load)
{
    if(_parent.availColors.length >= 3)
    {
        this.gotoAndStop(_parent.availColors[2])
    }
    else
    {
        this._visible = false;
    }
}
```

8. Now, click on the colored square just to the right. Its name is colorSquare3.

9. Open its Object Actions panel and enter this code:

```
// colorSquare3
onClipEvent(load)
{
    if(_parent.availColors.length >= 4)
    {
        this.gotoAndStop(_parent.availColors[3])
    }
    else
    {
        this._visible = false;
    }
}
```

10. Now, click on the colored square just to the right. Its name is colorSquare4.

11. Open its Object Actions panel and enter this code:

```
// colorSquare4
onClipEvent(load)
{
    if(_parent.availColors.length >= 5)
    {
        this.gotoAndStop(_parent.availColors[4])
    }
    else
    {
        this._visible = false;
    }
}
```

12. Test the movie! Since we haven't chosen any colors, the array `availColors` is empty, and all the colored square movie clips are invisible.

ABOUT THE CODE

We're deciding on a case-by-case basis whether a color square should be visible or not. We're deciding this by determining whether there's a matching element in the `availColors` array or not. If we're looking at square 1, we make sure that there's something in `availColors[1]`. If there is something, then we take the playhead of that instance to whatever the value of `availColors[1]` is. Again, we're using `_parent` because we need to look up one level.

Now let's set some colors.

1. Go back to Scene 1.
2. Click on the `allClothes` instance.
3. Delete it and drag a new one from the Library.
4. Window ⟶ Panels ⟶ Clip Parameters.
5. Double-click on " (`Array[]`) ".
6. Enter three values: gray, yellow, and orange.
7. Test the movie! Did the colors show up? Only three squares, hopefully.

Whew. That was a lot of work, but we plowed our way through a lot of Smart Clips. This movie is complete, but there's even *more* we can do. You know the interface of the clip

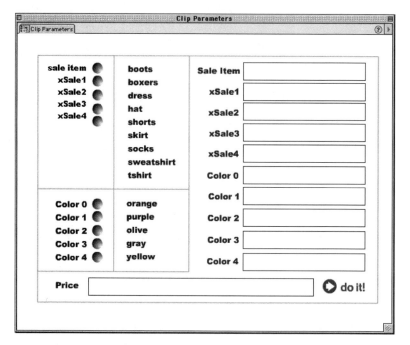

FIGURE 4–22 Our finished Clip Parameters panel

parameters panel? We can customize that to look like whatever we want.

To learn more about Smart Clips (and ActionScript in general), I strongly recommend you poke through the Smart Clips Library that comes with Flash 5. Go to Window ➠ Common Libraries ➠ Smart Clips. They've provided some excellent examples, and dissecting them will teach you much.

Creating a Custom Interface for Clip Parameters

We're going to create a custom interface for the Clip Parameters panel. It'll end up look like Figure 4-22.

You can create a custom interface by creating a specially constructed SWF file and tying that into your clip parameters.

The key is to create an empty symbol, create an instance of that empty symbol in your movie, and call that instance *xch*. When the user finishes entering all the required information, they'll hit some sort of button, and at that point, your code will have to transfer all the data into that xch instance. Don't worry—we'll build this step by step.

1. Open the *file chapter4/dexter-interface_0.fla*.
2. Insert ➠ New Symbol.
3. Call this new symbol *mc_exchangeclip*. Make it a Movie Clip.
4. Click OK.
5. Without putting anything in the symbol, go back to Scene 1.
6. Create a new layer called *Exchange Clip*.
7. If it isn't already, open the Library.
8. Drag the Exchange Clip symbol onto the Exchange Clip layer. It doesn't matter where—just someplace where it'll be easily visible. It will appear as a little dot.
9. Call the instance xch.

ABOUT OUR ACTIONS

The Exchange Clip symbol may seem pretty useless, but it's absolutely vital. That clip will act as the intermediary, or exchange, between this Flash file and the Clip Parameters panel. The panel can only look at the instance called xch, so creating xch simply has to happen.

Now we need to build the file so that it actually grabs the correct data. Here's how this thing works: the user first chooses one of the radio buttons in the first column. The user then clicks one of the values in the second column. The name-value pair then appears in the third column. The user can also enter any kind of text into the "price" text field. When the user has completed filling in all the fields they want, they click Do it!, and that should transfer all the data to the xch instance.

Let's start by making the radio buttons work. First, let's look at the two states of the radioButton symbol, shown in Figure 4-23 and Figure 4-24.

When the user clicks on this button, we want the button to move to the on state and we want all other buttons to be in the off state. Notice that there are two frame actions in this symbol: both are stop(), so the button doesn't loop from the off state to the on state and so on.

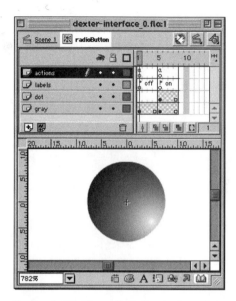

FIGURE 4–23 The radioButton in the off state

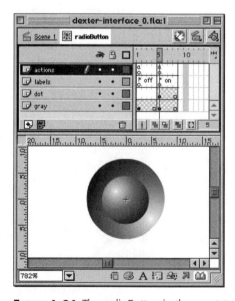

FIGURE 4–24 The radioButton in the on state

If you hide the transparent buttons layer and start clicking
on buttons, you'll notice that they're named *radioButtonN,*

where N is a number from 0 to 9. This becomes important later. For now, just note it.

You may have noticed that the radioButton symbol isn't actually a button. It's a movie clip. In order to make it respond like a button, we're going to cheat a little and place a transparent button on top of the movie clip. We get the best of both worlds that way—the easy scripting that's associated with a button and the controllable states of a movie clip.

In order to create the desired button, we're going to keep track of which button is on by creating an array called buttonOn[] . First, we're going to create this array, and then initialize all of its values to false.

1. Go back to Scene 1.
2. Click on the frame in the actions layer and open its Frame Actions panel.
3. Enter this code:

```
//set button array
buttonOn = new Array;
for (i=0; i<10; i++)
{
    buttonOn[i] = false;
}
```

ABOUT THE CODE

First, we create an array called buttonOn. Then, since there's a total of 10 buttons that we'll be using, we'll loop from 0 to 9 (remember that arrays start counting at 0, not 1) and make the value of each element in the array false. The value is false because none of the buttons have been pressed yet.

When a user clicks on one of the buttons, we want to make that button go to the on frame, and change all the other frames to off. We could do this by creating an Object Action for one button, and then copying and pasting that code nine times. However, there's a much better and more modular way to do this. We'll write a little function that turns on one button and turns off all the others. We'll place that function in one place, and then we'll have each radio button call that function.

Huh?, I hear you ask. Here's how—it's a neat trick.

1. Insert ➠ New Symbol.
2. Call the symbol *mc_switchButtons* and make it a Movie Clip.
3. Don't put anything in the symbol—just go back to Scene 1.
4. Open the Library, if it isn't already open.
5. Drag the switchButtons symbol onto the Stage. Drag it anywhere—it doesn't matter.
6. Click on the little dot that's the switchButtons symbol, and call the instance *switchButtons*.
7. Open its Object Actions panel, and enter this code:

```
onClipEvent(load)
{
    function switchButtons(buttonNum)
    {
        // turn on current button
        eval("_root.radioButton" +
buttonNum).gotoAndStop("on");
        _root.buttonOn[buttonNum] = true;

        // turn off all other buttons
        for(i=0; i<10; i++)
        {
            if(i != buttonNum)
            {
                eval("_root.radioButton" +
i).gotoAndStop("off");
                _root.buttonOn[i] = false;
            }
        }
    }
}
```

ABOUT THE CODE

Okay, we're doing a number of new things here. Most importantly, we're creating a new way of performing ActionScript in Flash. We've created something called a *constructor function*. This is a chunk of code that does something only when it's called. When the switchButtons symbol is loaded into the movie, the `switchButtons` function is loaded and just sits there, ready for action, ready to be called.

This function takes one argument or input variable, called `buttonNum`. Whatever code calls this function has to supply this input variable, or the function won't work. As it turns out, this will be a number from 0 to 9, corresponding to the names of the radioButton instances.

Once the function has the `buttonNum`, it sets that button's playhead to on. Notice that we're dynamically building the name of the symbol here, and we're doing it using the `eval` function.

For example, if we pass in 6 for `buttonNum`,

```
eval("_root.radioButton" + buttonNum)
```

results in

```
_root.radiobutton6
```

and Flash interprets the whole line as

```
_root.radioButton6.gotoAndStop("on");
```

resulting in button 6 flipping to the on position. It also would set `buttonOn[6]` to `true`.

The code then begins looping through the rest of the buttons. As long as `it` isn't the button we just turned on, we move its playhead to the off frame label, and set `buttonOn` to `false`.

Now that we've created the function, let's start coding the buttons that will call it.

1. Click on the turquoise rectangle over the top radio button. Remember, that's the transparent button.

2. Open the transparent button's Object Actions panel and enter this code:

```
on(release)
{
    _root.switchButtons.switchButtons(0);
}
```

ABOUT THE CODE

This is how we call our `switchButton` function—all we have to do is locate it and pass in the appropriate input variable. The name of the function is switchButtons; it lives inside the switchButtons instance on the root level.

Now let's add actions to all the other transparent buttons of the radio buttons.

Moving down the line of buttons, each one gets this code:

Transparent Button over Instance radioButton1

```
on(release)
{
    _root.switchButtons.switchButtons(1);
}
```

Transparent Button over Instance radioButton2

```
on(release)
{
    _root.switchButtons.switchButtons(2);
}
```

Transparent Button over Instance radioButton3

```
on(release)
{
    _root.switchButtons.switchButtons(3);
}
```

Transparent Button over Instance radioButton4

```
on(release)
{
    _root.switchButtons.switchButtons(4);
}
```

Transparent Button over Instance radioButton5

```
on(release)
{
    _root.switchButtons.switchButtons(5);
}
```

Transparent Button over Instance radioButton6

```
on(release)
{
    _root.switchButtons.switchButtons(6);
}
```

Transparent Button over Instance radioButton7

```
on(release)
{
    _root.switchButtons.switchButtons(7);
}
```

Transparent Button over Instance radioButton8

```
on(release)
{
    _root.switchButtons.switchButtons(8);
}
```

Transparent Button over Instance radioButton9

```
on(release)
{
    _root.switchButtons.switchButtons(9);
}
```

Feel free to test the movie. Your radio buttons should now work.

We're partway done. After the user uses the radio buttons to select the item or color they want to choose a value for, they have to actually choose that value. That value should then appear in the correct text field. So, we need a function that determines which radio button is pressed and what value was just pressed, and places the correct text in the correct text field. Fortunately, this isn't too hard.

We're going to use the same function trick to get this done as we did to make the radio buttons work.

1. Click on the `switchButtons` object and open its Object Actions panel.
2. Add this code inside the `onClipEvent(load)` curly braces:

```
function fillTextField(textVal)
{
    //loop through buttons
    for(i=0; i<10; i++)
    {
        if(_root.buttonOn[i])
        {
```

```
                eval("_root.text" + i) = textVal;
                break;
            }
        }
    }
```

ABOUT THE CODE

We're creating a new function called `fillTextField`, and it takes one argument, `textVal`. Simply, it cycles through the `buttonOn` array and sees which one is `true`, that is, which button is currently on. Once it finds the on button, it fills the corresponding text field with the passed argument. The key to this code's simplicity is in the naming of the text fields. Note that they're all named `textN`, where N is a value from 0 to 9. It's a boring naming scheme, but a useful one. Once we find the correct text field and fill it, we use `break` to exit the `for` loop. We already found the text field we were looking for, so we don't need to continue looping and looking.

Now that we've created the needed function, we need to add some actions to buttons so that the function gets called. Again, we're going to use the same method we did with the radio buttons. We've placed transparent buttons over the top of all the values in the second column. Let's start adding actions to those buttons.

1. Click on the rectangle over the `"boots"` text.
2. Open its Object Actions panel and enter this code:

```
on(release)
{
    _root.switchButtons.fillTextField("boots");
}
```

ABOUT THE CODE

Pretty similar to the radio buttons' code, isn't it? The only difference is that we're calling a different function, and since we're passing a string instead of a number, we have to enclose the value in quotes.

Now let's do the rest of them.

Transparent Button over `boxers`

```
on(release)
{
    _root.switchButtons.fillTextField("boxers");
}
```

Transparent Button over `dress`

```
on(release)
{
    _root.switchButtons.fillTextField("dress");
}
```

Transparent Button over `hat`

```
on(release)
{
    _root.switchButtons.fillTextField("hat");
}
```

Transparent Button over `shorts`

```
on(release)
{
    _root.switchButtons.fillTextField("shorts");
}
```

Transparent Button over `skirt`

```
on(release)
{
    _root.switchButtons.fillTextField("skirt");
}
```

Transparent Button over `socks`

```
on(release)
{
    _root.switchButtons.fillTextField("socks");
}
```

Transparent Button over `sweatshirt`

```
on(release)
{
    _root.switchButtons.fillTextField("sweatshirt");
}
```

Transparent Button over `orange`

```
on(release)
{
    _root.switchButtons.fillTextField("orange");
}
```

Transparent Button over `purple`

```
on(release)
{
    _root.switchButtons.fillTextField("purple");
}
```

Transparent Button over `olive`

```
on(release)
{
    _root.switchButtons.fillTextField("olive");
}
```

Transparent Button over `gray`

```
on(release)
{
    _root.switchButtons.fillTextField("gray");
}
```

Transparent Button over `yellow`

```
on(release)
{
    _root.switchButtons.fillTextField("yellow");
}
```

Great! Test the movie. Does the text appear in the right place? Notice that if there's a problem, we only have to change the code in one place: the function. We don't have to make a change in one place and then copy that change 10 times.

There's only one more step to take. We have to add some actions to the Do it! button, so that all the data gets transferred correctly to the xch instance. Let's go ahead and do that.

1. Click on the arrow button next to the Do it! text.
2. Open its Object Actions panel and enter this code:

```
on(release)
{
    // set pricing
    _root.xch.price = _root.price;

    //set clothing values
    _root.xch.saleItemName = _root.text0;
    _root.xch.xSale1Name = _root.text1;
    _root.xch.xSale2Name = _root.text2;
    _root.xch.xSale3Name = _root.text3;
    _root.xch.xSale4Name = _root.text4;

    // set color values
    _root.xch.availColors = new Array;
    for (i=0; i<5; i++)
    {
        if(eval("_root.text"+(i+5)).length > 0)
        {
            _root.xch.availColors[i] =
eval("_root.text"+(i+5));
        }
        else
        {
            break;
        }
    }
}
```

ABOUT THE CODE

Setting the price and clothing values is pretty straightforward. We assign values to new variable in the xch instance that have the same names as the values in our Clip Parameters. Setting the color values is a little trickier, for a few reasons. First, we're building an array. Second, that array has a variable length—we don't know how many elements it has. We deal with this by looking at text fields 5 through 9. Since our counter is counting from 0 to 4, we add 5 to our counter (i + 5) to look at the right text fields. If the length of that text field is greater than 0 (i.e., there's a value there), we then assign that value to an element in the availColors array. If there's no value, then we assume that we've reached the end of the list, and we remove ourselves from the loop and stop looking at text fields. The one problem with this method is that it assumes that the user has filled in the color text fields sequentially. If the user has filled in, say, Color 0 and Color 4, the code will never see Color 4 because it will see that Color 1 is blank and will stop looking further.

The next step is to export the movie. Choose File ⟶ Export Movie... and click OK until you're done. Name the file *dexter-interface.swf* and place it wherever you want.

Now we're going load this SWF file into our Dexter Dean movie as the desired interface.

1. Open *chapter4/dexter-dean_done.fla*.
2. Open the Library and click on the mc_clothes_all symbol.
3. Choose Define Clip Parameters... from the Options menu.
4. Click on the little folder icon under the Link to Custom UI header.
5. Find and choose the SWF file you just created *(dexter-interface.swf)*.
6. Click OK.
7. Go back to the Stage and click the all clothes instance.
8. Window ⟶ Panels ⟶ Clip Parameters.
9. Fill in the information and click Do it!
10. Test the movie! Woo hoo!

Conclusion

Congratulations! You really took Flash to the next level in this chapter. And here's the good news: you just finished the hardest part of this book. The next chapter on XML isn't this complicated.

So give yourself a good pat on the back, and be proud.

Ready for some XML? Everyone's talking about it...

Flash and XML

ne of the great new features of Flash 5 is its ability to understand and build XML. While its capabilities aren't perfect, they're quite powerful. If you're using XML for any backend data transfers, you can use Flash just like more common middleware, such as PHP or Cold Fusion.

If you don't know what XML is or why this is a big deal, don't worry. I'll explain.

What Is XML?

XML is structured data. It's a bunch of text that can describe an article, a shopping order, a spaceship, a multidimensional array, just about anything. Let's use an article as an example. Say you have an article entitled "Soupy Sales: Godfather of the Sitcom." You're the author, and your name is Irving Archbite. Let's turn that much into XML. Here's one way to do it:

```
<xml>
<article type="magazine">
     <headline>Soupy Sales</headline>
     <subhead>Godfather of the Sitcom</subhead>
     <byline>
          <author>
               <firstName>Irving</firstname>
               <lastName>Archbite</lastname>
          </author>
     </byline>
     <body>Blah blah blah</body>
</article>
</xml>
```

If you've ever coded any HTML, this should look familiar to you. XML contains tags that can be nested within each other. Just as HTML is Hypertext Markup Language, XML stands for Extensible Markup Language. It's the "Markup Language" part that makes them look so similar. Also, both XML and HTML come from the same parent, SGML. We won't go into that further, though.

Here's another example. This XML document contains just a string and a small array.

```
<xml>
     <string>hi there</string>
     <array length="4">
          <element />56
          <element />75
          <element />3
          <element />345.6
     </array>
</xml>
```

All elements in XML have to be closed; that is, `<tag>` must have a `</tag>`. The only way around this is to use `<tag />`, which eliminates the need for a `</tag>`. However, `<tag />` is only used for single-element nodes.

XML is extremely flexible, because you decide how to mark it up. You could create a perfectly valid XML document that looks like this:

```
<xml>
    <dogbite>arrf arf arf!</dogbite>
    <cat breed="siamese">meow meow. Hiss!!</cat>
    <owner>Bad Barney! Bad</owner>
</xml>
```

You could conceivably create an XML document that had nothing but nonsense words in it, and it would be a perfectly valid, working XML document. No one could understand it, but it'd be valid.

You may be asking yourself, "If I can create an XML document of a bunch of made-up stuff, why is that useful? What is this XML for?"

XML's purpose in life is to package data from one source and send it to another source. The thing that makes XML useful is that it can act as a language that all machines can understand. It would allow, say, Microsoft Word to exchange information with a video game you're playing. Or, a digital camera could communicate with your laptop and PDA. XML's promise is that it could be become the one language that all computers, large or small, can understand. It could simplify the electronic communication of information enormously, not just on the Web, but in all electronic devices. This is such a big, exciting deal that everyone wants XML to be adopted as quickly as possible, from mom-and-pop Web shops to Microsoft.

HOW IS THIS DONE?

Let's review what we know. XML is a markup language in which everyone can make up their own tags. And it's supposed to be the one thing that all machines understand. How is that possible?

It's possible because there's one part that I haven't mentioned yet. In addition to your XML document, you have to create something called a *document type definition,* or DTD. This DTD explains the overall hierarchy of your XML markup and what kinds of data go where. We won't be dealing with DTDs in this section—we'll only be looking at raw XML.

The XML Object

Even though XML is just a text string, Flash can take that XML and turn it into an object. This makes the XML easier to deal with, read, and manipulate.

The parts of XML's structure are something you'll have to know. Each tag is known as a *node.* If there's a tag nested inside another tag, the inside tag is known as a *child node.* If your tag looks like this:

```
<cat breed="siamese">meow meow. Hiss!!</cat>
```

then `breed` is known as an *attribute* of the `<cat>` node (or element). Also using this example, the text `meow  meow. Hiss!!` is a called a *text node* within the `<cat>` node. The text node is technically a child node of the `<cat>` node.

The Screenplay Example

For the rest of this chapter, we'll be dissecting (and then building from scratch) a medium-sized XML document. It's a very brief XMLization of the screenplay of *Three Days of the Condor,* a great movie starring Robert Redford and Faye Dunaway.

Here's what the screenplay example looks like:

```
<screenplay title="Three Days of the Condor">
    <author>Lorenzo Semple, Jr.</author>
    <author>David Rayfiel</author>
    <character type="main">Turner</character>
    <character type="major">Kathy</character>
    <character type="major">Higgins</character>
    <character type="major">Jobert</character>
    <character type="major">Mr. Wabash</character>
```

```
<act number="1">
    <dramaticNeed>Who's trying to kill Turner
and why?</dramaticNeed>
    <plotPoint>Turner returns from lunch to find
everyone in his bookish CIA office dead.</plotPoint>
  </act>

  <act number="2">
    <obstacle description="Turner tries to get
to a safe place">
        <sequence>Turner calls HQ.</sequence>
        <sequence>Turner is betrayed in alley.</
sequence>
    </obstacle>
    <obstacle description="Mailman/assasin
attacks Turner">
        <sequence>Turner and mailman fight.
Turner wins.</sequence>
    </obstacle>
    <plotPoint>Turner captures head CIA deputy
and becomes attacker instead of victim.</plotPoint>
  </act>

  <act number="3">
    <resolution>Turner finds the man who ordered
the murders, and why they were done.</resolution>
    <tagScene>Turner gives his story to the NY
Times, and wonders if they will print it.</tagScene>
  </act>

</screenplay>
```

However, Flash can't read XML documents that have carriage returns or extra spaces. Since this makes life much more annoying for programmers, I'm assuming this is a bug that will be fixed by the time you read this book. The Flash file (in case the bug hasn't been fixed) needs to look like this:

```
<screenplay title="Three Days of the
  Condor"><author>Lorenzo Semple, Jr.</
  author><author>David Rayfiel</author><character
  type="main">Turner</character><character
  type="major">Kathy</character><character
  type="major">Higgins</character><character
  type="major">Jobert</character><character
  type="major">Mr. Wabash</character><act num-
```

```
ber="1"><dramaticNeed>Who's trying to kill Turner and
why?</dramaticNeed><plotPoint>Turner returns from
lunch to find everyone in his bookish CIA office
dead.</plotPoint></act><act number="2"><obstacle
description="Turner tries to get to a safe
place"><sequence>Turner calls HQ.</
sequence><sequence>Turner is betrayed in alley.</
sequence></obstacle><obstacle description="Mailman/
assasin attacks Turner"><sequence>Turner and mailman
fight. Turner wins.</sequence></obstacle><plot-
Point>Turner captures head CIA deputy and becomes
attacker instead of victim.</plotPoint></act><act
number="3"><resolution>Turner finds the man who
ordered the murders, and why they were done.</resolu-
tion><tagScene>Turner gives his story to the NY Times,
and wonders if they will print it.</tagScene></act></
screenplay>
```

We'll start by loading this file into an XML object in Flash, and we'll use Flash commands to read through the document.

1. Create a folder somewhere on your hard drive called *Flash & XML*.
2. Copy *chapter5/screenplay_space.xml* to that folder.
3. Open Flash and create a new file called *xml1.fla*. Save this file to the Flash & XML folder.
4. Go back to the *xml1_done.fla* file in Flash.
5. Click on the single frame on layer 1 and open its Frame Actions panel.
6. Enter this code:

```
//create XML object
screenplayXML = new XML();

// load external file into XML object
screenplayXML.load("screenplay_space.xml");

// when loading is complete, go to a special function
screenplayXML.onLoad = loadedXML;

function loadedXML()
{
    trace("the XML object is loaded")
}
```

7. Test the movie. A blank Flash player should appear, along with the output window, with the expected message.

ABOUT THE CODE

We start by creating an XML object called `screenplayXML`. We then use the `load` method to load an XML document into that object. This method takes the long string of text that is our XML document and arranges it into the nodes, child nodes, attributes, and so on that comprise the XML object `screenplayXML`.

Since this loading of an external file isn't instantaneous, we have to give Flash some time to finish the job. To do that, we tell Flash where to go once the loading is completed. In this case, we're telling Flash to go to the function named `loadedXML` once the loading is finished.

Inside the `loadedXML` function, we have only one command, a simple `trace` action. So, we're able to create an empty XML object, load it with something, and go to a certain function once the loading is complete.

This is good, but now we need to be able to use Flash to look at the different parts of `screenplayXML`. We'll start by looking at child nodes. Referring to the original XML document, let's see what child nodes we're looking for.

```
<screenplay title="Three Days of the Condor">
    <author>Lorenzo Semple, Jr.</author>
    <author>David Rayfiel</author>

    ...

</screenplay>
```

Well, it looks like the `<author>` elements are child nodes of `<screenplay>`. So it seems that if we looked at the first child node of `screenplayXML`, we'd see `<author>Lorenzo Semple, Jr.</author>`, right?

Almost. Not quite. The first child node of `screenplayXML` is the entire XML document. Imagine it like this: `screenplayXML` is a container, and the actual XML—the text itself—is a child node of the `screenplayXML` object.

Let's see this in code. The way to access the first child node of an XML object is xmlObj.firstChild.

1. Open the Frame Actions panel for *xml1.fla*.
2. Change the loadedXML function to this:

```
function loadedXML()
{
  trace(screenplayXML.firstChild)
  trace(screenplayXML.firstChild.firstChild)
  trace(screenplayXML.firstChild.firstChild.firstChild)
}
```

3. Test the movie. You should see three lines of text in the Output window. The first is the whole XML document. The second is Lorenzo's author node, and the third is Lorenzo's name only.

ABOUT THE CODE

We access the whole of the XML with screenplayXML.firstChild, which results in the first child node of the screenplayXML object. An important thing to understand at this point is that screenplayXML.firstChild by *itself* is an XML object, and it can be treated as such. Thus, we can take the first child node of that object as well (screenplayXML.firstChild.firstChild).

Now, it may appear that the <author> nodes have no more child nodes. However, the text Lorenzo Semple, Jr. is a special kind of node, called a text node, and it can be a child node as well.

Let's rephrase this code somewhat in order to emphasize that child nodes can be XML objects of their own right.

1. Open the Frame Actions panel and replace the function with this code:

```
function loadedXML()
{
  // set sub-objects
  allText = screenplayXML.firstChild;
  author1Node = screen-playXML.firstChild.firstChild;
  author1Name = author1Node.firstChild;
  // display nodes
  trace(allText);
```

```
  trace(author1Node);
  trace(author1Name);
}
```

2. Test the movie. The output should be exactly the same
    as before.

ABOUT THE CODE

Before we display anything, we're creating three new
objects, all based on `screenplayXML`. `allText` is simply the
first child node of `screenplayXML`. `author1Node` is then the
first child node of that child node. We then take a little twist
and make `author1Name` the first child node of `author1Node`.

```
author1Name =
author1Node.firstChild =
allText.firstChild.firstChild =
screenplayXML.firstChild.firstChild.firstChild
```

All of these statements are equal and have the same value.

Now let's assume that your Flash code knows it's loading a
XMLized screenplay, but it doesn't know for which movie. You
know that the `<screenplay>` node has a `title` attribute, so
let's look for that.

1. Open the Frame Actions panel and add this code to the
    `loadedXML` function:

```
//dissect
movieTitle = allText.attributes.title
trace(movieTitle)
```

2. Test the movie. You should see another line appear:
    `"Three Days of the Condor"`.

ABOUT THE CODE

Remember, the `allText` object is this:

```
<screenplay title="Three Days of the Condor">
  … everything else …
</screenplay>
```

The code looks for the attribute named `title` (since a node can have more than one attribute) and places that value in `movieTitle`, which is then displayed.

Let's move on to checking out all the elements within the `<screenplay>` node. Because we've seen it, we know the file is structured like this:

```
<screenplay title="Three Days of the Condor">
    <author>...author>
    <author>...</author>
    <character type="main">...</character>
    <character type="major">...</character>
    <character type="major">...</character>
    <character type="major">...</character>
    <character type="major">...</character>
    <act number="1">...</act>
    <act number="2">...</act>
    <act number="3">...</act>
</screenplay>
```

However, it's possible that we may not know how many authors, characters, or acts this screenplay may have when it's first loaded. We can find this out by using a few new methods and properties: `childNodes`, `nodeName`, and `nextSibling`.

1. Open the Frame Actions panel and replace the `loadedXML` function with this:

```
function loadedXML()
{
    // set sub-objects
    allText = screenplayXML.firstChild;
    c = allText.firstChild;

    //dissect
    movieTitle = allText.attributes.title
    trace(movieTitle)

    // finding number of child nodes
    allTextChildren = allText.childNodes;
    numChildren = allTextChildren.length;

    for (i=0; i<numChildren; i++)
    {
        // display name of node
```

```
            trace(c.nodeName)
            c = c.nextSibling;
        }
    }
```

2. Test the movie. You should see the name of the screen-play, two <author>s, five <character>s and three <act>s.

ABOUT THE CODE

The first new thing we introduced is the XML object c, which is the first child of allText. That is, c is the first <author> element. I'll repeat, because it's important: c is a child node of allText.

The next new thing is childNodes. The action xmlObject.childNodes returns an array of the specified XML object's children. Thus, allText.childNodes returns an array of all of the child nodes of <screenplay>. We then deduce how many of these children there are by examining the length of the array numChildren.

Once we know the number of children, we start a loop. First, we display the name of node c. Remember, c is the child of allText, so its nodeName is <author>. Next, we update the value of c by looking at the next node in the document. These adjacent nodes are known as *siblings*. Hence, we update c to be c.nextSibling. We do this for the length of the loop, which is as long as there are child nodes in allText (that is, within <screenplay>).

Just listing the node names isn't particularly useful information. Let's add some more info to this list to make it more meaningful.

1. Open the Frame Actions panel and replace the for statement in the loadedXML function with this:

```
for(i=0; i<numChildren; i++)
{
    // find number of authors
    if(c.nodeName == "author")
    {
        authorName = c.firstChild.nodeValue;
        trace("author: " + authorName);
```

```
    }
    else if(c.nodeName == "character")
    {
        typeChar = c.attributes.type;
        characterName = c.firstChild.nodeValue;
        trace("character: " + typeChar + ": " +
characterName);              }
    else if(c.nodeName == "act")
    {
        actNum = c.attributes.number
        trace("act" + actNum);
    }
    c = c.nextSibling;
}
```

2. Test the movie.

3. The expected result is

```
Three Days of the Condor
author: Lorenzo Semple, Jr.
author: David Rayfiel
character: main: Turner
character: major: Kathy
character: major: Higgins
character: major: Jobert
character: major: Mr. Wabash
act1
act2
act3
```

ABOUT THE CODE

The first thing we're doing is testing for the value of the node names and then looking deeper into the elements. In the first section, we're looking for the authors. We're starting with c (which for the first child node is <author>), then looking at the first child (which is the text node), and then looking at the value of that first child. Please note that for the purposes of display, the nodeValue isn't required—delete it and the text will display just fine without it. It's in the code here just to teach you of its existence, since if you wanted to read that text into a string variable, or change that node's value, it's best to use nodeValue.

The rest of the code is nothing precisely new—we're just adding more techniques to the commands we already know. Now let's add a few more twists to the code.

1. Open the Frame Actions panel and replace the `for` statement with the following:

```
for (i=0; i<numChildren; i++)
{
    cNodeStr = c.firstChild.nodeValue.toString();

    // find number of authors
    if (c.nodeName == "author")
    {
        if(cNodeStr.indexOf("Lorenzo") != -1)
        {
            c.firstChild.nodeValue = "Clark Kent";
        }
        authorName = c.firstChild;
        trace("author: " + authorName);
    }
    else if (c.nodeName == "character")
    {
        if(cNodeStr.indexOf("Wabash") != -1)
        {
            d = c.previousSibling;
            c.removeNode();
            c = d;
        }
        else
        {
            typeChar = c.attributes.type;
            characterName = c.firstChild.nodeValue;
            trace("character: " + typeChar + ": " +
characterName);
        }
    }
    else if (c.nodeName == "act")
    {
        actNum = c.attributes.number
        trace("act" + actNum);
    }

    c = c.nextSibling;
}
```

2. Test the movie. The results should be

```
Three Days of the Condor
author: Clark Kent
author: David Rayfiel
character: main: Turner
character: major: Kathy
character: major: Higgins
character: major: Jobert
act1
act2
act3
```

ABOUT THE CODE

We're doing two things in this code: changing the name of one of the authors and removing one of the characters.

We've decided that Lorenzo didn't cowrite this screenplay, but rather, David's partner was Clark Kent. So, we're going to search for the name Lorenzo in the author's names, and when we find it, replace it with Clark Kent.

We begin this search by creating a new variable:

```
cNodeStr = c.firstChild.nodeValue.toString();
```

This cNodeStr looks at the value of the text node and changes it into a string. So, when c is <author>Lorenzo Semple, Jr.</author>, cNodeStr will be Lorenzo Semple, Jr.

We then test cNodeStr to see if Lorenzo is anywhere in that string. To do this, we're using one of the string functions, indexOf. If Lorenzo is in the string, we change the value of that node to Clark Kent.

```
c.firstChild.nodeValue = "Clark Kent";
```

Our next task is to remove Mr. Wabash as one of the major characters. We've decided he doesn't have enough lines, or impact the main character enough, to qualify as a major character. This one is a little more involved.

We look for Wabash in the text node. If we find it, we create a new XML object called d, which is the previous sibling to c: that is, d is the node that appears before the node with Wabash. In this case, d becomes <character

type="major">Jobert</character>. We then remove c completely with the removeNode() method. When we invoke this method, the c object disappears entirely—it doesn't exist anymore. If we tried to find a sibling or a child of c after removing it, nothing would happen. Thus we re-create c as d, or the node just previous to the one containing poor Mr. Wabash. The code continues along its merry way, and when it has to find the next sibling to c, it goes directly from the node carrying Jobert to the first <act> node, since the character node containing Mr. Wabash no longer exists.

For reference, here's all of the code for *xml1.fla*:

```
//create XML object
screenplayXML = new XML();

// load external file into XML object
screenplayXML.load("screenplay_space.xml");

// when loading is complete, go to a special function
screenplayXML.onLoad = loadedXML;

function loadedXML()
{
    // set sub-objects
    allText = screenplayXML.firstChild;
    c = allText.firstChild;

    //dissect
    movieTitle = allText.attributes.title
    trace(movieTitle)

    // finding number of child nodes
    allTextChildren = allText.childNodes;
    numChildren = allTextChildren.length;

    for(i=0; i<numChildren; i++)
    {
        cNodeStr = c.firstChild.nodeValue.toString();

        // find number of authors
        if(c.nodeName == "author")
        {
            if(cNodeStr.indexOf("Lorenzo") != -1)
            {
```

```
                    c.firstChild.nodeValue = "Clark
                        Kent";
            }
            authorName = c.firstChild;
            trace("author: " + authorName);
        }
        else if(c.nodeName == "character")
        {
            if(cNodeStr.indexOf("Wabash") != -1)
            {
                d = c.previousSibling;
                c.removeNode();
                c = d;
            }
            else
            {
                typeChar = c.attributes.type;
                characterName = c.firstChild.nodeValue;
                trace("character: " + typeChar + ": " +
characterName);
            }
        }
        else if(c.nodeName == "act")
        {
            actNum = c.attributes.number
            trace("act" + actNum);
        }

        c = c.nextSibling;
    }
}
```

That's all we're going to do as far as reading an imported
XML document goes. Our next task is to create from scratch,
using only Flash, the XML that you see in *screenplay.xml*.

Creating XML

The key to creating XML in Flash is that creating a node in an
XML object is a two-step process. First, an element must be
created. Then it must be placed. You can't do both at once. Let's
begin, and you'll see exactly what I mean.

Creating the Object

1. Create a new Flash file called *xml2.fla*.
2. Click on the frame in layer 1 and open its Frame Actions panel.
3. Enter this code:

```
// create XML object
screenplayXML = new XML();

// create screenplay element/node
screenElement =
screenplayXML.createElement("screenplay");

// place the screenplay element
screenplayXML.appendChild(screenElement);
screenElement.attributes.title = "Three Days of the
Condor";

// display
trace(screenplayXML.firstChild);
```

4. Test the movie. The result should be

```
<screenplay title="Three Days of the Condor" />
```

ABOUT THE CODE

As you can tell, we're starting small. We're creating an empty XML object called `screenplayXML`. Then, we create an element (or node) of that XML object, and we call that element `screenElement`. At this point, that element has no parent and no child—it's just kind of floating around in the ether. We give this roaming element a home by appending (or adding) it as a child to the `screenplayXML` object. `screenElement` is now a child node of `screenplayXML`. We finish this off by adding an attribute to `screenElement` and displaying the result.

ABOUT THE RESULT

We're not seeing a `<screenplay></screenplay>` because there's nothing inside the node yet. When that happens, Flash uses the XML shorthand of ending a tag in `/>` to indicate that there's no closing tag.

Creating the Authors

Now let's add the first author element.

1. In the frame actions, just above the section of code that displays the XML (the `trace` statement), and below the code that creates and places the screenplay element, add this code:

```
//create first author element
authorElement =
screenplayXML.createElement("author");
authorName = screenplayXML.createTextNode("Lorenzo
Semple, Jr.")

//place first author element
screenElement.appendChild(authorElement);
authorElement.appendChild(authorName);
```

2. Test the movie. The result should be

```
<screenplay title="Three Days of the Con-
dor"><author>Lorenzo Semple, Jr.</author></screenplay>
```

ABOUT THE CODE

In creating the first `<author>` element, we use `createEle-ment` just as we did to create the `<screenplay>` node. In addition, we create a text node, which is just like a regular node, but instead of having tags, it's just a text string. We then place the two elements: We place the `<author>` element inside of the `<screenplay>` node, and we place the text node (the name of the author) inside the `<author>` element.

Since there are two authors, let's give the second one his due. But since we've already created an `<author>` element, all we have to do is copy that one and change the name. Copying a node is known as *cloning* in Flash.

1. Insert this code after placing the first author statement, but before displaying the XML:

```
// create and place second author element
authorElem2 = authorElement.cloneNode(true);
screenElement.appendChild(authorElem2);
authorElem2.firstChild.nodeValue = "David Rayfiel";
```

2. Test the movie. The result should be:

```
<screenplay title="Three Days of the
   Condor"><author>Lorenzo Semple, Jr.
   </author><author>David Rayfiel</author>
   </screenplay>
```

ABOUT THE CODE

We start by copying (or cloning) the first author element. The argument for `cloneNode` is either `true` or `false`, which means that either all the child nodes of the cloned node are copied as well (the argument is `true`), or the children are not clones (argument is `false`). We're setting it to `true` because we want the author's name copied as well. That way, we don't have to re-create another text node and append it to the cloned node—we can just change the value of the already present text node.

Creating the Characters

Creating the character nodes is more good practice in cloning nodes. The big things to take away from creating these nodes are more practice and learning that cloning nodes also clones the attributes of those nodes.

1. Add this code after that of the authors, but above the display:

```
//create a character element
charElement = screenplayXML.createElement("character");
charName = screenplayXML.createTextNode("Turner");

//place main character element
screenElement.appendChild(charElement);
charElement.appendChild(charName);
charElement.attributes.type = "main";

//create remaining character elements
charElement2 = charElement.cloneNode(true);
charElement2.attributes.type = "major";
charElement2.firstChild.nodeValue = "Kathy";

charElement3 = charElement2.cloneNode(true);
charElement3.firstChild.nodeValue = "Higgins";
```

```
charElement4 = charElement2.cloneNode(true);
charElement4.firstChild.nodeValue = "Jobert";

charElement5 = charElement2.cloneNode(true);
charElement5.firstChild.nodeValue = "Mr. Wabash";

// place character elements
screenElement.appendChild(charElement2);
screenElement.appendChild(charElement3);
screenElement.appendChild(charElement4);
screenElement.appendChild(charElement5);
```

2. Test the movie. The result should look like this:

```
<screenplay title="Three Days of the
  Condor"><author>Lorenzo Semple, Jr.</
  author><author>David Rayfiel</author><character
  type="main">Turner</character><character
  type="major">Kathy</character><character
  type="major">Higgins</character><character
  type="major">Jobert</character><character
  type="major">Mr. Wabash</character></screenplay>
```

ABOUT THE CODE

Creating the main character and the first major character is nothing new. Just notice that we start cloning the second <character> element in order to copy its type="major" attribute, so we don't have to reset it for each <character> node.

The Whole Thing

The rest of the code to create the full screenplay XML document is pretty similar to what we've been looking at. I'll place everything here.

```
// create XML object
screenplayXML = new XML();

// create screenplay element/node
screenElement =
screenplayXML.createElement("screenplay");

// place the screenplay element
```

```
screenplayXML.appendChild(screenElement);
screenElement.attributes.title = "Three Days of the
Condor";

//create first author element
authorElement = screenplayXML.createElement("author");
authorName = screenplayXML.createTextNode("Lorenzo
Semple, Jr.")

//place first author element
screenElement.appendChild(authorElement);
authorElement.appendChild(authorName);

// create and place second author element
authorElem2 = authorElement.cloneNode(true);
screenElement.appendChild(authorElem2);
authorElem2.firstChild.nodeValue = "David Rayfiel";

//create a character element
charElement = screenplayXML.createElement("character");
charName = screenplayXML.createTextNode("Turner");

//place main character element
screenElement.appendChild(charElement);
charElement.appendChild(charName);
charElement.attributes.type = "main";

//create remaining character elements
charElement2 = charElement.cloneNode(true);
charElement2.attributes.type = "major";
charElement2.firstChild.nodeValue = "Kathy";

charElement3 = charElement2.cloneNode(true);
charElement3.firstChild.nodeValue = "Higgins";

charElement4 = charElement2.cloneNode(true);
charElement4.firstChild.nodeValue = "Jobert";

charElement5 = charElement2.cloneNode(true);
charElement5.firstChild.nodeValue = "Mr. Wabash";

// place character elements
screenElement.appendChild(charElement2);
screenElement.appendChild(charElement3);
screenElement.appendChild(charElement4);
screenElement.appendChild(charElement5);
```

```
//create the acts
actElement = screenplayXML.createElement("act");
actElement.attributes.number = "1";

actElement2 = actElement.cloneNode(true);
actElement2.attributes.number = "2";

actElement3 = actElement.cloneNode(true);
actElement3.attributes.number = "3";

//place the acts
screenElement.appendChild(actElement);
screenElement.appendChild(actElement2);
screenElement.appendChild(actElement3);

//create act 1 elements
dramaNeedElement =
screenplayXML.createElement("dramaticNeed");
dramaNeedText = screenplayXML.createTextNode("Who's
trying to kill Turner and why?")
plotPointElement =
screenplayXML.createElement("plotPoint");
plotPointText = screenplayXML.createTextNode("Turner
returns from lunch to find everyone in his bookish
CIA office dead");

//place act 1 elements
actElement.appendChild(dramaNeedElement);
actElement.appendChild(plotPointElement);
dramaNeedElement.appendChild(dramaNeedText);
plotPointElement.appendChild(plotPointText);

//create act 2 elements
obstacleElement1 =
screenplayXML.createElement("obstacle");
obstacleElement1.attributes.description = "Turner
tries to get to a safe place"

obstacleElement2 = obstacleElement1.cloneNode(true)
obstacleElement2.attributes.description = "Mailman/
assasin attacks Turner";

sequenceElement1 =
screenplayXML.createElement("sequence");
sequenceText1 = screenplayXML.createTextNode("Turner
calls HQ");
sequenceElement1.appendChild(sequenceText1);
```

```
sequenceElement2 = sequenceElement1.cloneNode(true);
sequenceElement2.firstChild.nodeValue = "Turner is
betrayed in alley"

sequenceElement3 = sequenceElement1.cloneNode(true);
sequenceElement3.firstChild.nodeValue = "Turner and
mailman fight. Turner wins";

plotPointElement2 = plotPointElement.cloneNode(true);
plotPointElement2.firstChild.nodeValue = "Turner
captures head CIA deputy and becomes attacker instead
of victim";

//place act 2 elements
actElement2.appendChild(obstacleElement1);
actElement2.appendChild(obstacleElement2);
actElement2.appendChild(plotPointElement2);

obstacleElement1.appendChild(sequenceElement1);
obstacleElement1.appendChild(sequenceElement2);
obstacleElement2.appendChild(sequenceElement3);

// create act 3 elements
resolutionElement =
screenplayXML.createElement("resolution");
tagElement = screenplayXML.createElement("tagScene");

resolutionText = screenplayXML.createTextNode("Turner
finds the man who ordered the murders, and why they
were done");
tagSceneText = screenplayXML.createTextNode("Turner
gives his story to the NY Times, and wonders if they
will print it");

//place act 3 elements
actElement3.appendChild(resolutionElement);
actElement3.appendChild(tagElement);

resolutionElement.appendChild(resolutionText);
tagElement.appendChild(tagSceneText);

// display
trace(screenplayXML.firstChild)
```

If you go through this example and understand every line, you'll be able to whip up almost any kind of XML document out there. If you're feeling especially energetic, start altering the placement of the statements. Put all of the create-Element statements together, and then mix up all the placement statements, and see what happens. Mostly, the XML will stay the same, but occasionally, it'll change. Seeing when it changes and when it doesn't will hone your XML skills.

Now we'll briefly look at XMLSocket, which is a way to open a connection to a server that stays open.

The XMLSocket Object

Using XMLSocket, you can create a continuous connection between your Flash movie and a server. This can be useful in applications such as chat rooms, where the server can send data to your Flash movie as soon as it's available, instead of waiting for an HTTP request from your movie (which is how most of the Web works).

While a continuous open connection can be useful, it's pretty tricky to set up. There has to be a special application on the server that will allow a connection to be open. That means you can't just use XMLSocket in your Flash file and expect it to somehow connect to your ISP and give you a continuously open connection. XMLSocket requires a specific setup in order to work properly. You'll have to check with your ISP to see if they have that setup available (chances are they don't, so don't hold your breath). The server must run a daemon that understands the protocol used by the XMLSocket object.

If you do get lucky enough to have access to that kind of connection, then you can use the connect method to do the actual connecting, and send to send your XML to the server.

Macromedia has installed a couple of security features onto XMLSocket:

1. XMLSocket can only connect to port numbers equal to or greater than 1024. This was done because other system services, like FTP, telnet, and HTTP, often run on

below-1024 port numbers. By forcing XMLSocket to live above 1024, there's less of a chance that someone will use it for hacking purposes.

2. XMLSocket can only connect to a server in the same subdomain as the SWF file that contains the XMLSocket object. This is the same restriction as for loadVariables.

That's the extent that we'll be looking at XMLSocket in this book. Chances are, most of you will be using loadVariables or XML.sendAndLoad to get your data.

Conclusion

If this was your first visit, welcome to XML! XML has already started to figure prominently in the plans from startup dot-coms like *icplanet.com* to the biggest of the big, Microsoft. It will always be a good thing to know XML, and if you've gone through this chapter, you've taken a big step.

Next, we'll look at way to figure what's happening in your Flash movie if something's wrong. Knowing how to trouble-shoot is almost as important as knowing how to code.

Troubleshooting ActionScript

Being a good troubleshooter can be as important as being a good coder, since chances are your code isn't perfect the first time you write it. In this chapter, we'll discuss some tools Flash has available to make troubleshooting easier, and we'll take a general look at troubleshooting for those of you just beginning your programming careers.

General Troubleshooting

Your biggest obstacle to finding out what's wrong with your code is usually yourself. Most people tend to get wrapped up in what they've done, how cool it is, that they did it right, and it should work, darn it! There's a tendency to blame everything else except your code. While this is sometimes true—a related program has a bug, or someone else messed up—most of the time the fault lies in your code, so that's a good place to start looking.

After you calm down from seeing a bug in your magnificent code, it's important to divorce yourself from your ego and your expectations and approach what's happening as logically and objectively as you can. This may sound blindingly obvious, but it's easy to forget when you're in the moment. Coding may seem like an unemotional task, but most programmers are quite emotional about what they're building, and when it goes wrong, it can sometimes be difficult to step back from your creation and look objectively at what's happening.

So, to be a good troubleshooter, emotionally step back from the code and look at it as objectively as you can.

Debugger

The Debugger window is a panel that you only need open when your Flash movie is playing. The Debugger is handy because it allows you to look at and alter certain parts of your movie while it's playing. You can

- Watch the values of all the variables in the movie and see how they change while the movie plays.
- Change some properties of movie clips while they play.
- Change the values of variables.
- Create a list of watched variables (helpful if you have a lot of variables but are curious about only a few of them).
- Change the values of watched variables.

In order to view and use the Debugger window, we're going to use a movie that features a baby bird trying to fly over

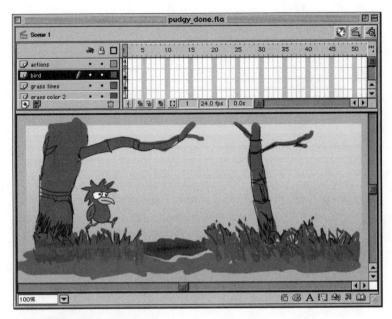

FIGURE 6–1 The bird movie

a puddle. Let's see some parts of the movie that we're going to be looking at and changing.

The Pudgy Bird Movie

Go ahead and open the movie *chapter6/pudgy_done.fla*. We'll be looking at this movie in more detail in the next chapter, but for now, let's just see what it does. See Figure 6-1.

The little bird is a movie clip that has four sections: standing, running, flying, and falling. Depending on what keys the user is pressing and where the bird is on the screen, those different sections are played. If the user isn't pressing any keys, the bird is stationary (standing), as shown in Figure 6-2.

If the right or left keys are being pressed, the bird is moved and is placed in the "running" frames, as shown in Figure 6-3.

If the up arrow is pressed, the bird takes off in flight, as shown in Figure 6-4.

If the user runs Pudgy into the puddle, he falls into it, as shown in Figure 6-5.

FIGURE 6–2 Standing Pudgy

FIGURE 6–3 Running Pudgy

FIGURE 6–4 Flying Pudgy

FIGURE 6–5 Falling Pudgy

FIGURE 6–6 Splashing puddle

The puddle also splashes, as shown in Figure 6-6.

This movie uses a number of variables to keep track of what's going on during the movie, such as `fallingNow`, `runningNow`, `jump`, `rightArrowDown`, `leftArrowDown`, and others. We can also set the height and distance of Pudgy's jumps.

Opening the Debugging Window

This is more complicated than it should be, and more so than Macromedia intended, I think. On both Macintosh and Windows, this requires more steps than the manual says it should, so I think there's a wee bug involved in opening up the debugging window—it's no big deal, but the steps to make it work will seem odd to you without this explanation.

1. Open the file *chapter6/pudgy_done.fla* from the CD.
2. Control ➠ Debug Movie.
    The movie and the Debugger window will appear. It'll look like Figure 6-7.
    There's supposed to be some useful information in that window.

FIGURE 6–7 The movie and Debugger window

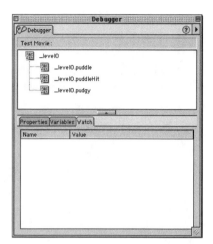

FIGURE 6–8 The active and working Debugger window

3. Close the Debugger window.

4. Control-click (Mac users) or right-click (Windows folk) on the movie and choose Debugger from the contextual menu that pops up.

5. A new Debugger window should appear that looks like Figure 6-8.

6. Notice that all the symbols in the movie are listed in the Display window, preceded by _level0 or possibly by _root. Click on the pudgy instance (_level0.pudgy).

7. Click on the Variables tab. It should look like Figure 6-9.

8. Click back on the movie and start pressing arrow keys (except the down arrow—that one doesn't do anything).

Notice that the variables are changing as the movie plays. Keeping the Debugger window open may slow down your movie somewhat.

Did you notice that once you started pressing keys, more variables appeared? When a Flash movie creates new variables, those appear in the Debugger as well, as shown in Figure 6-10.

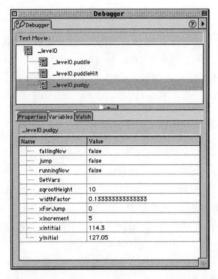

FIGURE 6–9 The Debugger with initial variables

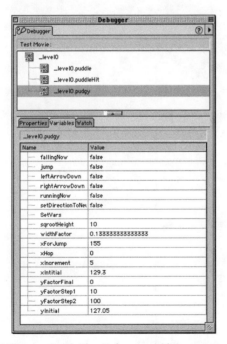

FIGURE 6–10 The Debugger with just-created variables

Watching Variables

Let's say this long list of variables is good, but we're only interested in a few of them. We can separate one or more variables from different levels or movie clips and watch them all in one place. Let's choose five variables from the long list and watch just those.

1. Play the Pudgy game for a few seconds by pressing the arrow keys (this initializes some variables).
2. Control-click (Mac) or right-click (Windows) on `fallingNow` in the `_level0.pudgy` variable list (click on the Variables tab if it isn't highlighted).
3. Choose Watch. It's the only option. Note that a blue dot appears next to the variable name.
4. Do the same for `jump`, `leftArrowDown`, `right-ArrowDown`, and `runningNow`.
5. Notice that the variable list should now look like Figure 6-11.

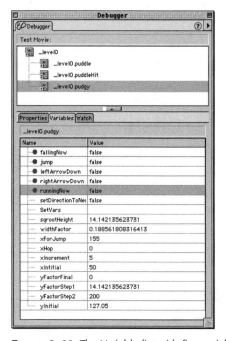

FIGURE 6–11 The Variable list with five variables marked as Watched

FIGURE 6–12 The Watch list

6. Click on the Watch tab. It should look something like Figure 6-12.

7. Notice something odd? The variables are listed using what's called *slash syntax* (as opposed to the dot syntax Flash 5 uses). Slash syntax is left over from Flash 4, so if you've used Flash before, this is probably familiar to you. If not, don't worry: the meaning is the same. `_level0/pudgy:jump` is the same thing as `_level0.pudgy.jump`. In slash syntax, levels of hierarchy are denoted by slashes and variables are preceded by a colon.

8. Click back on the movie and start using the arrow keys again. Notice how the variables change as you move Pudgy about the screen.

Changing Properties

You can also change some properties of the movie clips on the running movie.

1. Click on `_level0.pudgy` in the Debugger window's display list.

2. Click on the Properties tab.

3. Try double-clicking some of the property values and changing them. The ones you can change are colored black. The others are gray.

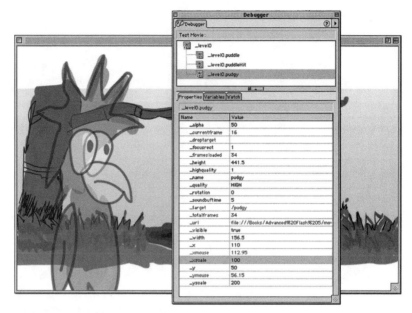

FIGURE 6–13 The property-tweaked Pudgy

4. Double-click the value next to _alpha. Enter *50* and press enter.

5. Double-click the value next to _xscale. Enter *100* and press enter.

6. Double-click the value next to _yscale. Enter *200* and press enter.

7. Double-click the value next to _y. Enter *50* and press enter.

You get the idea. The tweaked movie should look something like Figure 6-13.

Changing Variables

An impressive feature of the Debugging window is its ability to change variables on the fly, without altering any of the underlying code. Let's look at an example.

1. Close the Debugger and the SWF file.

2. Open Scene 1.

3. Click on the frame in the actions layer and open the Frame Actions panel.
4. The code is

```
// Set global values for how high and how far
// Pudgy will jump when he does jump.
// These are the values we'll change
// in the Debugger window.
distance = 150;
height = 100;
```

5. Close the Actions panel.
6. Control ➡ Debug Movie.
7. Close the Debugger.
8. Open a new Debugger by control-clicking or right-clicking on the movie and choosing Debugger.
9. In the Display list, click on `_level0`.
10. Click the Variables tab.
11. Change the `height` value to 250.
12. Change the `distance` value to 150.
13. Click on the SWF movie.
14. Pudgy flies much higher and further now.

Now let's try to change some of the variables for Pudgy.

1. Click on `_level0.pudgy`.
2. Click the Variables tab.
3. Change the values of any of the variables.
4. Click back on the movie and start playing. Note that the values of the variables go back to their original values. This is happening because those values are continually set by the movie. You did change their values, but the movie then changed them back.

One final note: when you're changing the value of variables with the Debugger, you have to use constants like `7` and `fringe`. You can't use expressions like `x * 7` or `toString(followNum)`.

So, that's the story for the Debugger. It can definitely be useful, but I find I use `trace` more than anything else to debug my movies.

Trace

You've seen `trace` used repeatedly in this book. It's a simple command, but it can be powerful if you show the right information at the right time. `trace` has an advantage over the Debugger in that it always prints on the next line, instead of constantly updating a single line, as the Debugger does. This allows you to see a history of the movie, instead of just one point in time.

For example, in creating this little Pudgy movie, crude though it may be, it was somewhat challenging to move Pudgy's playhead to the right place at all the right times. For example, if the user let go of one of the right or left arrow keys while the bird was in the air, when the bird landed, it kept moving in the direction of the key that had been released, flapping madly on the ground, even though no key was being pressed. I ended up using `trace` extensively to figure out what was happening at which point.

Let's get into some code to look at this a little closer.

1. In the Pudgy movie, click on the bird.
2. Open the Object Actions panel.

There's a lot here. We are going to look at one part of the code inside the `onClipEvent(enterFrame)` chunk. Here's the whole section:

```
onClipEvent(enterFrame)
{
    if((this.jump) && (xForJump <= _root.distance)
      && (!fallingNow))
    {
        // set jumping height
        yFactorStep1 = (widthFactor * xForJump) -
          sqrootHeight;
        yFactorStep2 = Math.pow(yFactorStep1, 2);
        yFactorFinal = _root.height - yFactorStep2;

        // actually move the object
        this._y = yInitial - yFactorFinal;
        this._x = this._x + xHop;
```

```
        // prepare for next loop
        xForJump = xForJump + 5;
}
else if(this.hitTest(_root.puddleHit))
{
        // the bird is falling
        if(!fallingNow)
        {
            //move Pudgy to the center of the
            // puddle, so he's falling in the water
            // so 1) the splash will make sense and
            // 2) he doesn't fall in the middle of
            // some grass
            fallingNow = true;
            this._x = _root.puddle._x;
            this.gotoAndPlay("falling");
        }

}
else
{
        // turn off jumping
        jump = false;

        //turn off falling
        fallingNow = false;

        // if user let go of a direction key while
        // in flight, reset it now
        if(setDirectionToNeutral)
        {
            leftArrowDown = false;
            rightArrowDown = false;
            xHop = 0;

            // this variable's job is done
            setDirectionToNeutral = false;
        }
        else if(rightArrowDown || leftArrowDown)
        {
            // allows the user to move Pudgy in
            // different directions without jumping
            this._x = this._x + xHop;
            runningNow = true;
        }
```

```
        else
        {
            // Pudgy is standing still
            this.gotoAndStop("standing");
            runningNow = false;
        }
    }
}
```

We're going to look at just one part of this:

```
if(setDirectionToNeutral)
{
    leftArrowDown = false;
    rightArrowDown = false;
    xHop = 0;

    // this variable's job is done
    setDirectionToNeutral = false;
}
```

As it is right now, it works as it should. That is, when the bird lands, it stops flying. Let's break the code, and then fix it, using `trace` to help us.

1. Change the code to:

```
if(setDirectionToNeutral)
{
    //leftArrowDown = false;
    //rightArrowDown = false;
    //xHop = 0;

    // this variable's job is done
    setDirectionToNeutral = false;
}
```

2. Test the movie.

Imagine you're trying to fix this problem. You've created this variable called `setDirectionToNeutral` and you think you've put it in the right places, but you don't know what to do with it yet. Before you start coding, test to see if it's being called at the right times. We want to stop the bird when it lands, and only if the user lets go of the right or left arrow key while the bird is in the air. We'll use `trace` to see if we're on the right track (we know we are, but pretend we don't).

1. Change the code to

```
if(setDirectionToNeutral)
{
        trace("land and chill");
        //leftArrowDown = false;
        //rightArrowDown = false;
        //xHop = 0;

        // this variable's job is done
        setDirectionToNeutral = false;
}
```

2. Test the movie. It looks like the message is appearing at the right time in the movie, so we can now start coding to make Pudgy stop flapping and moving once he hits the ground.

3. Change the code to

```
if(setDirectionToNeutral)
{
    leftArrowDown = false;
    rightArrowDown = false;
    xHop = 0;

    // this variable's job is done
    setDirectionToNeutral = false;
}
```

4. Test the movie again to make sure it works.

Comments

Odd as it may sound, using comments appropriately can be one of the easiest troubleshooting tools you have. Once your movies start to get complicated, it gets harder to understand what's going on by simply reading the code. The only way to show this is to show a sample of code with comments next to

one without comments. Let's look at all of the Object Actions
for Pudgy. First, let's look at them without comments:

```
onClipEvent(load)
{
    SetVars();
    this.gotoAndStop("standing");
    function SetVars()
    {
        sqrootHeight = Math.sqrt(_root.height);
        widthFactor = (2 * sqrootHeight) /
            _root.distance;
        yInitial = this._y;
        xIntitial = this._x;
        xForJump = 0;
        xIncrement = 5;
    }
}


onClipEvent(keyDown)
{
    if(!fallingNow)
    {
        if(Key.getCode() == Key.RIGHT)
        {
            rightArrowDown = true;
            this._xscale = 40;
            if((!runningNow) && (!jump))
            {
                this.gotoAndPlay("running");
                runningNow = true;
            }

            leftArrowDown = false;
            setDirectionToNeutral = false;
            xHop = 1 * xIncrement;
        }
        else if(Key.getCode() == Key.LEFT)
        {
            leftArrowDown = true;
            this._xscale = -40;
            if((!runningNow) && (!jump))
            {
                this.gotoAndPlay("running");
                runningNow = true;
            }
```

```
              rightArrowDown = false;
              setDirectionToNeutral = false;
              xHop = (-1) * xIncrement;
          }
          else if((Key.getCode() == Key.UP) && (!jump))
          {
              jump = true;
              this.gotoAndPlay("flying");
              SetVars();
          }
      }
}


onClipEvent(keyUp)
{
    if(!fallingNow)
    {
        if(Key.getCode() == Key.RIGHT)
        {
            runningNow = false;
            if(this.jump)
            {
                setDirectionToNeutral = true;
            }
            else
            {
                this.gotoAndStop("standing");
                rightArrowDown = false;
                xHop = 0;
            }
        }
        else if(Key.getCode() == Key.LEFT)
        {
            runningNow = false;
            if(this.jump)
            {
                setDirectionToNeutral = true;
            }
            else
            {
                this.gotoAndStop("standing");
                runningNow = false;
                leftArrowDown = false;
                xHop = 0;
            }
        }
    }
}
```

```
onClipEvent(enterFrame)
{
    if((this.jump) && (xForJump <= _root.distance)
      && (!fallingNow))
    {
        yFactorStep1 = (widthFactor * xForJump) -
          sqrootHeight;
        yFactorStep2 = Math.pow(yFactorStep1, 2);
        yFactorFinal = _root.height - yFactorStep2;
        this._y = yInitial - yFactorFinal;
        this._x = this._x + xHop;
        xForJump = xForJump + 5;
    }
    else if(this.hitTest(_root.puddleHit))
    {
        if(!fallingNow)
        {
            fallingNow = true;
            this._x = _root.puddle._x;
            this.gotoAndPlay("falling");
        }

    }
    else
    {
        jump = false;
        fallingNow = false;
        if(setDirectionToNeutral)
        {
            leftArrowDown = false;
            rightArrowDown = false;
            xHop = 0;
            setDirectionToNeutral = false;
        }
        else if(rightArrowDown || leftArrowDown)
        {
            this._x = this._x + xHop;
            runningNow = true;
        }
        else
        {
            this.gotoAndStop("standing");
            runningNow = false;
        }
    }
}
```

The names of the variables help a little in figuring out what's going on, but if there was something wrong in the code, it'd take a while to figure out what's happening where. Compare that with this commented code (this is an okay commenting job):

```
onClipEvent(load)
{
    // set variables for jumping
    // this calls the function a few lines down.
    SetVars();

    //set bird at right frame
    this.gotoAndStop("standing");

    function SetVars()
    {
        // set variables for jumping
        // these variables are based
        // on the x-y equation
        // y = h - (2*sqrt(h)x/d - sqrt(h))^2, where
        // h = height of the jump and
        // d = distance of the jump
        // This is a variation of the equation
        // for a parabola, y = x^2
        sqrootHeight = Math.sqrt(_root.height);
        widthFactor = (2 * sqrootHeight) /
          _root.distance;
        yInitial = this._y;
        xIntitial = this._x;
        xForJump = 0;
        xIncrement = 5;
    }
}


onClipEvent(keyDown)
{
    // we don't want the bird responding to
    // directional commands if it's falling down
    if(!fallingNow)
    {
        //determine which arrow key, if any,
        // is pressed down
        if(Key.getCode() == Key.RIGHT)
        {
```

```
            // set the correct variable and
            // make sure the bird's facing
            // the right direction
            rightArrowDown = true;
            this._xscale = 40;

            // determine whether bird should be
            // running or not
            if((!runningNow) && (!jump))
            {
                this.gotoAndPlay("running");
                runningNow = true;
            }

            leftArrowDown = false;
            setDirectionToNeutral = false;
            xHop = 1 * xIncrement;
        }
        else if(Key.getCode() == Key.LEFT)
        {
            // set the correct variable and make sure
            // the bird's facing the left direction
            leftArrowDown = true;
            this._xscale = -40;

            //determine whether bird should be
            // running or not
            if((!runningNow) && (!jump))
            {
                this.gotoAndPlay("running");
                runningNow = true;
            }

            rightArrowDown = false;
            setDirectionToNeutral = false;
            xHop = (-1) * xIncrement;
        }
        else if((Key.getCode() == Key.UP) && (!jump))
        {
            // set the stage and begin the jump process
            jump = true;
            this.gotoAndPlay("flying");
            SetVars();
        }
    }
}
```

```
onClipEvent(keyUp)
{
    // we don't want the bird to be able to jump
    // while it's falling.
    if(!fallingNow)
    {
        if(Key.getCode() == Key.RIGHT)
        {
            // This section makes sure that the bird
            // doesn't land and run in place
            runningNow = false;
            if(this.jump)
            {
                setDirectionToNeutral = true;
            }
            else
            {
                this.gotoAndStop("standing");
                rightArrowDown = false;
                xHop = 0;
            }
        }
        else if(Key.getCode() == Key.LEFT)
        {
            // This section makes sure that the bird
            // doesn't land and run in place
            runningNow = false;
            if(this.jump)
            {
                setDirectionToNeutral = true;
            }
            else
            {
                this.gotoAndStop("standing");
                runningNow = false;
                leftArrowDown = false;
                xHop = 0;
            }
        }
    }
}
```

```
onClipEvent(enterFrame)
{
    if((this.jump) && (xForJump <= _root.distance)
      && (!fallingNow))
    {
        // set jumping height
        yFactorStep1 = (widthFactor * xForJump) -
          sqrootHeight;
        yFactorStep2 = Math.pow(yFactorStep1, 2);
        yFactorFinal = _root.height - yFactorStep2;

        // actually move the object
        this._y = yInitial - yFactorFinal;
        this._x = this._x + xHop;

        // prepare for next loop
        xForJump = xForJump + 5;
    }
    else if(this.hitTest(_root.puddleHit))
    {
        // the bird is falling
        if(!fallingNow)
        {
            // move Pudgy to the center of the puddle,
            // so he's falling in the water
            // so 1) the splash will make sense and
            // 2) he doesn't fall in the middle of
            // some grass
            fallingNow = true;
            this._x = _root.puddle._x;
            this.gotoAndPlay("falling");
        }
    }
    else
    {
        // turn off jumping
        jump = false;

        //turn off falling
        fallingNow = false;

        // if user let go of a direction key
        // while in flight, reset it now
        if(setDirectionToNeutral)
        {
            leftArrowDown = false;
```

```
                rightArrowDown = false;
                xHop = 0;

                // this variable's job is done
                setDirectionToNeutral = false;
        }
        else if(rightArrowDown || leftArrowDown)
        {
                // allows the user to move Pudgy in
                // different directions without jumping
                this._x = this._x + xHop;
                runningNow = true;
        }
        else
        {
                // Pudgy is standing still
                this.gotoAndStop("standing");
                runningNow = false;
        }
    }
}
```

It's much easier to tell what's going on here, even with a mediocre commenting job. If you comment your code, you'll be able to isolate problem areas much more quickly.

Listing Object and Variables

An occasionally helpful set of tools is available when you test the movie. You can list all of the objects and all of the variables in the Output window. Here's how:

1. Test the movie.
2. Choose Debug ➧ List Objects.
3. In the Output window, you should see

```
Level #0: Frame=1
  Shape:
  Movie Clip: Frame=1 Target="_level0.puddleHit"
    Shape:
  Movie Clip: Frame=1 Target="_level0.puddle"
    Label="still"
    Shape:
  Shape:
```

```
Movie Clip: Frame=16 Target="_level0.pudgy"
  Label="standing"
  Shape:
```

This lists all of the objects in the movie, along with their initial values.

4. Choose Debug ➠ List Variables.

5. In the Output window you should see:

```
Level #0:
  Variable _level0.$version = "MAC 5,0,30,0"
  Variable _level0.distance = 150
  Variable _level0.height = 100
Movie Clip:  Target="_level0.pudgy"
Variable _level0.pudgy.SetVars = [function]
Variable _level0.pudgy.sqrootHeight = 10
Variable _level0.pudgy.widthFactor = 0.133333333333333
Variable _level0.pudgy.yInitial = 127.05
Variable _level0.pudgy.xIntitial = 114.3
Variable _level0.pudgy.xForJump = 0
Variable _level0.pudgy.xIncrement = 5
Variable _level0.pudgy.jump = false
Variable _level0.pudgy.fallingNow = false
Variable _level0.pudgy.runningNow = false
```

This lists all of the variables that initially exist in the movie.

Conclusion

Being able to troubleshoot your movie is essential. Most importantly, relax and look at what's happening objectively. Next, use the tools above to assist in figuring out what's happening in your movie.

Our next chapter will examine several complex Flash movies and dissect them so you can see other ways of creating Flash movies and what unexpected things are possible with ActionScript.

Complex Scripting

n this chapter we'll examine three Flash movies that have a significant amount of scripting—they contain more interaction and reaction than other movies we've built. We'll start with the *Pudgy* movie, which you saw pieces of in the last chapter. We'll then move on to two pieces from the open-source brainchild of Joshua Davis, *praystation.com,* that create Flash versions of elasticity and inertia (very cool).

FIGURE 7-1 Pudgy timeline

Pudgy

This movie is a simple game. The only objective is to move a baby bird named Pudgy past a puddle by jumping over it. We don't keep score or allow a limited number of attempts. There are only two objects that have animations: the bird and the puddle. The bird has several states: running, standing, flying and falling. Figure 7-1 shows the Pudgy timeline.

The puddle has two states: still and splashing. The puddle timeline is shown in Figure 7-2.

Controls and Events

There are three controls: the left arrow, the right arrow, and the up arrow. The side arrows move the bird horizontally, and the up arrow causes the bird to jump.

Here are the events:

- When the bird is jumping, it is in the flying stage.
- When the bird is not moving, it is standing.

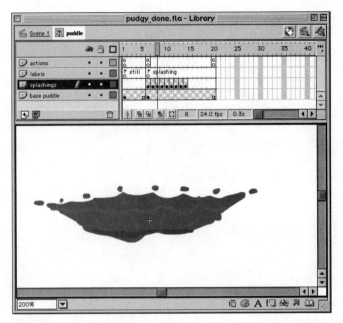

FIGURE 7–2 Puddle timeline

- When the bird is moving, but not jumping, it is running.
- The bird always faces the direction it is moving in.
- The bird can change direction mid-air.
- When the bird overlaps the puddle, it is falling.
- When the bird finishes falling, it disappears and the puddle splashes.
- When the puddle finishes splashing, the bird reappears and the puddle resets to still.

The Jump

Creating a jump that looks realistic forces us to get deeper into high school algebra than most of us would prefer. All jumps under gravity follow a parabolic path, as shown in Figure 7-3.

We don't want just any parabola, though; we want a parabola whose height and width can be manipulated, and that intersects (0,0), since that's our beginning point of when we'll be jumping.

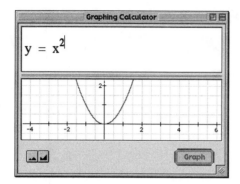

FIGURE 7-3 Basic parabola

I'll make it easy—the equation we want is

$$y = h - (2x/d * \_h - \_h)^2$$

where *h* is height of the jump and *d* is the distance of the jump. For example, if we wanted the jump to be 16 pixels high and 10 pixels wide, our equation (and graph) would look like Figure 7-4.

Let's start coding this thing.

1. Open the file *chapter7/pudgy1.fla* from the CD.
2. Click on the frame in the actions layer and open the Frame Actions panel.
3. Enter the following code:

```
// Set global values for how high and how far
// Pudgy will jump when he does jump.
distance = 150;
height = 100;
```

4. Now click on the `bird` instance on the Stage.
5. Open the Object Actions panel and enter the following code:

```
onClipEvent (load)
{
    // set variables for jumping
    // this calls the function a few lines down.
    SetVars();
```

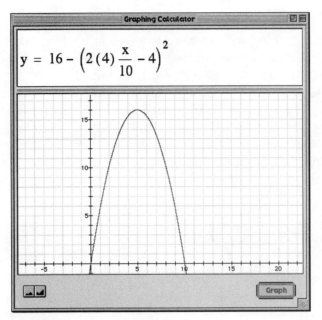

FIGURE 7-4 Our jumping parabola

```
//set bird at right frame
this.gotoAndStop("standing");

function SetVars()
{
    // set variables for jumping
    // these variables are based
    // on the x-y equation
    // y = h - (2*sqrt(h)x/d - sqrt(h))^2, where
    // h = height of the jump and
    // d = distance of the jump
    // This is a variation of the equation
    // for a parabola, y = x^2
    sqrootHeight = Math.sqrt(_root.height);
    widthFactor = (2 * sqrootHeight) /
      _root.distance;
    yInitial = this._y;
    xInitial = this._x;
    xForJump = 0;
    xIncrement = 5;
}
}
```

ABOUT THE CODE

The biggest thing we're building here is a function called Set-Vars, which initializes all the variables we'll eventually use for the jump. We're also setting the bird in the "standing" mode.

They way we'll deal with jumping is by using a variable called jump. If jump is true, then the bird's position is altered accordingly. Pressing the up arrow sets jump to true. We'll create a condition in an onClipEvent(enterFrame) that constantly looks for the value of jump, and takes appropriate action. Here's some pseudocode:

```
onClipEvent(keyDown)
{
    if Key == up arrow
    {
        jump = true
        initialize values for jumping (SetVars)
        set bird to "flying"
    }
}
```

Here's some more precise code for the enterFrame section.

```
onClipEvent(enterFrame)
{
    if jump is true and xForJump <= distance
    {
        set jumping height
        actually move the object
        prepare for next loop
    }
}
```

Now let's add some pseudocode that will cover the user moving the bird back and forth using the right and left arrows.

```
onClipEvent(keyDown)
{
    if Key == left
    {
        leftArrow = true
        rightArrow = false
        face the bird left
```

```
            if bird isn't jumping, set to running
            runningNow = true
        }
        else if Key == right
        {
            leftArrow = false
            rightArrow = true
            face the bird right
            if bird isn't jumping, set to running
            runningNow = true
        }
        else if Key == up arrow
        {
            jump = true
            initialize values for jumping (SetVars)
            set bird to "flying"
        }
    }


onClipEvent(keyUp)
{
    if Key == left
    {
        leftArrown = false
        runningNow = false
        set bird to standing
    }
    else if Key == right
    {
        leftArrown = false
        runningNow = false
        set bird to standing
    }
}


onClipEvent(enterFrame)
{
    if jump is true and xForJump <= distance
    {
        set jumping height
        actually move the object
        prepare for next loop
    }
```

```
        else
        {
            jump = false

            if leftArrowDown or rightArrowDown
            {
                move bird
                runningNow = true
            }
            else
            {
                make bird stand
                runningNow = false
            }
        }
    }
```

ABOUT THE PSEUDOCODE

The basic idea here is that the majority of real action takes place inside the enterFrame section. The other events serve to set the variables that the enterFrame section uses to make decisions about which action to take. The only real actions that occur outside of enterFrame are those that move the playhead of the Pudgy movie clip.

The only broad stroke we need to add now is the bird falling into the puddle. We'll handle that by placing a hitTest inside the enterFrame section. And since we want to disable the keys while the bird is falling (we don't want the bird to jump while it's falling), we'll add an if statement to the keyDown and keyUp sections, testing if the bird is falling or not. See if you can follow those in the pseudocode below.

```
onClipEvent (keyDown)
{
    if the bird is NOT falling
    {
        if Key == left
        {
            leftArrown = true
            rightArrow = false
            face the bird left
            if bird isn't jumping, set to running
            runningNow = true
        }
```

```
            else if Key == right
            {
                leftArrown = false
                rightArrow = true
                face the bird right
                if bird isn't jumping, set to running
                runningNow = true
            }
            else if Key == up arrow
            {
                jump = true
                initialize values for jumping (SetVars)
                set bird to "flying"
            }
        }
    }
}


onClipEvent (keyUp)
{
    if the bird is NOT falling
    {
        if Key == left
        {
            leftArrown = false
            runningNow = false
            set bird to standing
        }
        else if Key == right
        {
            leftArrown = false
            runningNow = false
            set bird to standing
        }
    }
}


onClipEvent (enterFrame)
{
    if jump is true and xForJump <= distance
    {
        set jumping height
        actually move the object
        prepare for next loop
    }
```

```
else if bird is over puddle
{
    fallingNow = true
    set bird playhead to "falling"
}
else
{
    jump = false

    if leftArrowDown or rightArrowDown
    {
        move bird
        runningNow = true
    }
    else
    {
        make bird stand
        runningNow = false
    }
}
}
```

The action of the last frame in the bird's "falling" section moves the puddle's playhead to "splashing". We'll be looking at real code for these actions instead of at pseudocode.

Frame Action for Last Frame of "falling"

```
stop();
_root.puddle.gotoAndPlay("splashing");
```

The frame actions of "splashing" then control the bird, the bird's properties, and the bird's variables.

Frame Action for First Frame of "splashing"

```
// Move Pudgy outside the puddle and hide him
// so the falling isn't triggered again
_root.pudgy._visible = false;
_root.pudgy._x = 50;
```

ABOUT THE CODE

The comments say it all: we move Pudgy outside the puddle so that he won't trigger the hitTest anymore. However, in practice, there were still a few situations where that didn't work—

Pudgy was falling over and over into the puddle in an almost endless loop. By making Pudgy invisible, the problem was solved.

Frame Action for the Last Frame in the `"splashing"` section

```
// Reset Pudgy's stats and position
_root.pudgy._visible = true;
_root.pudgy._xscale = 40;
_root.pudgy.fallingNow = false;
_root.pudgy.rightArrowDown = false;
_root.pudgy.leftArrowDown = false;

// set Pudgy to be standing still
_root.pudgy.gotoAndPlay("standing");

// move the puddle's playhead to calmness once again
gotoAndStop("still");
```

ABOUT THE CODE

When the splashing finishes, we want everything to return to normal, like it was when the movie first loaded. We make the bird visible again and set all the Boolean values to `false`. We set the bird facing right by setting its `xscale` to 40. We then set Pudgy to a standing position and move the puddle's playhead to `"still"`.

TWEAKING THE JUMP

To keep the bird from landing and running if the user lets go of the arrow keys in a certain way, we create a new variable called `setDirectionToNeutral` that we set if the user lets go of a left or right arrow while the bird is jumping. Let's go back to the pseudocode—here are the changes we'll make to the pseudocode:

```
onClipEvent(keyUp)
{
    if the bird is NOT falling
    {
        if Key == left
        {
            if bird is jumping
```

```
                    {
                            setDirectionToNeutral = true
                    }
                    else
                    {
                        leftArrown = false
                        runningNow = false
                        set bird to standing
                    }
                }
                else if Key == right
                {
                    if bird is jumping
                    {
                        setDirectionToNeutral = true
                    }
                    else
                    {
                        leftArrown = false
                        runningNow = false
                        set bird to standing
                    }
                }
            }
        }
}

onClipEvent(enterFrame)
{
    if jump is true and xForJump <= distance
    {
        set jumping height
        actually move the object
        prepare for next loop
    }
    else if bird is over puddle
    {
        fallingNow = true
        set bird playhead to "falling"
    }
    else
    {
        jump = false
        if setDirectionToNeutral
        {
            leftArrowDown = false
            rightArrowDown = false
```

```
                    setDirectionToNeutral = false
                }
                else if leftArrowDown or rightArrowDown
                {
                    move bird
                    runningNow = true
                }
                else
                {
                  make bird stand
                  runningNow = false
                }
            }
        }
```

All the Code

Now that we've gone over what the program will do and how it will work, let's unveil all the major code in the program. Here are the object actions for the bird:

```
onClipEvent(load)
{
    // set variables for jumping
    // this calls the function a few lines down.
    SetVars();

    //set bird at right frame
    this.gotoAndStop("standing");

    function SetVars()
    {
        // set variables for jumping
        // these variables are
        // based on the x-y equation
        // y = h - (2*sqrt(h)x/d - sqrt(h))^2, where
        // h = height of the jump and
        // d = distance of the jump
        // This is a variation of the equation
        // for a parabola, y = x^2
        sqrootHeight = Math.sqrt(_root.height);
        widthFactor = (2 * sqrootHeight) /
          _root.distance;
        yInitial = this._y;
        xInitial = this._x;
```

```
            xForJump = 0;
            xIncrement = 5;
    }
}

onClipEvent(keyDown)
{
    // we don't want the bird responding
    // to directional commands if it's falling down
    if(!fallingNow)
    {
        // determine which arrow key, if any,
        // is pressed down
        if(Key.getCode() == Key.RIGHT)
        {

            // set the correct variable and make sure
            // the bird's facing the right direction
            rightArrowDown = true;
            this._xscale = 40;

            // determine whether bird
            // should be running or not
            if((!runningNow) && (!jump))
            {
                this.gotoAndPlay("running");
                runningNow = true;
            }

            leftArrowDown = false;
            setDirectionToNeutral = false;
            xHop = 1 * xIncrement;
        }
        else if(Key.getCode() == Key.LEFT)
        {
            // set the correct variable and make sure
            // the bird's facing the left direction
            leftArrowDown = true;
            this._xscale = -40;

            // determine whether bird
            // should be running or not
            if((!runningNow) && (!jump))
            {
                this.gotoAndPlay("running");
```

```
                    runningNow = true;
                }

                rightArrowDown = false;
                setDirectionToNeutral = false;
                xHop = (-1) * xIncrement;
            }
            else if((Key.getCode() == Key.UP) && (!jump))
            {
                // set the stage and begin the jump process
                jump = true;
                this.gotoAndPlay("flying");
                SetVars();
            }
        }
    }
}


onClipEvent(keyUp)
{
    // we don't want the bird to be able to jump
    // while it's falling.
    if (!fallingNow)
    {
        if(Key.getCode() == Key.RIGHT)
        {
            // This section makes sure that the bird
            // doesn't land and run in place
            runningNow = false;
            if(this.jump)
            {
                setDirectionToNeutral = true;
            }
            else
            {
                this.gotoAndStop("standing");
                rightArrowDown = false;
                xHop = 0;
            }
        }
        else if(Key.getCode() == Key.LEFT)
        {
            // This section makes sure that the bird
            // doesn't land and run in place
            runningNow = false;
            if (this.jump)
```

```
                    {
                        setDirectionToNeutral = true;
                    }
                    else
                    {
                        this.gotoAndStop("standing");
                        runningNow = false;
                        leftArrowDown = false;
                        xHop = 0;
                    }
                }
            }
        }
    }


onClipEvent(enterFrame)
{
    if((this.jump) &&
        (xForJump <= _root.distance) &&
        (!fallingNow))
    {
        // set jumping height
        yFactorStep1 = (widthFactor * xForJump) -
sqrootHeight;
        yFactorStep2 = Math.pow(yFactorStep1, 2);
        yFactorFinal = _root.height - yFactorStep2;

        // actually move the object
        this._y = yInitial - yFactorFinal;
        this._x = this._x + xHop;

        // prepare for next loop
        xForJump = xForJump + 5;
    }
    else if(this.hitTest(_root.puddleHit))
    {
        // the bird is falling
        if(!fallingNow)
        {
            // move Pudgy to the center of the puddle,
            // so he's falling in the water
            // so 1) the splash will make sense and
            // 2) he doesn't fall in the middle of
            // some grass
            fallingNow = true;
```

```
                    this._x = _root.puddle._x;
                    this.gotoAndPlay("falling");
            }

    }
    else
    {
        // turn off jumping
        jump = false;

        //turn off falling
        fallingNow = false;

        // if user let go of a direction key
        // while in flight, reset it now
        if(setDirectionToNeutral)
        {
            leftArrowDown = false;
            rightArrowDown = false;
            xHop = 0;

            // this variable's job is done
            setDirectionToNeutral = false;
        }
        else if(rightArrowDown || leftArrowDown)
        {
            // allows the user to move Pudgy in
            // different directions without jumping
            this._x = this._x + xHop;
            runningNow = true;
        }
        else
        {
            // Pudgy is standing still
            this.gotoAndStop("standing");
            runningNow = false;
        }
    }
}
```

You can use this method in a number of situations—if you have a movie clip that needs to respond to user commands in numerous ways and needs to affect another movie clip on the stage, you can use the techniques outlined here.

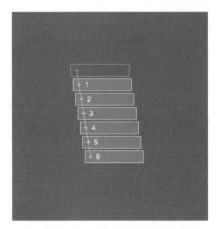

FIGURE 7–5 Screenshot of the *elasticity* movie

Elasticity

The next two movies are great: innovative, well-executed, and just darn cool. They're based on the open-source machinations of Joshua Davis and are available on his Web site, *www.praystation.com*. The movies we examine here are almost identical to the one on praystation—I've modified them slightly for teaching purposes.

You have to open the movie and play with it to get a real idea of what it does (*chapter7/elasticity.fla* on the CD). The movie (see Figure 7-5) contains several links in a chain, with each link connected by separate thin lines.

The user can drag the first link in the chain, which we'll call the anchor. When that happens, the other links in the chain move towards the anchor as if the lines are made of rubber.

Action-only Movie Clips

The big thing to keep in mind is that this movie is based on objects and their relationships to each other rather than on one central section of code that controls everything, as in the Pudgy example. One of the ways we'll be creating this object–object relationship is to create a special kind of movie clip. This movie clip will have no physical presence; that is, there aren't any

FIGURE 7–6 The two boxes

FIGURE 7–7 The dot of the auto-build instance

lines or squares or color. It's an empty movie clip. There are, however, two frames in this movie. These frames have actions. The first frame has a series of actions, and the second frame has only one action: `gotoAndPlay(1)`. That way, we have a constantly recurring set of actions. This method can take a little getting used to, but it's a great way to create modular, easily reused code.

AUTO-BUILD MOVIE CLIP

The first action-only movie clip we'll look at is *action—auto-build*. The purpose of this clip is to create the boxes in the chain. The chain begins with two boxes: the anchor and the first box, shown in Figure 7-6. The name of the anchor (shown in Figure 7-7) is *0* and the name of the first box is *1*.

The auto-build symbol is placed outside the Stage's limits—we've placed it just beyond the upper left corner. The action-only instance appears as a small dot. Here's the code for the action—auto-build symbol:

```
if(_root.currentClip < 6)
{
    duplicateMovieClip("_root." + _root.currentClip,
      _root.currentClip+1, _root.currentClip+1);
    _root.currentClip = _root.currentClip+1;
}
```

```
else
{
    stop();
}
```

ABOUT THE CODE

This code creates the six boxes, based on duplicating the first one. The initial value of currentClip is set by the main movie's frame actions:

```
// set variables
currentClip = 1;
```

When the movie starts playing, so does the auto-build instance; its code is run continuously, and five more boxes are created. When the boxes are created, they are placed on top of each other. The chain symbol, which creates the elastic-like motion, moves the boxes into position.

THE CHAIN MOVIE CLIP

This movie clip is another empty two-frame movie clip. This clip contains the meat of the movie. The movie clip does several things:

- Creates a duplicate of the *line* movie clip.
- Positions the duplicated line onto the appropriate box.
- Angles the duplicated *line* clip.
- Moves the box according to the elasticity rules.

The movement of the boxes and the placement of lines depends on the position of the previous box; for example, if you look at the box named 5, that box's position is based solely on the position of the box named 4.

Each box instance contains an instance of the chain movie clip. Thus, each box is constantly correcting its own position in relation to the box above it, as well as constantly redrawing the line connecting it to its predecessor.

Here's the actual code:

```
// This is the code that really creates the elasticity

// The line in question is duplicated,
// moved to the position of the box,
```

```
// and stretched appropriately.
// Then, the box is moved according to
// some math that determines the elasticity

// The previous clip is the one above the current clip.
// That is, if this is box #2, its
// name is "2" and the one above it is "1"
// Predictably, the top box - the one the user can drag,
// is named "0"
// Since each "chain" clip is inside a box clip,
// we have to look at the box clip's
// name, and then take one from that to get
// the name of the next box

boxNumber = _parent._name;
thisLineName = "_root.line" + boxNumber;

boxX = _parent._x;
boxY = _parent._y

previousBox = "_root." + (boxNumber - 1);

previousBoxX = getProperty(previousBox, _x)
previousBoxY = getProperty(previousBox, _y)


// Now, we'll modify the line that connects
// this box to the previous one
// this line creates a new movie clip and
// places it on a high level
duplicateMovieClip("_root.line", "line" + boxNumber,
boxNumber + 100);

// Now we'll set the properties of the line:
// its x and y position, and
// its xscale and yscale
// We have to use setProperty, because
// we're dynamically figuring out which clip this is,
// and we have to use boxName to figure that out.

// First, we set the x and y coordinates
// to be the same as the box's
setProperty(thisLineName, _x, _parent._x);
setProperty(thisLineName, _y, _parent._y);
// Now, we set the xscale and yscale of this line,
// so that it's the right shape
```

```
// and facing in the right direction
setProperty(thisLineName, _xscale, previousBoxX - boxX);
setProperty(thisLineName, _yscale, previousBoxY - boxY);

// Move the box
// The numbers here determine the
// elastic properties of the movie
// Increase the divisor to slow down the elasticity
// Decrease the divisor to speed up the elasticity
// The best way to understand what's going on here
// is to play with the numbers
setProperty(_parent, _x, (boxX + (previousBoxX - boxX)/
    2) + 2);
setProperty(_parent, _y, (boxY + (previousBoxY - boxY)/
    2) + 12);
```

ABOUT THE CODE

The parts of this code are discussed above. The best way to understand this script is to look closely at what's going on and to comment out, and possibly change, some of the lines and see the effect. Have fun with this one.

Inertia

This movie clip looks simpler than the elastic one, but it's no less interesting. This movie allows the user to drag a little box, and when the mouse button is released, the box continues moving at the same speed the user was dragging it, except that it slows gradually until it stops (see Figure 7-8). Check out *chapter7/inertia.fla* to see what it acts like. As with the elastic movie clip, this one comes from the brain of Joshua Davis, creator of *praystation.com*.

This movie has only one action-only movie clip, called *inertia*. The *inertia* clip is placed inside the box symbol, which is the little square with the crosshairs in it. The inertia clip has three sections: "stop", "map", and "coast". The "stop" section is only one frame and does exactly that—stop(). The "map" section is activated when the user is dragging the box instance, and its function is to set two variables: the horizontal and vertical speed the user is dragging the box at. When the user

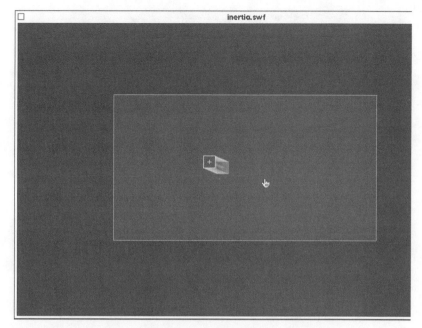

FIGURE 7–8 The coasting box after being released by a user

releases the mouse button, the `"coast"` section is called, and that code does several things:

- Determines the new position of the box, based on the horizontal and vertical speed it was moving at.
- Adjusts the box's speed, based on the inertia rules.
- Sees if the box has traveled beyond the boundaries; if so, makes it appear at the opposite side.

In other words, `"map"` sets the stage for the inertial part of the code, and `"coast"` implements it.

Let's start looking at this thing in more detail.

The Box Clip

Figure 7-9 shows what the box clip looks like.

There are several parts to the box clip.

- The box frame and the crosshairs (the `"content"` layer)
- A transparent button

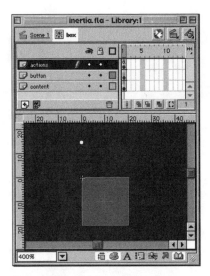

FIGURE 7–9 The box movie clip

- The inertia movie clip
- Some frame actions

Let's look at the box's frame actions first.

```
// set variables for dragging and inertia

// edges of box
left = 3;
top = 3;
bottom = 220;
right = 425;

sizeOfTarget = 22;
minX = left - sizeOfTarget;
maxX = right + sizeOfTarget;
minY = top - sizeOfTarget;
maxY = bottom + sizeOfTarget;

// Set factor of decreasing speed
// if this is greater than 1, the box
// will endlessly accelerate.
friction = 0.96;
```

ABOUT THE CODE

Like the first line implies, this section of the code's only purpose in life is to set the values that will be used to limit dragging by the *inertia* movie clip. The first four lines of real code set the limits of where the user can drag the box (we'll be seeing the `startDrag` where this is implemented soon). The next set of variables is used to determine if the box has traveled outside of the boundaries or not. The `sizeOfTarget` is just a few pixels bigger than the box image. And the last line of code is the actual coefficient that we'll use to slow down the coasting box.

A transparent button with these object actions covers the box itself.

```
on(press)
{
    startDrag(this, false, left, top, right, bottom);

    // start setting the horizontal speed and
    // vertical speed as determined by the user
    // dragging the box.
    inertia.gotoAndPlay("map");
}


on(release, releaseOutside)
{
    stopDrag();

    // initiate the coasting to a stop
    inertia.gotoAndPlay("coast");
}
```

ABOUT THE CODE

As you can see, each of these event handlers has only two lines of real code. They either start or stop dragging, and they move the *inertia* clip's playhead to the appropriate position. If the user is dragging the box, we want to set the stage for when the user lets go of the mouse button. When they do let go, we want the inertia code to take over, so we move the play head to `"coast"`.

Let's look at the *inertia* movie clip a little more closely.

FIGURE 7–10 The *inertia* movie clip

The *Inertia* Movie Clip

Figure 7-10 shows what this clip looks like.

MAP

Let's start by looking at the `"map"` part of the code. This section has only two frames: the frame with all the code and the next frame with `gotoAndPlay("map")`, which ensures that the code is constantly run. Here's the juicy part:

```
// get current coordinates of the box
newX = _parent._x;
newY = _parent._y;

// set horizontal and vertical speed
_parent.xspeed = (newX - oldX)*0.5;
_parent.yspeed = (newY - oldY)*0.5;

// prepare for next movement
oldX = newX;
oldY = newY;
```

ABOUT THE CODE

The only thing this section of code does is set the values of xspeed and yspeed, which stand for the horizontal and vertical speed of the box. When the user lets go of the mouse button, we need to know how fast that box is being dragged, and in which direction, in order to make it coast properly. To do this, we look at the current position of the box. Then, xspeed and yspeed are set by finding the average of the horizontal and vertical positions. For example, if the user dragged the box from (10,10) to (25,30) in the space of one frame, then xspeed would be 7.5 and yspeed would be 10. Then, the current position becomes the old position and the cycle is repeated. The only purpose for this code is to constantly update xspeed and yspeed.

COAST

The "coast" part of the code is also a two-frame section. The first frame has the interesting code, while the next just says gotoAndPlay("coast"). The "coast" section contains all the code for making the box travel in the direction it was going in, gradually coming to a stop. Here's some pseudocode:

```
Move the box to the new position, based on current
speed.
Change speed based on how much friction exists
If the box has moved too far right, move it to the
left edge.
If the box has moved too far left, move it to the
right edge.
If the box has moved too far down, move it to the top
edge.
If the box has moved too far up, move it to the
bottom edge.
```

That's it! Here's the actual code:

```
// set new position of square
_parent._x = _parent._x + _parent.xspeed;
_parent._y = _parent._y + _parent.yspeed;

// adjust speed according to friction rules
_parent.xspeed = _parent.xspeed * _parent.friction;
_parent.yspeed = _parent.yspeed * _parent.friction;

// wrap-around effect
if(_parent._x > _parent.maxX)
{
     _parent._x = _parent.minX;
}
```

```
else if(_parent._x < _parent.minX)
{
    _parent._x = _parent.maxX;
}
else if(_parent._y > _parent.maxY)
{
    _parent._y = _parent.minY;
}
else if(_parent._y < _parent.minY)
{
    _parent._y = _parent.maxY;
}
```

ABOUT THE CODE

We start by setting the position of the box to its current position plus the appropriate speed value. We then adjust the speed according to the friction variable. Finally, we look to see if the box has traveled outside its boundaries and, if so, transport it to the opposite side.

Conclusion

That's it! That's the tutorial section of the book. Congratulations for making it so far! We've gone from "An action is what?" to some pretty complicated scripts in just a few hundred pages. If you've understood what's going on in this book, there's no script anywhere that you can't handle (though I would challenge you to create a little movie that combines elasticity and inertia—you might end up with something looking like celestial gravity).

I hope you've enjoyed learning Flash, and that you have tons of great ideas you want to try out. Feel free to drop me a line with something cool you've done, or just something you've seen that you think is truly great. Also, email me at *flash@wire-man.com* with any questions you have and feel free to check out my site at *www.wire-man.com/flash5*.

Flash and Usability

lash is the most accessible animation program on the market. It's a wonderful combination of ease of use and power. And while this has led to some wonderful movies and animations being created (some by people who otherwise never would've been able to experiment so much), it has also led to serious abuse. If you're on a modem, you know what I'm talking about. The experience of waiting 30 seconds for a mildly interesting 2-second introductory splash screen is a frustrating one.

Many people who are creating Flash are not thinking about the user. It's clear that they're trying to make the Web more like TV with its constantly moving images. Let me be clear on this: The Web is not TV. They are fundamentally different. TV is a passive medium. People turn on the TV to escape, to be entertained without doing anything.

What Most Users Want

The vast majority of people on the Web are looking through Web sites to find *specific bits of information*. Entertainment is usually not their primary goal. Most surfers are goal-oriented, and anything that stands between them and the information they want is bad design. Unfortunately, much of the Flash out there is bad design, in that it keeps users from getting the information they want.

There are so many things Flash can do well, but they have to be done well in the right place. I would challenge you, the Flash wizard, to create Flash movies that enhance user experience not by throwing more flying text onto the screen, but rather by getting users to their information faster and more accurately than they would without Flash.

What to Do

I encourage you to create less animation (or, at the least, more strategic animation) than most Flash designers, and to use your development time to create a system, whether it's with Flash, JavaScript or whatever, that gets the user to the information they want *faster* than an all-text HTML-only site would. Given all of Flash's abilities to react to user input, I think there's a huge potential here now to create the world's fastest, most usable sites, using Flash. But it will take discipline and thinking about Flash and usability in a new way.

If you're creating a navigation scheme, do not make a 10-second movie. Create a user-centered system that does precisely what it's supposed to do—usually, to get users to the information they want as fast and as easily as possible.

For some sites, a lengthy Flash animation may be appropriate. Some sites are entertainment sites, and those could certainly benefit from some fancy Flash.

Make sure you know what kind of site you're creating, and that you know precisely what the users are looking for. If you don't know, conduct quick usability tests to find out. If done correctly, I guarantee it'll be worth the time you put into it.

ActionScript Reference

H ere's all the ActionScript. Everything here has at least one example except for the Date methods and the bitwise operators (honestly, I haven't used the bitwise operators or run into anyone who has, and I can't offer more of an explanation than exists in the Flash documentation). We'll start with a list of bitwise operators, then a list of deprecated functions, and then a bunch of reference entries for Flash 5 ActionScript.

Bitwise Operators

The bitwise operators are listed in Table B.1.

TABLE B.1 Bitwise Operators

OPERATOR	OPERATION
&	AND
&=	AND assignment
^	XOR
^=	XOR assignment
|	OR
|=	OR assignment
~	NOT
<<	left shift

(continued)

TABLE B.1 Bitwise Operators (continued)

OPERATOR	OPERATION
<<=	left shift and assignment
>>	right shift
>>=	right shift assignment
>>>	unsigned right shift
>>>=	unsigned right shift and assignment

Deprecated Functions

Deprecated means that these functions exist in Flash 4 and will still work in Flash 5, but only because they're leftovers from Flash 4. In future versions of Flash, the deprecated functions will probably disappear and no longer work. Thus, it's recommended to start coding in nondeprecated functions. Table B.2 lists alternatives to the deprecated functions.

TABLE B.2 Replacements for Deprecated Functions

DEPRECATED FUNCTION	SHOULD BE REPLACED WITH
<>	!=
and	&&
call	function
chr	String.fromCharCode
eq	==
ge	>=
gt	>
ifFrameLoaded	_framesloaded
int	Math.floor
le	<=
length	String.length
lt	<
mbchr	String.fromCharCode
mblength	String object and methods

(continued)

TABLE B.2 Replacements for Deprecated Functions (continued)

DEPRECATED FUNCTION	SHOULD BE REPLACED WITH
mbord	String.charCodeAt
mbsubstring	String.substr
ne	!=
not	!
or	||
ord	String object and methods
random	Math.random
substring	String.substring
tellTarget	with

ActionScript Reference

You might notice that I've added something here that's not in most reference sections: *Uses*. I've included some information about why you might use a certain method or property. Hopefully, this will make this reference a little more useful and educational than simply a dry listing of syntax conventions and simple examples.

-- (decrement)

SYNTAX	-- expression expression --
ARGUMENTS	The expression can be a variable, number, element in an array, or the property of an object.
DESCRIPTION	This operator subtracts 1 from the expression. Depending on the syntax used, it's either a pre-decrement or a post-decrement. A pre-decrement (--expression) subtracts 1 from the expression and returns the result. A post-decrement (expression--) subtracts 1 from the expression and returns the initial value of the expression.
PLAYER	Flash 4 or later

EXAMPLES	Pre-decrement
	x = 3;
	y = --x;
	Both x and y now have value of 2.
	Post-decrement
	x = 3;

(continued)

-- (decrement) (continued)

EXAMPLES (CONT.)	`y = x--;`
	x has a value of 2, but y has a value of 3.
	`for (i=10; i>0, i--)`
	`{`
	    `statements`
	`}`
	The variable i decrements from 10 down to 1.

USES	Use decrementing to subtract 1 from any variable. You'll find decrementing used most often in loops, as in the example. They're good for updating counters or indices.

++ increment

SYNTAX	`++ expression` `expression ++`
ARGUMENTS	The expression can be a variable, number, element in an array, or the property of an object.
DESCRIPTION	This operator adds 1 to the expression. Depending on the syntax used, it's either a pre-increment or a post-increment. A pre-increment (`++expression`) adds 1 to the expression and returns the result. A post-increment (`expression++`) adds 1 to the expression and returns the initial value of the expression.
PLAYER	Flash 4 or later

EXAMPLES	**Pre-increment**
	`x = 3;`
	`y = ++x;`
	Both x and y now have value of 4.
	`x = 3;`
	`x = ++x;`
	This results in x = 4.
	Post-increment
	`x = 3;`
	`y = x++;`
	x has a value of 4, but y has a value of 3.
	`x = 3;`
	`x = x++;`
	This results in x= 3.
	`for (i=0; i<10, i++)`
	`{`
	    `statements`
	`}`
	The variable i decrements from 10 down to 1.

(continued)

++ increment (continued)

USES	Use incrementing to add 1 to any variable. You'll find incrementing used most often in loops, as in the example. They're good for updating counters or indices.

! (logical NOT)

SYNTAX	!expression
ARGUMENTS	expression – A variable or evaluated expression.
DESCRIPTION	The ! operator (often called *bang*) inverts the Boolean value of the expression. A Boolean value is either true or false. Placing a ! in front of a true expression returns a false value, and placing a ! in front of a false expression returns a true value. This is easier to understand in practice.
PLAYER	Flash 4 or later
EXAMPLES	You probably won't use these exact examples in your code, but it should clarify the purpose of the ! operator. ```\nsheIsSingle = false;\nif (!sheIsSingle)\n{\n hitOnHer = "no";\n}\n\nenoughTequila = false\nif (!enoughTequila)\n{\n isHeHandsomeYet = "no";\n}\n```
USES	Using logical NOT is a convenient shorthand in coding, and it can make your code easier to read.

!= (inequality)

SYNTAX	expression1 != expression2
ARGUMENTS	expression1, expression2 – A variable, number, element in an array, or the property of an object.
DESCRIPTION	Operator that tests to see if the two expressions are not equal to each other—the opposite of the == operator.
PLAYER	Flash 5

(continued)

!= (inequality) (continued)

EXAMPLES	`if (5 != 8)`
	`{`
	`      trace("of course 5 isn't equal to 8")`
	`}`
	
	`if (password != "tinkerbell")`
	`{`
	`      trace("Access denied.")`
	`}`

% (modulo)

SYNTAX	`expression1 % expression2`
ARGUMENTS	`expression1, expression2` – A variable, number, element in an array, or the property of an object.
DESCRIPTION	This operator does a few things. First, it divides `expression1` by `expression2`. It then figures out what the remainder is and returns that value.
PLAYER	Flash 4+. Note: The Flash 4 player translates `x%y` to `x - int(x/y) * y`, and according to Macromedia, this may not be as fast or as accurate as the Flash 5 player.
EXAMPLES	`5 % 2 returns 1` `22 % 5 returns 2`

%= (modulo assignment)

SYNTAX	`expression1 %= expression2`
ARGUMENTS	`expression1, expression2` – Integers and variables.
DESCRIPTION	This operator assigns `expression1` the value of `expression1 % expression2`. `a %= b` is the same thing as `a = a % b`.
PLAYER	Flash 4 or later
EXAMPLES	If `a=5` and `b=2` then `a %= 2` would make a equal to 1.

&& (short-circuit AND)

SYNTAX	expression1 && expression2
ARGUMENTS	expression1, expression2 – Numbers, strings, variables, or functions.
DESCRIPTION	This operator determines if either of the expressions is false. If one of them is false, the condition as a whole is false. In greater detail, && performs a Boolean operation on expression1. If expression1 evaluates to false, then the whole of (expression1 && expression2) is considered false. Furthermore, if the first expression is false, the second expression isn't evaluated. That's why it's called short-circuit.
PLAYER	Flash 4 or later

EXAMPLES	`if ((highScore < 10000) && (timePlaying > 30))`
	`{`
	`    _root.message = "Too bad. You played long but not well.";`
	`}`
	`else if ((highScore > 10000) && (timePlaying < 30))`
	`{`
	`    _root.message = "Great job! That's a fast high score!";`
	`}`

USES	This is a necessary operator if you're going to use if statements of any level of complexity.

( ) (parentheses)

SYNTAX	(expression1, expression2) and function(argument1, …, argumentN)
ARGUMENTS	expression1, expression2 – Numbers, strings, variables, and text. function – The name of the function to be performed. argument1, …, argumentN – The values to pass to the function.
DESCRIPTION	This operator acts to group arguments and expressions together. It forces a precedence of evaluation.
PLAYER	Flash 4 or later
EXAMPLES	Usage 1: Use parentheses much like you've seen in math classes from junior high. This use causes grouping to override usual operator precedence; that is, it controls which numbers get operated on first. `(x * y) / (a + b)`

(continued)

( ) (parentheses) (continued)

EXAMPLES (CONT.)	Usage 2: Group together arguments to pass into a specified function. `screenplayXML.cloneNode(true);` `stopDrag();` `switchButtons(5);`
USES	Since parentheses are a basic part of many arithmetic techniques, as well as most methods and functions, it'd be hard to write some actions without them.

- (minus)

SYNTAX	`-(expression)` and `expression1 - expression2`
ARGUMENTS	`expression1, expression1` – Any number.
DESCRIPTION	This operator can be used in two ways: negation and subtraction. You can reverse a value sign by negating it (changing plus to minus and minus to plus). The minus operator also subtracts one numerical value from another.
PLAYER	Flash 4 or later
EXAMPLES	Negation `-(1+10) results in -11` `-(5-10) results in 5 (positive)` Subtraction `20 - 4 results in 16` `3.75 - 1.05 results in 2.7`
USES	In my experience, I use subtraction much more than negation, and usually to find out certain coordinates on the movie.

* (multiplication)

SYNTAX	`expression1 * expression2`
ARGUMENTS	`expression1, expression2` – Numbers.
DESCRIPTION	This operator multiplies two numerical expressions.
PLAYER	Flash 4 or later
EXAMPLES	`4 * 7 results in 28` `2 * 1.4 results in 2.8`
USES	You know, multiplying stuff.

*= (multiplication assignment)

SYNTAX	expression1 *= expression2
ARGUMENTS	expression1, expression2 – Numbers.
DESCRIPTION	This operator assigns expression1 the value of expression1 * expression2. That is, a *= b is the same as a = a*b.
PLAYER	Flash 4 or later
EXAMPLES	If a=3 and b=5, a *= b results in a=15

, (comma)

SYNTAX	expression1,expression2
ARGUMENTS	expression1, expression2 – Any data (numbers, variables, strings, etc.).
DESCRIPTION	This operator simply tells Flash to evaluate expression1, then expression2.
PLAYER	Flash 4 or later
EXAMPLES	_root.jumpFunction(page1, page2);

. (dot operator)

SYNTAX	object.property object.method object.childObject instanceName.variable instanceName.childInstance.variable
ARGUMENTS	object – Any instance of an object. property – Any property associated with the object (or instance). method – Any method associated with the object. childObject – Any object that's a part of another object. instanceName – Any instance of a movie clip. childInstance – Any instance of a movie clip that's a part of another movie clip. variable – Any variable in a movie clip.
DESCRIPTION	The operator's purpose in life is to provide a way to denote hierarchical relationships among objects, variables, methods, etc. You can also use dot syntax to call a method.
PLAYER	Flash 4 or later

(continued)

. (dot operator) (continued)

EXAMPLES	`screenplayXML.appendChild(author)`
	`this.dog.gotoAndPlay("drool")`
	`_root.fish._y`

USES	Dot syntax is inescapable—you need it to call other movie clips, variables, methods, etc.

?: (conditional)

SYNTAX	`expression1 ? expression2 : expression3`
ARGUMENTS	`expression1` — Any expression that can be evaluated to either `true` or `false`; usually some kind of comparison. `expression2, expression3` — Expressions of any sort.
DESCRIPTION	Using this operator causes Flash to evaluate `expression1`. If `expression1` is `true`, then the value of `expression2` is returned. If `expression1` is `false`, the value of `expression3` is returned.
PLAYER	Flash 4 or later

EXAMPLES	`a = true;`
	`b = a ? 3 : 40;`
	`trace (b)`
	This would result in 3 appearing in the Output window.

USES	You can use this as a short for a longer `if` statement. Personally, I find `if` statements a little easier to read, so I tend to use those instead of `?:`.

/ (division)

SYNTAX	`expression1 / expression2`
ARGUMENTS	`expression1, expression2` — Numbers.
DESCRIPTION	This operator divides the first expression by the second. That's it.
PLAYER	Flash 4 or later
EXAMPLES	`40 / 8` returns 5. `90.7 / 24.5` returns `3.7020408163`.

// (single-line comment delimiter)

SYNTAX	`// comment`
ARGUMENTS	comment – Any text that is for you, i.e., text that is not part of the code and should not be executed.
DESCRIPTION	The double slashes indicate to Flash that the rest of the line can be ignored.
PLAYER	Flash 1 or later

EXAMPLES	Here's an example from Chapter 5, "Flash and XML."
	`// create XML object`
	`screenplayXML = new XML();`
	
	`// create screenplay element/node`
	`screenElement = screen-`
	`playXML.createElement("screenplay");`
	
	`// place the screenplay element`
	`screenplayXML.appendChild(screenElement);`
	`screenElement.attributes.title = "Three Days of the`
	`Condor";`

USES	Comments are extremely useful to help organize your code and to describe to yourself what it is you're trying to do (because sometimes you look at your own code and wonder what in the world you were thinking. Comments can tell you). Also, if someone else looks at your code, they'll need your comments to follow the code's logic.

/* ... */ (multiline comment delimiters)

SYNTAX	`/* comment */`
	`/*`
	`    comments`
	`*/`

ARGUMENTS	comment – Any text that's for your benefit and that shouldn't be executed by Flash.
DESCRIPTION	This comment delimiter is good for starting and stopping comments that last for multiple lines. When Flash sees a `/*`, it starts ignoring everything it sees until it sees a `*/`.
PLAYER	Flash 5

(continued)

/* ... */ (multiline comment delimiters) (continued)

EXAMPLES	`/*`
	    `Here's where we initialize all the variables`
	    `for the Pudgy character, including, size,`
	    `speed, and facial expressions.`
	`*/`

USES	This is useful if you have a big block of text you need to use for a comment.

/= (division assignment)

SYNTAX	`expression1 /= expression2`
ARGUMENTS	`expression1, expression2` – Numbers.
DESCRIPTION	This operator assigns to `expression1` the value of `expression1` divided by `expression2`. That is, `a/= b` is the same as `a = a/b`.
PLAYER	Flash 4 or later
EXAMPLES	If `a = 12` and `b=3`, `a /= b` results in `a=4`.
USES	Why use this thing?

[ ] (array access operator)

SYNTAX	`myArray["value1","value2",…,"valueN"]`
	`myArray[elementNumber]`
	`object[propertyName]`

ARGUMENTS	`myArray` – The name of an array. `value1` – Any value. `object` – Any object. `elementNumber` – An integer.
DESCRIPTION	This operator is required in order to access a certain element in an array. The square brackets can also be used to create an array or to assign values to the array.
PLAYER	Flash 4 or later

EXAMPLES	Creating an Array
	`bigFatArray = [];`
	is the same as
	`bigFatArray = new Array();`

(continued)

[ ] (array access operator) (continued)

EXAMPLES (CONT.)	Assigning Values to an Array
	`bigFatArray = ["cheeseburger","pie","fries","oatmeal stout"];`
	`bigFatArray[4] = "root beer float"`

USES	If you ever use an array for anything, you'll need those little square brackets.

{} (object initializer)

SYNTAX	`object`
	`{`
	    `name1: value1,`
	    `name2: value2`
	    `...`
	    `nameN: valueN`
	`}`

ARGUMENTS	`object` – The object you want to create. `nameN` – The name of the property of the object. `valueN` – The value of that property of the object.
DESCRIPTION	The curly braces can be used to create a new object from scratch. Anything inside the { } represents the initial values of the properties of the object. You can add more properties later, too.
PLAYER	Flash 5

EXAMPLES	Creating an Object
	`treeObject = {};`
	`treeObject = new Object();`
	Assigning Values to an Object
	`treeObject = {`
	`branches: "4",`
	`leaves: "20,004",`
	`kind: "oak"`
	`};`
	You can also create an array inside an object using this method:
	`treeObject = {`
	`branches: "14",`
	`leaves: "20,004",`
	`kidsInTree: ["Bob","Mary","Damien"]`
	`};`

|| (OR)

SYNTAX	`expression1 || expression2`
ARGUMENTS	`expression1, expression2` – Any value, expression, etc. that can be converted to a Boolean value (`true` or `false`).
DESCRIPTION	This logical operator returns `true` if either of the expressions is `true`. It begins by evaluating `expression1`. If `expression1` is `true`, the code returns `true` for (`expression1 || expression2`). If `expression1` is `false`, `expression2` is evaluated.
PLAYER	Flash 4 or later
| **EXAMPLES** | ```
physicalAction = true;
emotionalAction = false
if (physicalAction || emotionalAction)
{
     trace("this screenplay has potential");
}
``` |
| **USES** | Just as with `&&`, the `||` operator will come in handy the more code you write and the more complicated your `if` statements become. |

+ (addition)

SYNTAX	`expression1 + expression2`
ARGUMENTS	`expression1, expression2` – Numbers or strings.
DESCRIPTION	This operator either adds numbers together or concatenates (that's computer talk for "joins together") strings. If you try to add a string and a number, Flash changes the number into a string and concatenates the two strings.
PLAYER	Flash 4, Flash 5. In Flash 4, + was just a numeric operator.

EXAMPLES	Let's say `a = "cat"`, `b="dog"`, `c=5`, and `d=82`.
	`newAnimal = a + b // returns "catdog"`
	`newNumber = c + d // returns 87`
	`whichCat = a + c // returns "cat5"`
	`lastCat = a + (c + d) // returns "cat87"`

USES	Use this to add numbers or concatenate strings.

+= (addition assignment)

SYNTAX	`expression1 += expression2`
ARGUMENTS	`expression1, expression2` – Numbers or strings.

(continued).
```

+= (addition assignment) (continued)

DESCRIPTION	This operator assigns to expression1 the value of expression1 plus expression2. That is, a =+ b is the same thing as a = a + b.
PLAYER	Flash 4 or later
EXAMPLES	If a=6 and b= 17 a += b returns 23.

< (less than)

SYNTAX	expression1 < expression2
ARGUMENTS	expression1, expression2 – Numbers or strings.
DESCRIPTION	This operator sees if the first expression is less than the second. If the expressions are strings, the comparison is alphabetical.
PLAYER	Flash 4, Flash 5. In Flash 4, < could only handle numeric comparisons.

EXAMPLES	`act1pages = 30;`
	`act2pages = 60;`
	`act3pages = 45;`
	`if (act2pages < act3pages)`
	`{`
	`    trace("act is too short or act 3 is too long.");`
	`}`
	
	`for( i=0, i<10, i++)`
	`{`
	`    trace("i: " + i);`
	`}`

USES	Like other comparison operators, you'll need this to adequately use if statements.

<= (less than or equal to)

SYNTAX	expression1 <= expression2
ARGUMENTS	expression1, expression2 – Numbers or strings.
DESCRIPTION	This comparison operator determines whether expression1 is less than, or has the same value as, expression2. If strings are compared, the comparison is alphabetical.
PLAYER	Flash 4, Flash 5. In Flash 4, <= only worked for numerical comparisons.

(continued)

<= (less than or equal to) (continued)

EXAMPLES	Let's say a="Syd", b="Field", c=4000000 and d=9.
	
	``
	if(a <= b)
	{
	    // this code would not be executed
	    trace("a is not greater than b");
	}
	
	if (d <= c)
	{
	    // this code would be executed
	    trace("d is not greater than c");
	}
	``

= (assignment)

SYNTAX	expression1 = expression2
ARGUMENTS	expression1 – Variable, array element, or property. expression2 – Numbers, strings, values, Booleans, objects, arrays, etc.
DESCRIPTION	This operator simply assigns the value of expression2 to the container/property that is expression1.
PLAYER	Flash 4, Flash 5. In Flash 4, = was used as a numeric equality operator (it's == in Flash 5).
EXAMPLES	``` firstOffShip = "rats"; weirdFishName = "sarcastic fringehead"; angelsOnPinhead = "90"; ```
USES	If you have variables (and you will), you'll need the assignment operator.

-= (negation assignment)

SYNTAX	expression1 -= expression2
ARGUMENTS	expression1, expression2 – Numbers or strings.
DESCRIPTION	This operator assigns the value of expression1 – expression2 to expression1. That is, a -= b is the same thing as a = a-b.
PLAYER	Flash 4 or later

EXAMPLES	```
	a = 5;
	b = 3
	a -= b;
	trace (a) // displays "2"
	``

== (equality)

SYNTAX	expression1 == expression2
ARGUMENTS	expression1, expression2 – Numbers, strings, Booleans, variables, objects, arrays, or functions.
DESCRIPTION	This equality operator tests the two expressions for equality and returns true if they are. Note that separate arrays are never considered equal. Two variables that point to the same array can be equal, though.
PLAYER	Flash 5

EXAMPLES	`if (whereverYouGo == thereYouAre)`
	`{`
	`      trace("Rock on, Buckaroo");`
	`}`

USES	Like other comparison operators, you'll need this to adequately use if statements.

> (greater than)

SYNTAX	expression1 > expression2
ARGUMENTS	expression1, expression2 – Numbers or strings.
DESCRIPTION	This operator determines whether expression1 is greater than expression2.
PLAYER	Flash 4, Flash 5. In Flash 4, > could only handle comparing numbers.

EXAMPLES	`if (commonCause > greaterGood)`
	`{`
	`      joinPeaceCorp = true;`
	`}`

USES	Like other comparison operators, you'll need this to adequately use if statements.

>= (greater than or equal to)

SYNTAX	expression1 >= expression2
ARGUMENTS	expression1, expression2 – Numbers or strings.
DESCRIPTION	This operator determines whether expression1 is greater than or equal to expression2.
PLAYER	Flash 4, Flash 5. In Flash 4, > could only handle comparing numbers.

(continued)

>= (greater than or equal to) (continued)

EXAMPLES	`if (romans >= greeks)`
	`{`
	      `trace("Toga! Toga!");`
	`}`

USES	Like other comparison operators, you'll need this to adequately use `if` statements.

_alpha

SYNTAX	`instanceName._alpha` `instanceName._alpha = value`
ARGUMENTS	`instanceName` – The name of any movie clip. `value` – A number between 0 and 100.
DESCRIPTION	The property both reads and sets a movie clip's alpha transparency. A value of 0 is completely transparent. A value of 100 is completely opaque. Elements with an alpha setting are still active and respond to user events. For example, an invisible movie clip can still detect `onClipEvent(mouseDown)`.
PLAYER	Flash 4 or later

EXAMPLES	`onClipEvent(enterFrame)`
	`{`
	      `_root.gash._alpha = 40;`
	`}`

USES	Altering a movie clip's alpha setting is a nice way to achieve fading effects. However, changing alpha settings is processor-intensive, and if there's a way to change a movie clip's tint instead of changing the alpha setting to achieve the same effect, that's recommended.

Array (object)

The Array object allows you to create and manipulate arrays. An Array object is composed of a number of pieces, or properties, like most objects, but an array's constituents are placed in sequentially numbered containers called elements. For example,

```
artArray[0]  =  "Picasso";
artArray[1]  =  "Hopper";
artArray[2]  =  "Miro";
artArray[3]  =  "Taylor";
```

All arrays in Flash start at element zero. Table B.3 describes the methods for the Array object, and Table B.4 describes its property.

TABLE B.3 Methods for the Array Object

METHOD	DESCRIPTION
concat	Concatenates the arguments and creates a new array from those arguments.
join	Joins all the elements of an array into a string.
pop	Removes the last element of an array and returns that last element's value.
push	Adds one or more new elements to an array and returns the array's new length.
reverse	Reverses the direction of an array. The last element in the array becomes the first, and so on.
shift	Similar to pop, this method removes the first element from an array and returns that first element's value.
slice	Copies a section of an array and returns that section as a new array. The original array is not modified.
sort	Sorts an array in a few simple ways.
toString	Returns a string with all the elements of the array.
unshift	Similar to shift, unshift adds one or more elements to the beginning of an array and returns the array's new length.

TABLE B.4 Property for the Array Object

PROPERTY	DESCRIPTION
length	Returns the number of elements in an array.

Constructing an Array

SYNTAX	`arrayName = new Array()`
	`arrayName = new Array(length)`
	`arrayName = new Array(element0, element1, …, elementN)`
	`arrayName = []`

ARGUMENTS	`arrayName` – The name of your array. It doesn't have to include the word *array*, but sometimes the code is easier to read if it does. `length` – The number of elements in the array. `element0`, etc. – A list of values.
DESCRIPTION	This constructor creates a new Array object.

(continued)

Constructing an Array (continued)

PLAYER	Flash 5

EXAMPLES	`marinArray = new Array(4);`
	`marinArray[0] = "Fairfax";`
	`marinArray[1] = "Ross";`
	`marinArray[2] = "San Rafael";`
	`marinArray[3] = "San Anselmo";`
	
	`myCatArray = new Array("Issa","Tycho");`

USES	Arrays are incredibly useful for maintaining lists of related items—similar movie clips, Web pages, etc. Being able to access those list items by number (i.e., their element number) makes arrays a very handy thing to have. If you're unfamiliar with arrays, I strongly recommend you practice using them—they're a powerful tool.

Array.concat

SYNTAX	`arrayName.concat(value0,value1,...valueN)`
ARGUMENTS	`arrayName` – The name of your array. `valueN` – Numbers, elements, or strings.
DESCRIPTION	This method combines all of the values listed into a single new array. The original arrays and/or values are not affected.
PLAYER	Flash 5

EXAMPLES	`colors = new Array("blue","cyan","red");`
	`nums = new Array(1, 2, 3);`
	`letters = new Array("A","B","C")`
	`newArray = colors.concat(nums,letters);`
	`// this created array is`
	`// ["blue","cyan","red",1, 2, 3, "A", "B", "C"];`

USES	If you have several arrays with similar information, this can be a good method to consolidate similar bits of information with each other.

Array.join

SYNTAX	`arrayName.join()` `arrayName.join(separator)`
ARGUMENTS	`arrayName` – The name of your array. `separator` – A character or a string that separates array elements from

(continued)

Array.join (continued)

ARGUMENTS (CONT.)	each other in the returned string. If you don't include a separator, a comma is used by default.
DESCRIPTION	This method turns all of the elements in your array to strings, and then concatenates them with the separator in between each element.
PLAYER	Flash 5
| EXAMPLES | ```
frogs = new Array("tree", "poison dart", "Kermit");
frogVar = frogs.join();
trace (frogVar) // displays "tree,poison dart,Kermit"

frogVar2 = frogs.join("--");
trace (frogVar2)
// displays " tree--poison dart--Kermit"
``` |
| USES | Sometimes, arrays have to be translated into lists like this in order to be transferred to other programs, like Excel or a database program. If your Flash gets serious, you might run into this issue. |

Array.length

SYNTAX	arrayName.length
ARGUMENTS	No arguments.
DESCRIPTION	This read-only property returns the number of elements in the specified array. It's automatically updated if you add or remove elements.
PLAYER	Flash 5
| EXAMPLES | ```
euro = new Array("Spain", "France", "Italy");
numCountries = euro.length;
trace(numCountries);
// displays "3"
``` |
| USES | This comes in most useful when you have to loop over an entire array, but you don't know how big it is. Set your loop counter to go from 0 to array.length-1. |

Array.pop

SYNTAX	arrayName.pop()
ARGUMENTS	No arguments.
DESCRIPTION	This method removes the last element from the array and returns the value of that array.

(continued)

Array.pop (continued)

PLAYER	Flash 5

EXAMPLES	```brooklyn = new Array("Guido","Carlo","Rocko");```
	```popped = brooklyn.pop();```
	```trace(popped);```
	```// displays "Rocko"```

Array.push

SYNTAX	```arrayName.push(value1,…,valueN)```
ARGUMENTS	value – Values to add to the end of the array.
DESCRIPTION	This method adds the listed values to the end of the specified array and returns the array's new length.
PLAYER	Flash 5

EXAMPLES	```colorSchemes = new Array("supernova", "astral");```
	```numSchemes = colorSchemes.push("radiant","urban");```
	```trace(numSchemes);```
	```// displays "4"```

Array.reverse

SYNTAX	```arrayName.reverse()```
ARGUMENTS	No arguments.
DESCRIPTION	This method reverses the array. The last element becomes the first, the first becomes last, and so on.
PLAYER	Flash 5

EXAMPLES	```letters = new Array("A","B","C","D","E");```
	```letters.reverse();```
	```// the new order of the letters array is```
	```// ["E","D","C","B","A"]```

Array.shift

SYNTAX	```arrayName.shift()```
ARGUMENTS	No arguments.
DESCRIPTION	This method removes the first element from the array and returns that element's value.

(continued)

Array.shift (continued)

PLAYER	Flash 5
EXAMPLES	```clubs = new Array("Metropolis","Uni-verse","Café","Mass");
shifted = clubs.shift();
trace (shifted);
// displays "Metropolis"```

Array.slice

SYNTAX	arrayName.slice(start [,end])
ARGUMENTS	start – A number: the starting element index of where you're taking the slice. end – An integer: the ending element index of the slice. This argument is optional.
DESCRIPTION	This method copies the elements from the specified array and creates a new array with those elements. If you omit the end integer, the slice is from the start index to the end of the array.
PLAYER	Flash 5
EXAMPLES	```jCrewColors = new Array("heather","forest","light steel");

fewColors = jCrewColors.slice(1);
// creates a new array called "fewColors":
// ["forest","light steel"]``` |
| USES | If you need to work on only a subsection of a large array, this method can be a good way to work quickly with only the subsection that you're currently interested in. You can always copy the values back over later. |

Array.sort

SYNTAX	arrayName.sort([orderfunction]);
ARGUMENTS	orderfunction – An optional function used to determine the sort order. You have to write the function yourself. When the function compares two elements, say X and Y, the function should perform a sort as follows: -1 if A comes before B 0 if A = B 1 if A comes after B

(continued)

Array.sort (continued)

DESCRIPTION	This method changes the order of the elements in the array. It modifies the original array without making a copy. If you don't call an `order` function, Flash sorts numbers in ascending order and text in alphabetical order.
PLAYER	Flash 5

EXAMPLES	`parties = new Array("republican","democrat","indie");`
	`parties.sort();`
	`// results in`
	`// ["democrat","indie","republican"]`

USES	If you're gathering information from different sources and need to consolidate it and present it to the user in a nice, neat fashion, this is a useful method. You don't need it often, but when you do, you really need it.

Array.splice

SYNTAX	`arrayName.splice(start, [deleteCount,] [value1,…,valueN])`
ARGUMENTS	`start` Integer – the element index to start deleting/inserting. `deleteCount` Integer – the number of elements to be deleted. If this is omitted, this method deletes everything to the end of the array. `valueN` Optional list of values to be inserted at the point where the deleting began.
DESCRIPTION	Method can both add and remove elements from an array.
PLAYER	Flash 5

EXAMPLES	`a = new Array("a","b","c","d","e","f");`
	`b = a.splice(3,2,"z","y");`
	
	`trace("a: " + a.join());`
	`trace("b: " + b.join());`
	`//here's what's displayed`
	`// a: a,b,c,z,y,f`
	`// b: d,e`

USES	This is a pretty powerful method: it can alter one array, take parts of it and create a new array, and add elements to the original array. Again, this is one of those methods that you don't need often, but it's great to have when you do need it.

Array.toString

SYNTAX	`arrayName.toString()`
ARGUMENTS	No arguments.
DESCRIPTION	Exactly like `arrayName.join()`. This method transforms the elements into strings, concatenates all the elements, and places a comma between them.
PLAYER	Flash 5

EXAMPLES	`people = new Array("friend", "enemy");`
	`trace(people.toString());`
	`// displays this`
	`// friend,enemy`

Array.unshift

SYNTAX	`arrayName(value1,…,valueN)`
ARGUMENTS	`value` – Numbers, strings, or elements.
DESCRIPTION	This method adds elements to the beginning of an array and returns the array's new length.
PLAYER	Flash 5

EXAMPLES	`people = new Array("friend", "enemy");`
	`peopleLength = people.unshift("bud","ex");`
	`trace(peopleLength);`
	`trace(people.join());`
	`//displays:`
	`// "4"`
	`// "bud,ex,friend,enemy"`

USES	This is definitely the best way to add elements to the beginning of an array.

Boolean (function)

SYNTAX	`Boolean(expression)`
ARGUMENTS	`expression` – The number or string to be converted.
DESCRIPTION	This function converts the expression into a Boolean value and returns the Boolean value.
PLAYER	Flash 5

(continued)

Boolean (function) (continued)

EXAMPLES	
| | ```
a = 1;
b = 0;
c = -1;
d = "hi there";
trace(Boolean(a)); // displays true
trace(Boolean(b)); // displays false
trace(Boolean(c)); // displays true
trace(Boolean(d)); // displays false
// displays this:
// true
// false
// true
// false
``` |

Boolean (object)

A Boolean object is a simple one: it's either true or false. You can use this object's methods to reveal the value of a Boolean object or to turn it into a string. Its methods are shown in Table B.5.

TABLE B.5 Methods for the Boolean Object

METHOD	DESCRIPTION
toString	Returns the string true or false, depending on the variable's value.
valueOf	Returns the value, true or false, of the specified Boolean.

Constructing a Boolean Object

SYNTAX	myBool = new Boolean([x]) myBool = true/false
ARGUMENTS	x – A number, string, expression, or object. This argument is optional.
DESCRIPTION	Creates a Boolean object. I recommend the second method, which is simply assigning true or false to a variable. The variable is technically a Boolean object at that point. If you use the first method, and omit the x, the object is initialized to false. If you do include x, here are the rules for whether that x is translated to true or false. • If x is a number, the function is false when x is 0. Otherwise, it's true.

(continued)
```

Constructing a Boolean Object (continued)

DESCRIPTION (CONT.)	• If x is an object or a movie clip, the function returns true as long as the object is not null. • If x is a string, the function returns true when Number(x) does not equal 0. Otherwise, the function returns false.
PLAYER	Flash 5
EXAMPLES	iCanFly = false; sheCanFly = new Boolean();

Boolean.toString

SYNTAX	myBoolean.toString()
ARGUMENTS	No arguments.
DESCRIPTION	Returns the string true or false, based on the value of the specified Boolean object.
PLAYER	Flash 5

EXAMPLES	goo = true;
	 trace(goo.toString());
	 // diplays "true"

USES	This can be useful for debugging certain variables, but I haven't found many other uses.

Boolean.valueOf

SYNTAX	myBoolean.valueOf()
ARGUMENTS	No arguments.
DESCRIPTION	This method returns the primitive value type, i.e., true or false, of the specified Boolean object.
PLAYER	Flash 5

EXAMPLES	goo = true;
	 trace(goo.valueOf());
	 // diplays "true"

USES	If you find one, let me know.

break

SYNTAX	break
ARGUMENTS	No arguments.
DESCRIPTION	This action is placed within a loop and is used to exit the loop. When Flash comes across break, it ignores the rest of the loop body and starts executing code after the last line of the loop code.
PLAYER	Flash 4 or later

EXAMPLES	`for(i=0; i<10; i++)`
	`{`
	    `if (i==5)`
	    `{`
	       `break;`
	    `}`
	    `trace(i);`
	`}`
	`//displays this:`
	`// 0`
	`// 1`
	`// 2`
	`// 3`
	`// 4`

USES	Sometimes breaking out of a loop can save processing time. Often, you'll be looking for something specific and using a loop to find it. Once you find it, you don't need to stay in the loop anymore, and break is a good way to get out of it.

Color (object)

This object allows you to get and set the RGB values of movie clips. Its methods are listed in Table B.6.

TABLE B.6 Methods for the Color Object

METHOD	DESCRIPTION
getRGB	Returns the numeric RGB value set by the last setRGB call.
getTransform	Returns the transformation last set by the setTransform call.
setRGB	Sets the RGB value of a Color object (hexadecimal).
setTransform	Returns the value, true or false, of the specified Boolean.

Constructing a Color Object

SYNTAX	new Color(movieClip)
ARGUMENTS	movieClip – The name of a movie clip.
DESCRIPTION	This constructor creates a Color object that will affect the targeted movie clip.
PLAYER	Flash 5
EXAMPLES	fishColor = new Color(jakeMoveClip);
USES	The Color object is useful if you want to change entire movie clips to a single color. My movies tend to be a little more complex, so I don't use the Color object very often.

Color.getRGB

SYNTAX	colorObj.getRGB()
ARGUMENTS	No arguments.
DESCRIPTION	This method returns the numeric values set by the last setRGB call.
PLAYER	Flash 5

EXAMPLES	If square is a movie clip in your movie:
	c = new Color(square);
	c.setRGB(0x00FF00); // sets square to light green
	trace(c.getRGB());
	// displays "65280"

Color.getTransform

SYNTAX	colorObj.getTransform()
ARGUMENTS	No arguments.
DESCRIPTION	This method returns the transform object created by the last setTransform call. Setting a color transformation is complicated, and those transformation values are placed inside a separate transformation object. getTransform returns that object.
PLAYER	Flash 5

EXAMPLES	t = new Object();
	t.ra = 100;
	t.rb = 255;
	c.setTransform(t);
	tObject = c.getTransform());

Color.setRGB

SYNTAX	`colorObj.setRGB(0xRRGGBB)`
ARGUMENTS	RRGGBB – The hexadecimal designation of the desired color.
DESCRIPTION	This method sets the entire color of the movie clip, not just a fill or a line. The entire clip changes to the single color designated.
PLAYER	Flash 5
EXAMPLES	`Syntax c = new Color(square);` `c.setRGB(0x00FF00); // sets square to light green`

Color.setTransform

SYNTAX	`colorObj.setTransform(transformObject)`
ARGUMENTS	`transformObject` – An object created to contain all of the color transformation information. The accepted values for this object are: `ra`, `rb`, `ga`, `gb`, `ba`, `bb`, `aa`, and `ab`.
DESCRIPTION	This method sets the color transformation as described by the information inside the `transformObject`. The parameters, meanings, and accepted values are listed in Table B.7.
PLAYER	Flash 5

EXAMPLES	If `square` is a movie clip in your movie:
	`c = new Color(square);`
	`t = new Object();`
	`t.ra = 100;`
	`t.rb = 255;`
	`t.ga = 30;`
	`t.gb = 7;`
	`t.ba = -50;`
	`t.bb = -200;`
	`t.aa = 100;`
	`t.ab = 25;`
	`c.setTransform(t);`
	`// displays an orangish-red color`

TABLE B.7 Object Transformation Parameters of Color.setTransform

PARAMETER	MEANING	ACCEPTED VALUES
ra	percentage for the red component	-100 to 100
rb	offset for the red component	-255 to 255
ga	percentage for the green component	-100 to 100

(continued)

TABLE B.7 Object Transformation Parameters of Color.setTransform (continued)

gb	offset for the green component	-255 to 255
ba	percentage for the blue component	-100 to 100
bb	offset for the blue component	-255 to 255
aa	percentage for alpha	-100 to 100
ab	offset for alpha	-255 to 255

continue

SYNTAX	continue
ARGUMENTS	No arguments.
DESCRIPTION	This action is placed inside a loop. When Flash reaches continue, it skips the rest of the loop, and begins the loop again.
PLAYER	Flash 4 or later

EXAMPLES	<pre>for (i=0; i<8; i++)
	{
	    if (i>5)
	    {
	        continue;
	    }
	    trace("i: " + i)
	}
	// this results in:
	// i: 0
	// i: 1
	// i: 2
	// i: 3
	// i: 4
	// i: 5</pre>

USES	This action is good for avoiding unnecessary computation. If you're at a point in the code where you need to continue looping, but don't need the rest of the looping code, continue will work well.

_currentframe

SYNTAX	instanceName._currentframe
ARGUMENTS	instanceName – The name of the movie clip's instance.
DESCRIPTION	This read-only property returns the frame number of where the playhead is on the indicated movie clip's timeline.

(continued)

_currentframe (continued)

PLAYER	Flash 4 or later

EXAMPLES	```
	if ((this._currentframe > 10) && (!foundTreasure))
	{
	      message = "Go back! You missed the gold!";
	}
	``

Date (object)

This object allows you to retrieve and create date and time values from either the clock on the local system where the Flash movie is playing or from Greenwich Mean Time (now called the more boring Universal Coordinated Time). To use any of the date methods, you have to create a Date object (just like with the Color object and methods). Table B.8 lists the methods for the Date object.

TABLE B.8 Methods for the Date Object

METHOD	DESCRIPTION
getDate	Returns the day of the month according to local time.
getDay	Returns the number of the day of the week according to local time. Monday is day 1.
getFullYear	Returns the four-digit year according to local time.
getHours	Returns the hour according to local time. Hours are from 0 to 23.
getMilliseconds	Returns the number of milliseconds elapsed since the last second began. Range of result is from 0 to 999.
getMinutes	Returns the number of minutes since the last hour began according to local time.
getMonth	Returns the number of the month according to local time. Range is from 0 to 11.
getSeconds	Returns the number of seconds elapsed since the last minute began according to local time.
getTime	Returns the number of milliseconds since midnight, January 1, 1970, according to local time.
getTimezoneOffset	Returns the difference in minutes between local time and Universal Coordinated Time.
getUTCDate	Returns the day of the month according to Universal Coordinated Time.

(continued)

TABLE B.8 Methods for the Date Object (continued)

METHOD	DESCRIPTION
getUTCDay	Returns the number of the day of the week according to Universal Coordinated Time. Monday is day 1.
getUTCFullYear	Returns the four-digit year according to Universal Coordinated Time.
getUTCHours	Returns the hour according to Universal Coordinated Time. Hours are from 0 to 23.
getUTCMilliseconds	Returns the number of milliseconds elapsed since the last second began. Range of result is from 0 to 999.
getUTCMinutes	Returns the number of minutes since the last hour began according to Universal Coordinated Time.
getUTCMonth	Returns the number of the month according to Universal Coordinated Time. Range is from 0 to 11.
getUTCSeconds	Returns the number of seconds elapsed since the last minute began according to Universal Coordinated Time.
getYear	Returns the year according to local time. Result is four-digit year minus 100.
setYear	Sets the year for a Date object, characterized as being in local time.
setDate	Sets the day of the month for a Date object, characterized as being in local time.
setFullYear	Sets the four-digit year for a Date object, characterized as being in local time.
setHours	Sets the hours for a Date object according to local time.
setMilliseconds	Sets the milliseconds for a Date object according to local time.
setMinutes	Sets the minutes for a Date object according to local time.
setMonth	Sets the month for a Date object according to local time.
setSeconds	Sets the seconds for a Date object according to local time.
setTime	Sets the time (in milliseconds) for a Date object according to local time.
setUTCDate	Sets the day of the month for a Date object, characterized as being in Universal Coordinated Time.
setUTCFullYear	Sets the four-digit year for a Date object, characterized as being in Universal Coordinated Time.
setUTCHours	Sets the hours for a Date object according to Universal Coordinated Time.

(continued)

TABLE B.8 Methods for the Date Object (continued)

METHOD	DESCRIPTION
setUTCMilliseconds	Sets the milliseconds for a Date object according to Universal Coordinated Time.
setUTCMinutes	Sets the minutes for a Date object according to Universal Coordinated Time.
setUTCMonth	Sets the month for a Date object according to Universal Coordinated Time.
setUTCSeconds	Sets the seconds for a Date object according to Universal Coordinated Time.
setUTCTime	Sets the time (in milliseconds) for a Date object according to Universal Coordinated Time.
setYear	Sets the year for a Date object according to local time.
toString	Returns a string containing the date and time information in a Date object
UTC	Returns the number of milliseconds between midnight, January 1, 1970, Universal Coordinated Time, and the specified Date object

Constructing a Date Object

SYNTAX	new Date([year[,month [,date [,hour [,minute [,second ,[millisecond]]]]]]]);
ARGUMENTS	year — An integer that's either the full four-digit year, or a value from 0 to 99 (for years starting in 19). This argument is optional. month — An integer from 0 to 11. This argument is optional. date — An integer from 1 to 31. This argument is optional. hour — An integer from 0 to 23. This argument is optional. minute — An integer from 0 to 59. This argument is optional. second — An integer from 0 to 59. This argument is optional. millisecond — An integer from 0 to 999. This argument is optional.
DESCRIPTION	Constructs a new Date object containing date and/or time.
PLAYER	Flash 5

EXAMPLES	now = new Date(); // returns the current date/time
	
	dayOfFreedom = new Date(2000, 8, 22);

USES	Creating dates is usually good for comparison—you're comparing one date to another. If your Flash movie is tied into a backend system, those often have dates and times that events occurred or data was updated, and it can be useful to compare or display those dates and times.

Date.getDate

SYNTAX	dateObject.getDate()
ARGUMENTS	No arguments.
DESCRIPTION	This method returns the day of the month (an integer from 1 to 31) of the specified Date object according to local time. Local time is determined by the computer system the Flash movie is currently playing on.
PLAYER	Flash 5

Date.getDay

SYNTAX	dateObject.getDay()
ARGUMENTS	No arguments.
DESCRIPTION	This method returns the day of the week (an integer from 0 to 6, with Sunday being day 0) of the specified Date object according to local time. Local time is determined by the computer system the Flash movie is currently playing on.
PLAYER	Flash 5

Date.getFullYear

SYNTAX	dateObject.getFullYear()
ARGUMENTS	No arguments.
DESCRIPTION	This method returns the four-digit year of the specified Date object according to local time. Local time is determined by the computer system the Flash movie is currently playing on.
PLAYER	Flash 5

Date.getHours

SYNTAX	dateObject.getHours()
ARGUMENTS	No arguments.
DESCRIPTION	This method returns the hour of the day (an integer from 0 to 11) of the specified Date object according to local time. Local time is determined by the computer system the Flash movie is currently playing on.
PLAYER	Flash 5

Date.getMilliseconds

SYNTAX	dateObject.getMilliseconds()
ARGUMENTS	No arguments.
DESCRIPTION	This method returns the number of milliseconds elapsed since the last second began of the specified Date object according to local time. Local time is determined by the computer system the Flash movie is currently playing on.
PLAYER	Flash 5

Date.getMinutes

SYNTAX	dateObject.getMinutes()
ARGUMENTS	No arguments.
DESCRIPTION	This method returns the number of minutes elapsed since the last hour began (an integer from 0 to 59) of the specified Date object according to local time. Local time is determined by the computer system the Flash movie is currently playing on.
PLAYER	Flash 5

Date.getMonth

SYNTAX	dateObject.getMonth()
ARGUMENTS	No arguments.
DESCRIPTION	This method returns the month of the current year (an integer from 0 to 11; January is month 0) of the specified Date object according to local time. Local time is determined by the computer system the Flash movie is currently playing on.
PLAYER	Flash 5

Date.getSeconds

SYNTAX	dateObject.getSeconds()
ARGUMENTS	No arguments.

(continued)

Date.getSeconds (continued)

DESCRIPTION	This method returns the number of seconds elapsed since the last minute began (an integer from 0 to 59) of the specified Date object according to local time. Local time is determined by the computer system the Flash movie is currently playing on.
PLAYER	Flash 5

Date.getTime

SYNTAX	dateObject.getTime()
ARGUMENTS	No arguments.
DESCRIPTION	This method returns the number of milliseconds passed since midnight, January 1, 1970, Universal Coordinated Time, for the specified Date object.
PLAYER	Flash 5

Date.getTimezoneOffset

SYNTAX	dateObject.getTimezoneOffset()
ARGUMENTS	No arguments.
DESCRIPTION	This method returns the difference in minutes between the specified Date object and Universal Coordinated Time.
PLAYER	Flash 5

Date.getUTCDate

SYNTAX	dateObject.getUTCDate()
ARGUMENTS	No arguments.
DESCRIPTION	This method returns the day of the month (an integer from 1 to 31) of the specified Date object according to Universal Coordinated Time.
PLAYER	Flash 5

Date.getUTCDay

SYNTAX	dateObject.getUTCDay()
ARGUMENTS	No arguments.
DESCRIPTION	This method returns the day of the week (an integer from 0 to 6, with Sunday being day 0) of the specified Date object according to Universal Coordinated Time.
PLAYER	Flash 5

Date.getUTCFullYear

SYNTAX	dateObject.getUTCFullYear()
ARGUMENTS	No arguments.
DESCRIPTION	This method returns the four-digit year of the specified Date object according to Universal Coordinated Time.
PLAYER	Flash 5

Date.getUTCHours

SYNTAX	dateObject.getUTCHours()
ARGUMENTS	No arguments.
DESCRIPTION	This method returns the hour of the day (an integer from 0 to 11) of the specified Date object according to Universal Coordinated Time.
PLAYER	Flash 5

Date.getUTCMilliseconds

SYNTAX	dateObject.getUTCMilliseconds()
ARGUMENTS	No arguments.
DESCRIPTION	This method returns the number of milliseconds elapsed since the last second began of the specified Date object according to Universal Coordinated Time.
PLAYER	Flash 5

Date.getUTCMinutes

SYNTAX	`dateObject.getUTCMinutes()`
ARGUMENTS	No arguments.
DESCRIPTION	This method returns the number of minutes elapsed since the last hour began (an integer from 0 to 59) of the specified Date object according to Universal Coordinated Time.
PLAYER	Flash 5

Date.getUTCMonth

SYNTAX	`dateObject.getMonth()`
ARGUMENTS	No arguments.
DESCRIPTION	This method returns the month of the current year (an integer from 0 to 11; January is month 0) of the specified Date object according to Universal Coordinated Time.
PLAYER	Flash 5

Date.getUTCSeconds

SYNTAX	`dateObject.getSeconds()`
ARGUMENTS	No arguments.
DESCRIPTION	This method returns the number of seconds elapsed since the last minute began (an integer from 0 to 59) of the specified Date object according to Universal Coordinated Time.
PLAYER	Flash 5

Date.getYear

SYNTAX	`dateObject.getYear()`
ARGUMENTS	No arguments.
DESCRIPTION	This method returns the year of the specified Date object according to local time. Local time is determined by the computer system the Flash movie is currently playing on. The number returned is the full year minus 1900. Thus, the year 2001 would be returned as 101.
PLAYER	Flash 5

Date.setDate

SYNTAX	dateObject.setDate(date)
ARGUMENTS	date – An integer from 1 to 31.
DESCRIPTION	This method sets the day of the month for the specified Date object according to local time. Local time is determined by the computer system the Flash movie is currently playing on.
PLAYER	Flash 5

Date.setFullYear

SYNTAX	dateObject.setFullYear(year[, month[, date]])
ARGUMENTS	year – A four-digit number. month – An integer from 0 to 11. This argument is optional. date – An integer from 1 to 31. This argument is optional.
DESCRIPTION	This method sets the year, and potentially the month and date, of the specified Date object according to local time. Local time is determined by the computer system the Flash movie is currently playing on.
PLAYER	Flash 5

Date.setHours

SYNTAX	dateObject.setHours(hour)
ARGUMENTS	hour – An integer from 0 to 23.
DESCRIPTION	This method sets the hour of the day for the specified Date object according to local time. Local time is determined by the computer system the Flash movie is currently playing on.
PLAYER	Flash 5

Date.setMilliseconds

SYNTAX	dateObject.setMilliseconds(milliseconds)
ARGUMENTS	milliseconds – An integer from 0 to 999.
DESCRIPTION	This method sets the number of milliseconds elapsed since the last second for the specified Date object according to local time. Local time is determined by the computer system the Flash movie is currently playing on.
PLAYER	Flash 5

Date.setMinutes

SYNTAX	`dateObject.setMinutes(minutes)`
ARGUMENTS	`minutes` – An integer from 0 to 59.
DESCRIPTION	This method sets the minutes for the specified Date object according to local time. Local time is determined by the computer system the Flash movie is currently playing on.
PLAYER	Flash 5

Date.setMonth

SYNTAX	`dateObject.setMonth(month)`
ARGUMENTS	`month` – An integer from 0 to 11.
DESCRIPTION	This method sets the month for the specified Date object (January is month 0) according to local time. Local time is determined by the computer system the Flash movie is currently playing on.
PLAYER	Flash 5

Date.setSeconds

SYNTAX	`dateObject.setSeconds(seconds)`
ARGUMENTS	`seconds` – An integer from 0 to 59.
DESCRIPTION	This method sets the seconds elapsed for the specified Date object according to local time. Local time is determined by the computer system the Flash movie is currently playing on.
PLAYER	Flash 5

Date.setTime

SYNTAX	`dateObject.setTime(milliseconds)`
ARGUMENTS	`milliseconds` – A large number.
DESCRIPTION	This method sets the number of milliseconds for the specified Date object, according to local time. Local time is determined by the computer system the Flash movie is currently playing on.
PLAYER	Flash 5

Date.setUTCDate

SYNTAX	dateObject.setUTCDate(date)
ARGUMENTS	date – An integer from 1 to 31.
DESCRIPTION	This method sets the day of the month for the specified Date object according to Universal Coordinated Time.
PLAYER	Flash 5

Date.setUTCFullYear

SYNTAX	dateObject.setUTCFullYear(year[, month[, date]])
ARGUMENTS	year – A four-digit number. month – An integer from 0 to 11. This argument is optional. date – An integer from 1 to 31. This argument is optional.
DESCRIPTION	This method sets the year, and potentially the month and date, of the specified Date object, according to Universal Coordinated Time.
PLAYER	Flash 5

Date.setUTCHours

SYNTAX	dateObject.setUTCHours(hour)
ARGUMENTS	hour – An integer from 0 to 23.
DESCRIPTION	This method sets the hour of the day for the specified Date object according to Universal Coordinated Time.
PLAYER	Flash 5

Date.setUTCMilliseconds

SYNTAX	dateObject.setUTCMilliseconds(milliseconds)
ARGUMENTS	milliseconds – An integer from 0 to 999.
DESCRIPTION	This method sets the number of milliseconds elapsed since the last second for the specified Date object according to Universal Coordinated Time.
PLAYER	Flash 5

Date.setUTCMinutes

SYNTAX	dateObject.setUTCMinutes(minutes)
ARGUMENTS	minutes – An integer from 0 to 59.
DESCRIPTION	This method sets the minutes for the specified Date object according to Universal Coordinated Time.
PLAYER	Flash 5

Date.setUTCMonth

SYNTAX	dateObject.setMonth(month)
ARGUMENTS	month – An integer from 0 to 11.
DESCRIPTION	This method sets the month for the specified Date object (January is month 0) according to Universal Coordinated Time.
PLAYER	Flash 5

Date.setUTCSeconds

SYNTAX	dateObject.setSeconds(seconds)
ARGUMENTS	seconds – An integer from 0 to 59.
DESCRIPTION	This method sets the seconds elapsed for the specified Date object, according to Universal Coordinated Time.
PLAYER	Flash 5

Date.setYear

SYNTAX	dateObject.setYear(year)
ARGUMENTS	year – A four-digit year.
DESCRIPTION	This method sets the year of the specified Date object in local time. Local time is determined by the computer system the Flash movie is currently playing on.
PLAYER	Flash 5

Date.toString

SYNTAX	dateObject.toString()
ARGUMENTS	No arguments.
DESCRIPTION	This method creates a string from the date and time values of a Date object.
PLAYER	Flash 5

EXAMPLES	now = new Date
	trace(now.toString());
	// displays:
	// Tue Nov 7 16:53:05 GMT-0800 2000

Date.UTC

SYNTAX	Date.UTC(year[,month[,date[,hour[,minute[,second [,millisecond]]]]]])
ARGUMENTS	year – An integer that's either the full four-digit year or a value from 0 to 99 (for years starting in 19). This argument is optional. month – An integer from 0 to 11. This argument is optional. date – An integer from 1 to 31. This argument is optional. hour – An integer from 0 to 23. This argument is optional. minute – An integer from 0 to 59. This argument is optional. second – An integer from 0 to 59. This argument is optional. millisecond – An integer from 0 to 999. This argument is optional.
DESCRIPTION	This method returns the number of milliseconds elapsed since midnight, January 1, 1970 to the time specified. Note that this is not specific to a certain Date object. Rather, this method allows you to create a date in Universal Coordinated Time as opposed to local time, which is assumed by the Date constructor.
PLAYER	Flash 5

delete

SYNTAX	delete(reference)
ARGUMENTS	reference – Any variable or object.
DESCRIPTION	This operator destroys the specified object or variable, and returns true if it was successfully destroyed. Otherwise, it returns false. Predefined objects and variables, as well as variables that are declared with var, cannot be deleted.
PLAYER	Flash 5

(continued)

delete (continued)

EXAMPLES	`mi = 2;`
	`delete mi;`
	`trace(mi);`
	`// displays nothing`

USES	Useful for freeing up memory if you create some especially large objects or variables.

do … while

SYNTAX	`do {`
	      `statements`
	`}`
	`while (condition)`

ARGUMENTS	`statements` – Lines of ActionScript. `condition` – Any condition to evaluate.
DESCRIPTION	This action executes a series of commands while a certain condition is true.
PLAYER	Flash 4 or later

EXAMPLES	`mi = 2;`
	`do {`
	      `mi = mi + 1;`
	      `trace("hi there");`
	`}`
	`while (mi<6);`
	`//displays:`
	`// hi there`
	`// hi there`
	`// hi there`
	`// hi there`

USES	If you need to run a loop based on conditions more complex than a simple counter, do...while can be useful.

_droptarget

SYNTAX	`draggableInstance._droptarget`
ARGUMENTS	`draggableInstance` – The name of the draggable instance movie clip.

(continued)

_droptarget (continued)

DESCRIPTION	This read-only property returns the name of the movie clip instance that draggableInstance has been dragged over by the user. The name of the movie clip being dragged over is always an absolute path in the old Flash 4 way—that is, it always begins with /. This property is different than hitTest in that for _droptarget to be true, the movie clips have to be directly over each other, not just overlapping.
PLAYER	Flash 4 or later

EXAMPLES	You can find this movie example on the CD in *reference/droptarget.fla*. It has two movie clips in it: s1 and s2. Below are the object actions for s1.
	
	```onClipEvent (enterFrame)```
	```{```
	    ```if (eval(this._droptarget) == _root.s2)```
	    ```{```
	        ```trace("zap");```
	    ```}```
	```}```
	
	```onClipEvent (mouseDown)```
	```{```
	    ```startDrag(this,true);```
	```}```
	```}```

USES	This property is good if you need to look for a more precise placement than hitTest can give you.

duplicateMovieClip

SYNTAX	duplicateMovieClip(target, newName, depth)
ARGUMENTS	target – The target path of the movie to duplicate. newName – The name of the duplicate movie clip. depth – The depth level of the movie clip. All Flash movies begin at level 0, and when creating duplicate movie clips, you must specify a level greater than 0, or the duplicate move clip will replace the root movie (whenever you place a movie clip on a level using duplicateMovieClip, it replaces any movie clips on that level).
DESCRIPTION	This action creates a new instance of a movie clip. The new movie clip always starts playing on frame 1, regardless of where the playhead of the original movie clip is. Any object actions on the original movie clip are copied onto the new movie clip, but any variable values of the current movie clip are not copied over. If the original movie clip is deleted, then all of its duplicates are deleted as well.
PLAYER	Flash 4 or later

(continued)

duplicateMovieClip (continued)

EXAMPLES	This example is on the CD at *reference/duplicatemovieclip1.fla*. There's a single movie clip in the movie called `oval0`. Below are the frame actions for frame 1 (the only frame in the movie).
	
	``
	for(i=1; i<5; i++)
	{
	    duplicateMovieClip(oval0, "oval" + i, i);
	    setProperty("oval"+i, _x, i*50);
	    setProperty("oval"+i, _y, i*50);
	}
	``

else

SYNTAX	`else { statements }`
ARGUMENTS	`statements` – Lines of ActionScript code.
DESCRIPTION	This action specifies which lines of code should be executed if the previous `if` statement's condition was not `true`.
PLAYER	Flash 4 or later

EXAMPLES	```
	if (value1 > value2)
	{
	    trace("value1 rules!");
	}
	else
	{
	    trace("value2 rules!");
	}
	``

escape

SYNTAX	`escape(expression)`
ARGUMENTS	`expression` – The expression to convert into a string and transform to a URL-encoded format.
DESCRIPTION	This function converts the argument into a string and encodes it in a URL-encoded format.
PLAYER	Flash 5

EXAMPLES	```
	a = "hi there#$%!!";
	trace(escape(a));
	// displays "hi%20there%23%24%25%21%21"
	``

USES	Good for creating strings that can be passed via the GET method, which uses the URL to transfer information.

eval

SYNTAX	`eval(expression)`
ARGUMENTS	`expression` – A string containing a variable, property, object, movie clip, etc.
DESCRIPTION	This function takes a string as its argument and returns a variable, a property, or a movie clip, depending on what's inside the expression.
PLAYER	Flash 4, Flash 5. Flash 4 requires slash notation, and only variables can be used.

EXAMPLES	The file for this example is on the CD at *reference/eval1.fla*. We have a movie with five instances of the `ball` movie clip.
	`for(i=1; i<6; i++)`
	`{`
	`        eval("ball"+i).gotoAndPlay(7);`
	`}`

USES	This is a great function, and very good for when you need to dynamically create object names or movie clip instance names.

_focusrect

SYNTAX	`_focusrect = Boolean`
ARGUMENTS	`Boolean` – `true` or `false`.
DESCRIPTION	This is a global property—it affects the entire Flash movie. It specifies whether a yellow rectangle appears around the button or text field that has the current focus when the user uses the Tab key to navigate.
PLAYER	Flash 4 or later

for

SYNTAX	`for( initialValue; condition; valueUpdate) {`
	`        statements`
	`}`

ARGUMENTS	`initialValue` – An expression that sets the initial value of the counter used to determine how many times the `for` loop runs. `condition` – An expression that uses the counter that can be evaluated to `true` or `false`, like a condition in an `if` statement. `valueUpdate` – An expression that is executed after each loop iteration; usually this changes the value of the counter. `statements` – ActionScript statements.

(continued)

for (continued)

DESCRIPTION	This action creates a loop that looks at the initialValue, which usually sets a counter, and then executes all of the statements in the loop (that is, all the statements inside the { }). Once those statements are executed, the valueUpdate expression is executed. Then, the condition is tested. If the condition is true, the statements in the loop are run again. The valueUpdate is then executed, the condition tested, and if true, the loop statements are run again.
PLAYER	Flash 4 or later

EXAMPLES	<pre>total = 0;
	for (i=0; i<10; i++)
	{
	      total = total + i;
	}
	trace(total);
	// displays: 45</pre>

USES	Loops in general are a mandatory part of anything that calls itself a computer language, whether you're using for loops or do...while. Anything that requires repetitive calculation or looking through a group of values for a specific bit can be used with a for loop.

for...in

SYNTAX	<pre>for(counter in object) {
	      statements
	}</pre>

ARGUMENTS	counter – The variable that acts as a placeholder, an iterant, to refer to the object's properties. object – The name of the object whose properties will be iterated over. statements – ActionScript statements.
DESCRIPTION	This action loops through all of the properties of an object or elements in an array. For each property or element, the statements are executed once.

EXAMPLES	You can see this example on the CD at reference/for-in.fla.
	<pre>wife = new Object();
	wife.name = "Tanya";
	wife.age = 26;
	wife.maidenName = "Muller";
	wife.job = "Usability Architect";</pre>

(continued)

for...in (continued)

EXAMPLES (CONT.)	```for(counter in wife)
{
objName = "wife." + counter + ": ";
objProp = eval("wife." + counter);
trace(objName + objProp);
}
// displays:
// wife.job: Usability Architect
// wife.maidenName: Muller
// wife.age: 26
// wife.name: Tanya```
PLAYER	Flash 5
USES	This action is good for looping over an object and getting its properties at the same time. You don't have to use this action to accomplish this, but it's the easiest way.

_framesloaded

SYNTAX	`instanceName._framesloaded`
ARGUMENTS	instanceName – The name of a movie clip instance.
DESCRIPTION	This read-only property returns the number of frames that have been loaded into the local system's memory.
PLAYER	Flash 4 or later
EXAMPLES	```if (_framesloaded == _totalframes)
{
_root.mainMove.gotoAndPlay(2);
}```
USES	This property is useful when downloading large movies—it can tell you whether all the frames of the movie have been loaded or not. A short preview movie can be shown until all the frames are loaded.

fscommand

SYNTAX	`fscommand(command, arguments)`
ARGUMENTS	command – A string passed to the host application (a browser, Director, etc.).
arguments – A string passed to the host application (a browser, Director, etc.).

(continued)

fscommand (continued)

DESCRIPTION	This action sends a message to the application holding the Flash Player. In a browser, `fscommand` calls the JavaScript function `movieName_DoFSCommand(command, args)`, where `movieName` is the name of the Flash movie.
PLAYER	Flash 3 or later
EXAMPLES	Chapter 4, "Serious Interactivity," is the best place to look for `fscommand` examples.
USES	If you'd like your HTML or JavaScript to respond to actions within your Flash movie, this is a way to do it. I prefer using `getURL` to call JavaScript functions.

function

| SYNTAX | ```
function [functionName] ([arguments])
{
        statements
}
``` |
ARGUMENTS	`functionName` – The name of the new function. Can be omitted (useful if you're creating a method for an object; see example). `arguments` – One or more input parameters: strings, numbers or objects. Arguments are optional. `statements` – ActionScript statements.
DESCRIPTION	This action allows you to define a certain set of actions and call on them on when you need to. Usually, functions are built to do a single thing well—you pass in a variable or two, and it either changes those variables or returns a new value. If you use a function name, the code in the function isn't executed until the function is called by name. If you don't use a function name, the code inside the function will be executed immediately. This is a useful way of creating methods for objects.
PLAYER	Flash 5
| EXAMPLES | Here's an example from Chapter 4: <br> ```
function fillTextField(textVal)
{
//loop through buttons
    for (i=0; i<10; i++)
    {
        if(_root.buttonOn[i])
        {
``` |

(continued)

function (continued)

EXAMPLES (CONT.)	```eval("_root.text" + i) = textVal;```
	```break;```
	`            }`
	`        }`
	`    }`
	And here's an example that uses the no-function-name usage. It creates a method called `firstSign` in the `wife` object.
	```wife.firstSight = function() { trace("Jon has a cute girlfriend!"); }```

USES	Functions are perfect for creating specific chunks of code that can be called upon at specific times. It's best if your functions do one thing, and do it well—it tends to make them more reusable by different parts of your movie.

getProperty

SYNTAX	`getProperty(instanceName, property)`
ARGUMENTS	`instanceName` – The name of the movie clip or object that we want to know about. `property` – The property we wish to know.
DESCRIPTION	This function returns the value of the property of the specified instance. It's most useful when you have to dynamically create your instance name. Otherwise, using `instanceName.property` works just fine.
PLAYER	Flash 4 or later

EXAMPLES	This example is on the CD at *reference/getproperty.fla*. There are four movie clip instances in the movie, named circle1, circle2, circle3 and circle 4. The code below is a frame action.
	```for(i=1; i<5; i++)```
	`{`
	`    xPosition = getProperty("circle"+i, _x);`
	`    trace(xPosition);`
	`}`
	`// displays`
	`// 90.5`
	`// 160.5`
	`// 296.5`
	`// 455.45`
	`//  or different values if you've moved the circles.`

USES	The only reason to use `getProperty` that I've found is if you're dynamically creating an instance name, i.e., part of the instance name is a variable.

getURL

SYNTAX	getURL(url [,window [,variableMethod]])
ARGUMENTS	url – The URL to take the user's browser to. The URL can also be a JavaScript function call. window – The name of the window or frame the new URL should be in. There are several predefined values that you can use (they're the same for HTML): • _self targets the current window. • _blank opens a new browser window. • _parent targets the frameset just above the current frame. • _top targets the whole of the browser window and wipes out any existing frames. variableMethod – Either GET or POST. Use this argument if you wish to send the movie's variables to the specified URL. This argument determines how they are sent: GET is through the URL and POST is through another HTTP header.
DESCRIPTION	This action loads a document from the specified URL into a browser window. It can also pass variables to an application at a certain location (an application being a page that has some server-side scriping in it, like Perl or PHP).
PLAYER	Flash 2 or later. The GET and POST options are available with Flash 4 and later.

EXAMPLES	getURL("chapter2/index.html");
	getURL("shoppingcart/validate.php3", "_self", "GET");
	getURL("javascript:back(3)");

USES	Sending the user to another Web page or calling a JavaScript function in the current page.

getVersion

SYNTAX	getVersion()
ARGUMENTS	No arguments.
DESCRIPTION	This functions returns, in string form, the version of Flash the user currently has installed.
PLAYER	Flash 5

EXAMPLES	trace(getVersion());
	// displays (on my PowerBook)
	// MAC 5,0,30,0

gotoAndPlay

SYNTAX	gotoAndPlay(scene, frame)
ARGUMENTS	scene – The name of the scene to move the main timeline's playhead to. frame – The frame number to move the main timeline's playhead to.
DESCRIPTION	This action sends the main timeline's playhead to the specified scene and frame, and plays from that point. If no scene is specified, the playhead goes to the specified frame in the current scene.
PLAYER	Flash 2 or later
EXAMPLES	Imagine this code as an object action on a "go forward" button. `on(release)` `{` `gotoAndPlay("Scene 6", 10);` `}`

gotoAndStop

SYNTAX	gotoAndStop(scene, frame)
ARGUMENTS	scene – The name of the scene to move the main timeline's playhead to. frame – The frame number to move the main timeline's playhead to.
DESCRIPTION	This action sends the main timeline's playhead to the specified scene and frame, and stops the playhead in its tracks, as if a stop() had been read. If no scene is specified, the playhead goes to the specified frame in the current scene.
PLAYER	Flash 2 or later
EXAMPLES	Imagine this code as an object action on a "go forward" button. `on(release)` `{` `gotoAndStop("Kale Finds Father", 10);` `}`

_height

SYNTAX	movieClip._height movieClip._height = value
ARGUMENTS	movieClip – The name of a movie clip instance. value – A number describing the new height of the movie clip in pixels.
DESCRIPTION	This property either returns the current height of the specified movie clip or sets the height of the movie clip.

(continued)

_height (continued)

PLAYER	Flash 4, Flash 5. In Flash 4, `_height` and `_width` were read-only.

EXAMPLES	Check out the file *reference/height.fla* on the CD to see this example.
	`onClipEvent (mouseDown)`
	`{`
	`    this._height = 50;`
	`}`

_highquality

SYNTAX	`_highquality = value`
ARGUMENTS	`value` – 0, 1, or 2. This is the level of anti-aliasing present in the movie. Level 2 (best) turns on bitmap smoothing. Level 1 (high) applies anti-aliasing. Level 0 (low) turns off anti-aliasing.
DESCRIPTION	This is a global property that determines the level of anti-aliasing in your Flash movie.
PLAYER	Flash 4 or later

if

SYNTAX	`if (condition) {`
	`      statements`
	`}`

ARGUMENTS	`condition` – Any expression that can be evaluated to `true` or `false`. Usually a comparison of some kind. `statements` – ActionScript statements. They'll be executed if the `condition` is `true`.
DESCRIPTION	This action evaluates a condition, and if it's `true`, executes the actions enclosed in the `{ }`.
PLAYER	Flash 4 or later

EXAMPLES	`if (romans >= greeks)`
	`{`
	`      trace ("Toga! Toga!");`
	`}`

USES	Most code requires some form of branching and conditional logic. The `if` statement is the way to do it.

#include

SYNTAX	`#include "filename"`
ARGUMENTS	`filename` – The name of the file containing the desired ActionScript. The recommend extension is `.as`.
DESCRIPTION	This action reads the text of the specified file, and Flash executes that text as if it were written inside the current Action. When the Flash movie is tested, exported, or published, the text in that external file is included in the resulting SWF file.
PLAYER	N/A

Infinity

SYNTAX	`Infinity`
ARGUMENTS	No arguments.
DESCRIPTION	This is a predefined variable with the value for infinity.
PLAYER	Flash 5
EXAMPLES	An example of infinity? Sorry; the book's not that long.

isFinite

SYNTAX	`isFinite(expression)`
ARGUMENTS	`expression` – No arguments.
DESCRIPTION	This function evaluates an expression and returns `true` if the expression is a finite number. Otherwise, it returns `false` (only if the value is infinity or negative infinity).
PLAYER	Flash 5
USES	Good to check if your code accidentally divided by zero.

isNan

SYNTAX	`isNan(expression)`
ARGUMENTS	`expression` – Any expression, number, string, Boolean, etc.
DESCRIPTION	This function evaluates the expression and returns `true` if the expression is not a number.
PLAYER	Flash 5

Key (object)

The Key object is a predefined object whose properties contain key codes for some commonly used keys, as well as methods that can scan the keyboard and see if the user presses any keys. The Key object is not constructed. Methods and properties for the Key object are listed in Tables B. 9 and B.10.

TABLE B.9 Methods for the Key Object

METHOD	DESCRIPTION
getASCII	Returns the ASCII value of the last key pressed.
getCode	Returns the key code of the last key pressed.
isDown	Returns true if the specified key is currently being pressed down.
isToggled	Returns true if the Caps Lock or Num Lock key is down.

TABLE B.10 Properties for the Key Object

PROPERTY	DESCRIPTION
BACKSPACE	Returns the key code value for the Backspace key (8).
CAPSLOCK	Returns the key code value for the Caps Lock key (20).
CONTROL	Returns the key code value for the Control key (17).
DELETEKEY	Returns the key code value for the Delete key (46).
DOWN	Returns the key code value for the Down Arrow key (40).
END	Returns the key code value for the End key (35).
ENTER	Returns the key code value for the Enter key (13).
ESCAPE	Returns the key code value for the Escape key (27).
HOME	Returns the key code value for the Home key (26).
INSERT	Returns the key code value for the Insert key (45).
LEFT	Returns the key code value for the Left Arrow key (34).
PGDN	Returns the key code value for the Page Down key (37).
PGUP	Returns the key code value for the Page Up key (33).
RIGHT	Returns the key code value for the Right Arrow key (39).
SHIFT	Returns the key code value for the Shift key (16).
SPACE	Returns the key code value for the Space key (32).

(continued)

TABLE B.10 Properties for the Key Object (continued)

PROPERTY	DESCRIPTION
TAB	Returns the key code value for the Tab key (9).
UP	Returns the key code value for the Up Arrow key (38).

Key.BACKSPACE

SYNTAX	Key.BACKSPACE
ARGUMENTS	No arguments.
DESCRIPTION	This read-only property returns the key code value associated with the Backspace key (8).
PLAYER	Flash 5

Key.CAPSLOCK

SYNTAX	Key.CAPSLOCK
ARGUMENTS	No arguments.
DESCRIPTION	This read-only property returns the key code value associated with the Caps Lock key (20).
PLAYER	Flash 5

Key.CONTROL

SYNTAX	Key.CONTROL
ARGUMENTS	No arguments.
DESCRIPTION	This read-only property returns the key code value associated with the Control key (17).
PLAYER	Flash 5

Key.DELETEKEY

SYNTAX	Key.DELETELKEY
ARGUMENTS	No arguments.

(continued)

Key.DELETEKEY (continued)

DESCRIPTION	This read-only property returns the key code value associated with the Delete key (46).
PLAYER	Flash 5

Key.DOWN

SYNTAX	Key.DOWN
ARGUMENTS	No arguments.
DESCRIPTION	This read-only property returns the key code value associated with the Down Arrow key (40).
PLAYER	Flash 5

Key.END

SYNTAX	Key.END
ARGUMENTS	No arguments.
DESCRIPTION	This read-only property returns the key code value associated with the End key (35).
PLAYER	Flash 5

Key.ENTER

SYNTAX	Key.ENTER
ARGUMENTS	No arguments.
DESCRIPTION	This read-only property returns the key code value associated with the Enter key (13).
PLAYER	Flash 5

Key.ESCAPE

SYNTAX	Key.ESCAPE
ARGUMENTS	No arguments.

(continued)

Key.ESCAPE (continued)

DESCRIPTION	This read-only property returns the key code value associated with the Escape key (27).
PLAYER	Flash 5

Key.getAscii

SYNTAX	`Key.getAscii()`
ARGUMENTS	No arguments.
DESCRIPTION	This method returns the ASCII code of the last key pressed. And, yes, the method is `getAscii` not `getASCII` as you might expect.
PLAYER	Flash 5

Key.getCode

SYNTAX	`Key.getCode()`
ARGUMENTS	No arguments.
DESCRIPTION	This method returns the key code of the last key pressed.
PLAYER	Flash 5

Key.HOME

SYNTAX	`Key.HOME`
ARGUMENTS	No arguments.
DESCRIPTION	This read-only property returns the key code value associated with the Home key (36).
PLAYER	Flash 5

Key.INSERT

SYNTAX	`Key.INSERT`
ARGUMENTS	No arguments.

(continued)

Key.INSERT (continued)

DESCRIPTION	This read-only property returns the key code value associated with the Insert key (45).
PLAYER	Flash 5

Key.isDown

SYNTAX	`Key.isDown(keyCode)`
ARGUMENTS	keyCode – The key code value assigned to the desired key.
DESCRIPTION	This method returns `true` if the specified key is pressed. If not, it returns `false`.
PLAYER	Flash 5

EXAMPLES	This example is on the CD at *reference/Key.isDown.fla*. Imagine we have a two-frame movie (so that the frame action on the first frame gets called repeatedly, and a text field called `handsOff`. We want some text to appear if the user holds down the space bar, and disappear when the space bar is released. Here's the code for the first frame:
	
	``
	if (Key.isDown(Key.SPACE))
	{
	    handsOff = "Let go of the space bar.";
	}
	else
	{
	    handsOff = "";
	}
	``

Key.isToggled

SYNTAX	`Key.isToggled(keyCode)`
ARGUMENTS	keyCode – The key code value assigned to the desired key.
DESCRIPTION	This method returns `true` if the Caps Lock or Num Lock keys are down/activated. On the Macintosh, the key code values for those keys are identical, so there's no way to tell them apart.
PLAYER	Flash 5
EXAMPLES	This example is on the CD at *reference/Key.isToggled.fla*. Imagine we have a two-frame movie (so that the frame action on the first frame gets called repeatedly) and a text field called `handsOff`. We want some text to appear if the user holds activates Caps Lock, and disappear when Caps Lock is turned off.

(continued)

Key.isToggled (continued)

EXAMPLES (CONT.)	Here's the code for the first frame:
| | ```
if (Key.isToggled(Key.CAPSLOCK))
{
      handsOff = "Undo the Caps Lock.";
}
else
{
      handsOff = "";
}
``` |

Key.LEFT

SYNTAX	Key.LEFT
ARGUMENTS	No arguments.
DESCRIPTION	This read-only property returns the key code value associated with the Left Arrow key (37).
PLAYER	Flash 5

Key.PGDN

SYNTAX	Key.PGDN
ARGUMENTS	No arguments.
DESCRIPTION	This read-only property returns the key code value associated with the Page Down key (34).
PLAYER	Flash 5

Key.PGUP

SYNTAX	Key.PGUP
ARGUMENTS	No arguments.
DESCRIPTION	This read-only property returns the key code value associated with the Page Up key (33).
PLAYER	Flash 5
```

Key.RIGHT

SYNTAX	Key.RIGHT
ARGUMENTS	No arguments.
DESCRIPTION	This read-only property returns the key code value associated with the Right Arrow key (39).
PLAYER	Flash 5

Key.SHIFT

SYNTAX	Key.SHIFT
ARGUMENTS	No arguments.
DESCRIPTION	This read-only property returns the key code value associated with the Shift key (16).
PLAYER	Flash 5

Key.SPACE

SYNTAX	Key.SPACE
ARGUMENTS	No arguments.
DESCRIPTION	This read-only property returns the key code value associated with the Space key (32).
PLAYER	Flash 5

Key.TAB

SYNTAX	Key.TAB
ARGUMENTS	No arguments.
DESCRIPTION	This read-only property returns the key code value associated with the Tab key (9).
PLAYER	Flash 5

Key.UP

SYNTAX	Key.UP
ARGUMENTS	No arguments.
DESCRIPTION	This read-only property returns the key code value associated with the Up Arrow key (38).
PLAYER	Flash 5

_level

SYNTAX	_levelN
ARGUMENTS	N – Any nonnegative integer. This specifies a depth, or level. All Flash movies by default load into level 0 (also denoted as _level0)
DESCRIPTION	This property refers to the movie with the timeline on level N. You must load a movie into Flash using loadMovie before you can look at its level. The root movie is loaded onto level 0.
PLAYER	Flash 4 or later

EXAMPLES	// this halts the movie playing on level 3
	_level3.stop();

loadMovie

SYNTAX	loadMovie (URL [,target/level [,"get"/"post"]])
ARGUMENTS	URL – The URL to load the movie from. The path must be relative from, and in the same subdomain as, the SWF doing the loading. For testing, all SWF files have to be in the same folder. target – The target of a movie is the name of another movie clip that the loaded movie will replace. The loaded movie inherits the position, scaling, and rotation of the movie it's replacing. You can also, in place of a movie clip name, specify a level as a target. You should not specify a movie clip name and a level—you must do neither (since the argument is optional) or either, but not both. level – The level of a movie is the level, or depth, that the loaded movie will load into. The loaded movie will replace any movie clip currently on that level, and will also inherit the position, scaling, and rotation of the movie it's replacing. You can also, in place of a level, specify a movie clip name (target) as a place for the loaded movie to load into. You should not specify a movie clip name and a level—you must do neither (since the argument is optional) or either, but not both.

(continued)

loadMovie (continued)

DESCRIPTION	This action loads additional SWF files into the Flash player without closing the player or taking the user to a new location. It can act the same as going to another Web page, except that it will load faster. Loaded movies can replace present movies, so you could conceivably create a whole site with a number of Flash movies, and have them all accessible through a single Web page. Don't worry about `"get"`/`"post"`. That sends variables to the movie to be loaded, but the loaded movie can't see those variables. It's best to keep your important variables on level 0, and then all movies can refer to `_level0.variableName`.
PLAYER	Flash 3 or later

EXAMPLES	<pre>on(release)
	{
	    // load a movie into level 1
	    loadMovie("act2.swf", 1);
	}</pre>

USES	This method is great for showing users only the information they asked for without their having to download several movies that they don't need.

loadVariables

SYNTAX	`loadVariables(URL, location [,"get"/"post"])`
ARGUMENTS	`URL` – The absolute or relative URL to the page where the variables are located. `location` – The level of the movie clip target to receive the loaded variables. `"get"`/`"post"` – You can also send the current movie's variables to the URL in question by including either of these arguments. This can be useful to send variables to a page of middleware (e.g., PHP, Cold Fusion, etc.), which can then spit out some variables that are sent back to the Flash movie.
DESCRIPTION	This action reads a list of variables and values from an external file. The variables and values have to be in URL-encoded format, with no whitespace or line breaks. This external file can generate this list of variables on the fly, and so the page can be a PHP or ASP page (or something like that). If you choose to send variables using `"get"` or `"post"`, the page can utilize those variables before creating its own list. This is a great way to dynamically alter Flash movies based on user actions.
PLAYER	Flash 4 or later

(continued)

loadVariables (continued)

EXAMPLES	`on(release)`
	`{`
	    `sendToExternalPage = "gad zooks!";`
	    `loadVariables("middle.cfm", 1, "post");`
	`}`

USES	This is a great way to both send and receive data from external sources, and it can happen while the Flash movie is still playing.

Math (object)

The Math object allows you to access and manipulate mathematical functions and constants. It doesn't have a constructor function.

All math constants are double-precision.

The Math object, fully supported in Flash 5, was only emulated in Flash 4, so you may get somewhat different answers, depending on which player you're using (chances are very good you won't notice anything, though). The methods and properties for the Math object are listed in Tables B.11 and B.12.

TABLE B.11 Methods for the Math Object

METHOD	DESCRIPTION
abs	Computes an absolute value.
acos	Computes an arc cosine.
asin	Computes an arc sine.
atan	Computes an arc tangent.
atan2	Computes an angle from the x-axis to the point.
ceil	Rounds a number up to the nearest integer.
cos	Computes a cosine.
exp	Computes an exponential value.
floor	Rounds a number down to the nearest integer.
log	Computes a natural logarithm.
max	Returns the largest of two integers.
min	Returns the smallest of two integers.
pow	Computes x raised to the power y.

(continued)

TABLE B.11 Methods for the Math Object (continued)

METHOD	DESCRIPTION
random	Returns a pseudo-random (random enough for most purposes) number between 0 and 1.
round	Rounds to the nearest integer.
sin	Computes a sine.
sqrt	Computes a square root.
tan	Computes a tangent.

TABLE B.12 Properties for the Math Object

PROPERTY	DESCRIPTION
E	Euler's constant—the base of natural logarithms (approx. 2.718).
LN2	The natural logarithm of 2 (approx. 0.693).
LOG2E	The base-2 logarithm of e (approx. 1.442).
LN10	The natural logarithm of 10 (approx. 2.302).
LOG10E	The base-10 logarithm of e (approx. 0.434).
PI	The ratio of a circle's circumference to its diameter (approx. 3.14159265).
SQRT1_2	The square root of .5 (approx. 0.707).
SQRT2	The square root of 2 (approx. 1.414).

Math.abs

SYNTAX	Math.abs(number)
ARGUMENTS	number – Any number.
DESCRIPTION	This method computes the absolute value of the specified number.
PLAYER	Flash 5. The Math methods and properties were only emulated in Flash 4, and may not be as accurate as the non-emulated ones used in Flash 5.

Math.acos

SYNTAX	Math.acos(number)
ARGUMENTS	number – A number from −1 to 1.

(continued)

Math.acos (continued)

DESCRIPTION	This method returns the arc cosine of the specified number in radians.
PLAYER	Flash 5. The Math methods and properties were only emulated in Flash 4, and may not be as accurate as the non-emulated ones used in Flash 5.

Math.asin

SYNTAX	`Math.asin(number)`
ARGUMENTS	`number` – A number from −1 to 1.
DESCRIPTION	This method returns the arc sine of the specified number in radians.
PLAYER	Flash 5. The Math methods and properties were only emulated in Flash 4, and may not be as accurate as the non-emulated ones used in Flash 5.

Math.atan

SYNTAX	`Math.atan(number)`
ARGUMENTS	`number` – Any number.
DESCRIPTION	This method returns the arc tangent of the specified number.
PLAYER	Flash 5. The Math methods and properties were only emulated in Flash 4, and may not be as accurate as the non-emulated ones used in Flash 5.

Math.atan2

SYNTAX	`Math.atan2(x, y)`
ARGUMENTS	`x` – Any number specifying the x-coordinate of the point. `y` – Any number specifying the y-coordinate of the point.
DESCRIPTION	This method returns the arc tangent of `y/x` in radians.
PLAYER	Flash 5. The Math methods and properties were only emulated in Flash 4, and may not be as accurate as the non-emulated ones used in Flash 5.

Math.ceil

SYNTAX	`Math.ceil(number)`
ARGUMENTS	`number` – Any number or expression.

(continued)

Math.ceil (continued)

DESCRIPTION	This method returns the closest integer that is equal to or greater than the specified number.
PLAYER	Flash 5. The Math methods and properties were only emulated in Flash 4, and may not be as accurate as the non-emulated ones used in Flash 5.

Math.cos

SYNTAX	`Math.cos(angle)`
ARGUMENTS	`angle` – An angle measured in radians.
DESCRIPTION	This method returns the cosine of the specified number.
PLAYER	Flash 5. The Math methods and properties were only emulated in Flash 4, and may not be as accurate as the non-emulated ones used in Flash 5.

Math.E

SYNTAX	`Math.E`
ARGUMENTS	No arguments.
DESCRIPTION	This constant returns Euler's constant, the base of natural logarithms— approx. 2.718.
PLAYER	Flash 5. The Math methods and properties were only emulated in Flash 4, and may not be as accurate as the non-emulated ones used in Flash 5.

Math.exp

SYNTAX	`Math.exp(number)`
ARGUMENTS	`number` – Any number or expression.
DESCRIPTION	This method returns the value of e (that is, `Math.E`), taken to the power of the specified number.
PLAYER	Flash 5. The Math methods and properties were only emulated in Flash 4, and may not be as accurate as the non-emulated ones used in Flash 5.

Math.floor

SYNTAX	`Math.floor(number)`
ARGUMENTS	`number` – Any number or expression.
DESCRIPTION	This method returns the closest integer equal to or less than the specified number.
PLAYER	Flash 5. The Math methods and properties were only emulated in Flash 4, and may not be as accurate as the non-emulated ones used in Flash 5.

Math.log

SYNTAX	`Math.log(number)`
ARGUMENTS	`number` – Any number or expression greater than 0.
DESCRIPTION	This method returns the natural logarithm of the specified number.
PLAYER	Flash 5. The Math methods and properties were only emulated in Flash 4, and may not be as accurate as the non-emulated ones used in Flash 5.

Math.LOG2E

SYNTAX	`Math.LOG2E`
ARGUMENTS	No arguments.
DESCRIPTION	This constant is the base-2 logarithm of e (`Math.E`), approx. 1.4427.
PLAYER	Flash 5. The Math methods and properties were only emulated in Flash 4, and may not be as accurate as the non-emulated ones used in Flash 5.

Math.LOG10E

SYNTAX	`Math.LOG10E`
ARGUMENTS	No arguments.
DESCRIPTION	This constant is the base-10 logarithm of the constant e (`Math.E`), approx. 0.4343.
PLAYER	Flash 5. The Math methods and properties were only emulated in Flash 4, and may not be as accurate as the non-emulated ones used in Flash 5.

Math.LN2

SYNTAX	Math.LN2
ARGUMENTS	No arguments.
DESCRIPTION	This constant is the natural logarithm of 2, approx. 0.6931.
PLAYER	Flash 5. The Math methods and properties were only emulated in Flash 4, and may not be as accurate as the non-emulated ones used in Flash 5.

Math.LN10

SYNTAX	Math.LN10
ARGUMENTS	No arguments.
DESCRIPTION	This constant is the natural logarithm of 10, approx. 2.302.
PLAYER	Flash 5. The Math methods and properties were only emulated in Flash 4, and may not be as accurate as the non-emulated ones used in Flash 5.

Math.max

SYNTAX	Math.max(number1, number2)
ARGUMENTS	number1 – Any number or expression. number2 – Any number or expression.
DESCRIPTION	This method evaluates both arguments and returns the larger value.
PLAYER	Flash 5. The Math methods and properties were only emulated in Flash 4, and may not be as accurate as the non-emulated ones used in Flash 5.

Math.min

SYNTAX	Math.min(number1, number2)
ARGUMENTS	number1 – Any number or expression. number2 – Any number or expression.
DESCRIPTION	This method evaluates both arguments and returns the smaller value.
PLAYER	Flash 5. The Math methods and properties were only emulated in Flash 4, and may not be as accurate as the non-emulated ones used in Flash 5.

Math.PI

SYNTAX	Math.PI
ARGUMENTS	No arguments.
DESCRIPTION	This constant is the ratio of a circle's circumference to its diameter.
PLAYER	Flash 5. The Math methods and properties were only emulated in Flash 4, and may not be as accurate as the non-emulated ones used in Flash 5.

Math.pow

SYNTAX	Math.pow(number1, number2)
ARGUMENTS	number1 – Any number. This is the number that will be raised to the power of number2. number2 – Any number. This is the number that will be the exponent of number1.
DESCRIPTION	This method returns the value of number1 taken to the power of number2.
PLAYER	Flash 5. The Math methods and properties were only emulated in Flash 4, and may not be as accurate as the non-emulated ones used in Flash 5.

Math.random

SYNTAX	Math.random()
ARGUMENTS	No arguments.
DESCRIPTION	This method returns a pseudo-random number between 0 and 1.
PLAYER	Flash 5. The Math methods and properties were only emulated in Flash 4, and may not be as accurate as the non-emulated ones used in Flash 5.

Math.round

SYNTAX	Math.round(number)
ARGUMENTS	number – Any number.
DESCRIPTION	This method returns the closest integer to the specified number.
PLAYER	Flash 5. The Math methods and properties were only emulated in Flash 4, and may not be as accurate as the non-emulated ones used in Flash 5.

Math.sin

SYNTAX	Math.sin(angle)
ARGUMENTS	angle – Any angle in radians.
DESCRIPTION	This method returns the sine of the specified angle.
PLAYER	Flash 5. The Math methods and properties were only emulated in Flash 4, and may not be as accurate as the non-emulated ones used in Flash 5.

Math.sqrt

SYNTAX	Math.sqrt(number)
ARGUMENTS	number – Any nonnegative number.
DESCRIPTION	This method returns the square root of the specified number.
PLAYER	Flash 5. The Math methods and properties were only emulated in Flash 4, and may not be as accurate as the non-emulated ones used in Flash 5.

Math.SQRT1_2

SYNTAX	Math.SQRT1_2
ARGUMENTS	No arguments.
DESCRIPTION	This constant is the square root of one-half (.5), approx. 0.707.
PLAYER	Flash 5. The Math methods and properties were only emulated in Flash 4, and may not be as accurate as the non-emulated ones used in Flash 5.

Math.SQRT2

SYNTAX	Math.SQRT2
ARGUMENTS	No arguments.
DESCRIPTION	This constant is the square root of 2, approx. 1.414.
PLAYER	Flash 5. The Math methods and properties were only emulated in Flash 4, and may not be as accurate as the non-emulated ones used in Flash 5.

Math.tan

SYNTAX	`Math.tan(angle)`
ARGUMENTS	`angle` – An angle measured in radians.
DESCRIPTION	This method returns the tangent of the specified angle.
PLAYER	Flash 5. The Math methods and properties were only emulated in Flash 4, and may not be as accurate as the non-emulated ones used in Flash 5.

maxscroll

SYNTAX	`variableName.maxscroll`
ARGUMENTS	`variableName` – The name of a variable associated with a text field.
DESCRIPTION	This read-only property returns the line number that is the maximum allowed for the `scroll` property, determined by the height of the text field.
PLAYER	Flash 4 or later

Mouse (object)

The mouse object is pretty simple—use it to hide and show the cursor in your movie. That's it. Its methods are listed in Table B.13.

TABLE B.13   Methods for the Mouse Object

METHOD	DESCRIPTION
hide	Hides the mouse cursor in the Flash player.
show	Displays the mouse cursor in the Flash movie (default).

Mouse.hide

SYNTAX	`Mouse.hide()`
ARGUMENTS	No arguments.
DESCRIPTION	This method hides the mouse cursor in a Flash movie.
PLAYER	Flash 5

(continued)

Mouse.hide (continued)

EXAMPLES	`onClipEvent(load)`
	`{`
	`        Mouse.hide();`
	`}`

USES	By hiding the mouse cursor and creating a small movie clip that can be dragged, you've created a custom cursor!

Mouse.show

SYNTAX	`Mouse.show()`
ARGUMENTS	No arguments.
DESCRIPTION	This method displays the mouse cursor in a Flash movie. This is the default, so you only need to use this code if the `Mouse.hide()` has been called previously.
PLAYER	Flash 5

MovieClip (object)

The methods of the MovieClip object provide much of the basic functionality of ActionScript. Movie clips have properties, but they aren't listed here—most of them begin with an underscore (_), so they're pretty easy to spot.

You don't use a constructor to create a movieClip object—the presence of a movie clip in the movie is all that's required. Table B.14 lists the methods for the MovieClip object.

TABLE B.14 Methods for the MovieClip Object

METHOD	DESCRIPTION
`attachMovie`	Attaches a movie from the Library to the active movie.
`duplicateMovieClip`	Creates a duplicate of the specified movie clip.
`getBounds`	Returns an object containing the minimum and maximum x- and y-coordinates of the movie within a specified space.
`getBytesLoaded`	Returns the number of bytes loaded for the specified movie clip.
`getBytesTotal`	Returns the size of the movie clip in bytes.

(continued)

TABLE B.14 Methods for the MovieClip Object (continued)

METHOD	DESCRIPTION
getURL	Retrieves a document from a URL and sends the user's browser there.
globalToLocal	Converts the point object from Stage (or _root) coordinates to the local coordinates of the specified movie clip.
gotoAndPlay	Sends the playhead to a specific scene and frame number and plays the movie.
gotoAndStop	Sends the playhead to a specific scene and frame number and stops the movie.
hitTest	Returns whether or not the specified movie is overlapping another specified movie clip.
loadMovie	Loads a movie into the specified movie clip.
loadVariables	Loads variables from an external data file.
localToGlobal	Converts the point object from the local coordinates to the Stage (or _root) coordinates.
nextFrame	Moves the playhead to the next frame of the movie clip.
play	Plays the specified movie clip.
prevFrame	Moves the playhead to the previous frame of the movie clip.
removeMovieClip	Removes a movie clip from the Stage if that clip was created by duplicateMovieClip or attachMovie.
startDrag	Starts dragging a movie clip.
stop	Stops the movie's playhead.
stopDrag	Stops dragging a movie.
swapDepths	Interchanges two movies at specified depths.
unloadMovie	Removes a movie clip that was brought onto the stage with loadMovie.

MovieClip.attachMovie

SYNTAX	movieClip.attachMovie(identifier, newName, depth)
ARGUMENTS	identifier – The name of the movie clip in the Library to attach. This value comes from the Identifier field in the Symbol Linkage Properties dialog box.

(continued)

MovieClip.attachMovie (continued)

ARGUMENTS (CONT.)	newName – A unique instance name for the attached movie clip. depth – The level/depth where the attached movie gets placed.
DESCRIPTION	This method creates a new instance of a movie clip from the Library and attaches it to the movieClip. You can remove the attached movie by using removeMovieClip or unloadMovie.
PLAYER	Flash 5
USES	This is the only way to pull a movie clip from a Library that isn't already in the movie.

MovieClip.duplicateMovieClip

SYNTAX	movieClip. duplicateMovieClip(newName, depth)
ARGUMENTS	newName – The name of the new instance of the duplicated movie clip. depth – The depth/level the new instance will be placed in.
DESCRIPTION	This method makes a copy of the specified movie clip, gives the copy a new name, and places it at the indicated depth. Duplicated movie clips start playing at frame 1, no matter what frame the original movie clip is on. Any object actions that are part of the original movie clip get duplicated and executed in the copy of the new movie clip.
PLAYER	Flash 5
EXAMPLES	fishClip.duplicateMovieClip("mackerel", 4)

MovieClip.getBounds

SYNTAX	movieClip.getBounds(targetCoordinateSpace)
ARGUMENTS	targetCoordinateSpace – The path to the movie clip to be used as the frame-of-reference coordinate space.
DESCRIPTION	This method returns an object with four properties representing the maximum and minimum x- and y-coordinates. The four properties of the returned object are: xMin, xMax, yMin, and yMax.
PLAYER	Flash 5

EXAMPLES	Here's an abridged example from the *Make Frank* movie:
	// see if user clicked on this image
	bounds = this.getBounds(_root);

(continued)

MovieClip.getBounds (continued)

EXAMPLES (CONT.)	```// see if the user clicked inside the body
if ((_root._xmouse <= bounds.xMax) &&
(_root._xmouse >= bounds.xMin) &&
(_root._ymouse <= bounds.yMax) &&
(_root._ymouse >= bounds.yMin))
{
trace("click.");
}```
USES	As in the example above, you can use getBounds to find the edges of a movie clip, and thus make it act like a button, since you can find out where the user clicked or moved the mouse.

MovieClip.getBytesLoaded

SYNTAX	movieClip.getBytesLoaded()
ARGUMENTS	No arguments.
DESCRIPTION	This method returns the number of bytes loaded of the movieClip so far.
PLAYER	Flash 5
USES	You can compare this value to getBytesTotal to see how much of a movie has loaded.

MovieClip.getBytesTotal

SYNTAX	movieClip.getBytesTotal()
ARGUMENTS	No arguments.
DESCRIPTION	This method returns the size of the movieClip in bytes.
PLAYER	Flash 5
USES	You can compare this value to getBytesLoaded to see how much of a movie has loaded.

MovieClip.getURL

SYNTAX	movieClip.getURL(url [,window [,variableMethod]])
ARGUMENTS	url — The URL to take the user's browser to. The URL can also be a JavaScript function call.

(continued)

MovieClip.getURL (continued)

ARGUMENTS (CONT.)	window – The name of the window or frame the new URL should be in. There are several predefined values that you can use (they're the same as for HTML):
	• _self targets the current window.
	• _blank opens a new browser window.
	• _parent targets the frameset just above the current frame.
	• _top targets the whole of the browser window and wipes out any existing frames.
	variableMethod – Either GET or POST. Use this argument if you wish to send the movie's variables to the specified URL. This argument determines how they are sent: GET is through the URL and POST is through another HTTP header
DESCRIPTION	This action loads a document from the specified URL into a browser window. It can also pass variables to an application at a certain location (an application being a page that has some server-side scripting in it, like Perl or PHP).
PLAYER	Flash 2 or later. The GET and POST options are available with Flash 4 and later.
EXAMPLES	`getURL("chapter2/index.html");`
	`getURL("shoppingcart/validate.php3", "_self", "GET");`
	`getURL("javascript:back(3)");`
USES	Sending the user to another Web page or calling a JavaScript function in the current page.

MovieClip.globalToLocal

SYNTAX	`movieClip.globalToLocal(point)`
ARGUMENTS	point – The name of an object created with the generic Object constructor, specifying the x- and y-coordinates as properties.
DESCRIPTION	This method converts the point object from Stage (global) coordinates to the movie clip's local coordinates.
PLAYER	Flash 5
EXAMPLES	Check out *reference/globalToLocal.fla* to see this example in action. See Figure B-1.
	We have a big square as our movie clip and three text fields: out, out2, and out3. The object action for the square is this:
	`onClipEvent(mouseMove)`
	`{`

(continued)

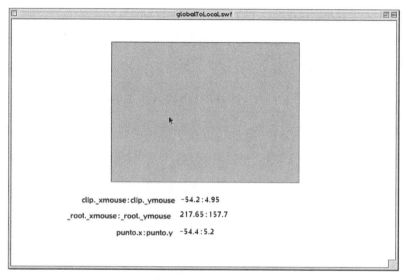

FIGURE B–1 *reference/globalToLocal.fla*

MovieClip.globalToLocal (continued)

EXAMPLES (CONT.)	`punto = new Object();`
	`punto.x = _root._xmouse;`
	`punto.y = _root._ymouse;`
	`this.globalToLocal(punto);`
	`_root.out = this._xmouse + " : " + this._ymouse;`
	`_root.out2 = _root._xmouse + " : " +`
	`_root._ymouse;`
	`_root.out3 = punto.x + " : " + punto.y;`
	
	`// causes display to update faster`
	`updateAfterEvent();`
	`}`
	Notice that even though we set `punto.x` and `punto.y` to be the root coordinates, those values are (nearly) the same as the local movie clip's coordinates. That's what `globalToLocal` did.

MovieClip.gotoAndPlay

SYNTAX	`movieClip.gotoAndPlay(frame)`
ARGUMENTS	`frame` – The frame number to send the playhead to, or the frame label.

(continued)

MovieClip.gotoAndPlay (continued)

DESCRIPTION	This method sends the playhead of the specified `movie` to the `frame` specified by the frame number.
PLAYER	Flash 5
| EXAMPLES | ```
if (answer != rightAnswer)
{
     _root.result.gotoAndPlay("wrong");
}
``` |
| USES | Great for manipulating multiple movie clips from a central point. |

MovieClip.gotoAndStop

SYNTAX	`movieClip.gotoAndStop(frame)`
ARGUMENTS	`frame` – The frame number to send the playhead to, or the frame label
DESCRIPTION	This method sends the playhead of the specified movie the `frame` number, and stops the movie.
PLAYER	Flash 5
| EXAMPLES | ```
if (answer == "halt")
{
     _root.result.gotoAndStop("frozen");
}
``` |
| USES | Great for manipulating multiple movie clips from a central point. |

MovieClip.hitTest

SYNTAX	`movieClip.hitTest(x, y, shapeFlag)` `movieClip.hitTest(target)`
ARGUMENTS	`x` – The x-coordinate of the hit area on the Stage. `y` – The y-coordinate of the hit area on the Stage. `shapeFlag` – A Boolean value. Make this `true` if you want to see if any of the shape of the `movieClip` is overlapping the (x,y) coordinate. Enter `false` if you want to only check the bounding box of the instance. `target` – The name (and path to) another movie clip. This will cause Flash to see if the `movieClip` is overlapping the `target`.

(continued)

MovieClip.hitTest (continued)

DESCRIPTION	This method determines whether the specified movieClip is overlapping either a point (specifying x, y and shapeFlag) or another movie clip (specifying target). If you specify a point and set the shapeFlag to true, hitTest will only check to see if the space actually occupied by the movie clip is overlapping the point. If you use target, hitTest evaluates whether the bounding boxes of the two movie clips overlap (there isn't a way to see if only the space occupied by the movie clips is overlapping, which is unfortunate).
PLAYER	Flash 5

EXAMPLES	Here's an example from the spaceship game *(chapter3/ space_game_done.fla)*. This is part of the object actions for the rocket ship, and it checks to see if one of the bad guys' shots have hit it.
	 ```// see if ourHero got nailed```
	 ```if ((this.hitTest(_root.mantaShot) ||```
	 ``` this.hitTest(_root.spikeShot)) &&```
	 ``` !_root.ourHeroDead)```
	 ```{```
	 ``` _root.ourHeroDead = true;```
	 ```}```

USES	This is a great way to test for interactions between different movie clips and then cause the movie to respond to those interactions.

MovieClip.loadMovie

SYNTAX	```movieClip.loadMovie(URL, ["get"/"post"])```
ARGUMENTS	URL — An absolute or relative path to a SWF file in the same subdomain as the currently playing movie. Remember, when you're testing movies, the SWF files have to be in the same folder. "get"/"post" — If you have variables to send, you can, but the movie being loaded can't see them. I recommend not sending variables, but rather storing them in level 0, where all movies can access them.
DESCRIPTION	This action loads additional SWF files into the Flash player without closing the player or taking the user to a new location. It can act the same as going to another Web page, except that it will load faster. Loaded movies can replace present movies, so you could conceivably create a whole site with a number of Flash movies and have them all accessible through a single Web page. Don't worry about "get"/"post". That sends variables to the movie to be loaded, but the loaded movie can't see those variables. It's best to keep your important variables on level 0, and then all movies can refer to _level0.variableName.
PLAYER	Flash 3 or later

(continued)

MovieClip.loadMovie (continued)

EXAMPLES	```on(release){ // load a movie into level 1 _root.dropMovieHere.loadMovie("act2.swf");}```
USES	This method is great for showing users only the information they asked for without their having to download several movies that they don't need.

MovieClip.loadVariables

SYNTAX	`movieClip.loadVariables(URL, [,"get"/"post"])`
ARGUMENTS	URL – The absolute or relative URL to the page where the variables are located. `"get"/"post"` – You can also send the current movie's variables to the URL in question by including either of these arguments. This can be useful to send variables to a page of middleware (e.g., PHP, Cold Fusion, etc.), which can then spit out some variables that are sent back to the Flash movie.
DESCRIPTION	This action reads a list of variables and values from an external file. The variables and values have to be in URL-encoded format, with no whitespace or line breaks. This external file can generate this list of variables on the fly, and so the page can be a PHP or ASP page (or something like that). If you choose to send variables using `"get"` or `"post"`, the page can utilize those variables before creating its own list. This is a great way to dynamically alter Flash movies based on user actions.
PLAYER	Flash 4 or later
EXAMPLES	```on(release){ sendToExternalPage = "gad zooks!"; _root.variableClip.loadVariables("middle.cfm", "post");}```
USES	This is a great way to both send and receive data from external sources, and it can happen while the Flash movie is still playing.

MovieClip.localToGlobal

SYNTAX	`movieClip.localToGlobal(point)`
ARGUMENTS	point – The name of an object created with the generic Object constructor, specifying the x- and y-coordinates as properties.
DESCRIPTION	This method converts the point object from the movie clip's local coordinates to the Stage (global) coordinates.
PLAYER	Flash 5

EXAMPLES	Check out *reference/localToGlobal.fla* to see this example in action. See Figure B-2.
	We have a big square as our movie clip and three text fields: out, out2 and out3. The object action for the square is this:
	<pre>onClipEvent (mouseMove)
	{
	    punto = new Object();
	    punto.x = this._xmouse;
	    punto.y = this._ymouse;
	    this.localToGlobal(punto);
	    _root.out = this._xmouse + " : " +
	      this._ymouse;
	    _root.out2 = _root._xmouse + " : " +
	      _root._ymouse;
	    _root.out3 = punto.x + " : " + punto.y;
	
	    // causes display to update faster
	    updateAfterEvent();
	}</pre>Notice that even though we set punto.x and punto.y to be the square's coordinates, those values are (nearly) the same as the Stage's coordinates. That's what localToGlobal did.

MovieClip.nextFrame

SYNTAX	`movieClip.nextFrame()`
ARGUMENTS	No arguments.
DESCRIPTION	This method sends the playhead of the specified movie clip to the next frame.
PLAYER	Flash 5

EXAMPLES	<pre>on(release)
	{
	    _root.counter.nextFrame();
	}</pre>

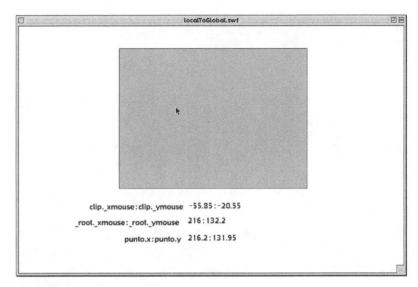

FIGURE B-2 *reference/localToGlobal.fla*

MovieClip.play

SYNTAX	movieClip.play()
ARGUMENTS	No arguments.
DESCRIPTION	This method plays the specified movie clip.
PLAYER	Flash 5

EXAMPLES	on(press)
	{
	    _root.smallAnim.play();
	}

MovieClip.prevFrame

SYNTAX	movieClip.prevFrame()
ARGUMENTS	No arguments.
DESCRIPTION	This method sends the playhead of the specified movie clip to the previous frame.
PLAYER	Flash 5

(continued)

MovieClip.prevFrame (continued)

EXAMPLES	on(release)
	{
	    _root.counter.prevFrame();
	}

MovieClip.removeMovieClip

SYNTAX	movieClip.removeMovieClip()
ARGUMENTS	No arguments.
DESCRIPTION	This method removes a movie clip brought into the movie via duplicateMovieClip or attachMovie.
PLAYER	Flash 5

EXAMPLES	if (bombDestroyed)
	{
	    _root.bomb.removeMovieClip();
	}

USES	Good for cleaning up your movie when you don't need a certain movie clip anymore. This saves more memory than simply making the clip invisible.

MovieClip.startDrag

SYNTAX	movieClip.startDrag([lock, [left,right,top,bottom]])
ARGUMENTS	lock – Boolean value: if true, the center of the specified movie clip moves to where the mouse cursor is (good for creating custom cursors). If false, the movie clip's motion simply mirrors that of the mouse, regardless of where the two are in relation to each other. This argument is optional. left, right, top, bottom – The bounding coordinates of where the movie clip can be dragged. The four values specify a rectangle. These arguments are optional.
DESCRIPTION	Allows the user to start dragging a specified movie clip. That is, the movie clip starts to move around the screen, following the user's mouse. Only one movie clip is draggable at a time.
PLAYER	Flash 5
EXAMPLES	Here's an abridged example from the space game (chapter3/space_game_done.fla).

(continued)

MovieClip.startDrag (continued)

| EXAMPLES (CONT.) | ```onClipEvent (load)
{
    // allows dragging to begin within a rectangle
    // on the lower part of the screen.
    this.startDrag (true, 50, 300, 500, 375);
}``` |
| --- | --- |
| USES | Allows the user to manipulate the motion on movie clips in the screen, adding a serious level of interactivity to your movie. |

MovieClip.stop

SYNTAX	`movieClip.stop()`
ARGUMENTS	No arguments.
DESCRIPTION	This movie clip stops the playhead of the indicated movie clip.
PLAYER	Flash 5
EXAMPLES	```if (stopMovieButton = "pressed")
{
_root.cartoon.stop();
}```

MovieClip.stopDrag

SYNTAX	`movieClip.stopDrag()`
ARGUMENTS	No arguments.
DESCRIPTION	Disables dragging of the specified movie clip.
PLAYER	Flash 5
EXAMPLES	```if (this.hitTest(_root.blackHoleOfDeath))
{
this.stopDrag();
}```

MovieClip.swapDepths

SYNTAX	`movieClip.swapDepths(depth)` `movieClip.swapDepths(target)`

(continued)

MovieClip.swapDepths (continued)

ARGUMENTS	depth – The depth or level to interchange with the specified movie clip. target – The name of the movie clip to exchange with movieClip. Both clips must have the same parent clip.
DESCRIPTION	This method swaps the stacking order of the movieClip with whatever is in the specified level, or with the movie that's specified by target. This has the effect of placing one movie clip behind another, when previously the reverse was true. Note that if either movie clip is in the middle of tweening when this method is called, the tweening is halted.
PLAYER	Flash 5

MovieClip.unloadMovie

SYNTAX	movieClip.unloadMovie()
ARGUMENTS	No arguments.
DESCRIPTION	This method removes the specified movie clip from the main movie. The movie clip must have been loaded via loadMovie or attachMovie.
PLAYER	Flash 5

_name

SYNTAX	instanceName._name instanceName._name = value
ARGUMENTS	instanceName – The name of a movie clip. value – A string of the instance's new name.
DESCRIPTION	This property specifies the instance's name (usually set in the Instances panel).
PLAYER	Flash 4 or later

NaN

SYNTAX	NaN
ARGUMENTS	No arguments.
DESCRIPTION	This predefined variable has a value of NaN (specified by the IEEE-754 value). NaN stands for *Not a Number*.
PLAYER	Flash 5

new

SYNTAX	`new constructor([arguments])`
ARGUMENTS	`constructor` – A function followed by optional `arguments`. This function is usually a type of object, like Object, Date, or Array.
DESCRIPTION	This operator creates a new object.
PLAYER	Flash 5
EXAMPLES	```function Ship(name, purpose)
{
    this.name = name;
    this.purpose = purpose;
}

ship1 = new Ship("Valkyrie","cargo");
ship2 = new Ship("Neptune", "passenger");``` |
| USES | You'll use this all the time to create any new object. |

nextFrame

SYNTAX	`nextFrame()`
ARGUMENTS	No arguments.
DESCRIPTION	This method moves the playhead to the next frame.
PLAYER	Flash 4 or later

nextScene

SYNTAX	`nextScene()`
ARGUMENTS	No arguments.
DESCRIPTION	This method moves the playhead to the beginning of the next scene.
PLAYER	Flash 4 or later

null

SYNTAX	`null`
ARGUMENTS	No arguments.

(continued)

null (continued)

DESCRIPTION	This keyword is a special value that can be assigned to variables. More often, the `null` value is returned by functions when no data is provided.
PLAYER	Flash 5
| EXAMPLES | ```
bob = new Object();
bob.jinx = null;
bob.jonx = bob.jinx + 5;
trace(bob.jinx + " : " + bob.jonx);
// displays: "null : 5"
``` |

Number (function)

SYNTAX	`Number(expression)`
ARGUMENTS	`expression` – A string, Boolean, or other expression to convert into a number.
DESCRIPTION	This function converts the expression into a number, according to these rules: If the expression is a number, the return value is the expression. If the expression is a Boolean, the return value is 1 for `true`, 0 for `false`. If the expression is a string, the function attempts to parse it as a decimal number. If the expression is undefined, the return value is 0.
PLAYER	Flash 4 or later

Number (object)

The Number object is a simple wrapper for a basic data type of a number. This was done so that you can use the methods and properties of the Number object with your basic numbers. The Number object functions identically to the JavaScript Number object.

When using Number methods, you have to first create a number object.

```
aNumber = Number(42);
aString = aNumber.toString();
```

Fortunately, you don't have to create a Number object in order to use the properties. Methods and properties for the Number object are listed in Tables B.15 and B.16.
```

TABLE B.15 Methods for the Number Object

METHOD	DESCRIPTION
toString	Returns a string representation of the number.
valueOf	Returns the primitive value of the number (i.e., the non-object version of the number).

TABLE B.16 Properties for the Number Object

PROPERTY	DESCRIPTION
MAX_VALUE	A constant representing the largest representable double-precision number (based on IEEE-754). This number is approximately 1.7976931348623158e+308.
MIN_VALUE	A constant representing the smallest non-negative, representable double-precision number (based on IEEE-754). This number is approximately 5e-324.
NaN	A constant representing Not a Number.
NEGATIVE_INFINITY	A constant representing negative infinity.
POSITIVE_INFINITY	A constant representing positive infinity.

Constructing a Number Object

SYNTAX	numName = new Number(value)
ARGUMENTS	value – An expression to be converted into a number.
DESCRIPTION	This constructor creates a new Number object. You have to use this constructor before you can use the toString or the valueOf methods. You do not have to use this constructor in order to create simple variables whose value is a number.
PLAYER	Flash 5

Number.MAX_VALUE

SYNTAX	Number.MAX_VALUE
ARGUMENTS	No arguments.
DESCRIPTION	This property is a constant that represents the largest representable double-precision number (based on IEEE-754). This number is approximately 1.7976931348623158e+308.
PLAYER	Flash 5

Number.MIN_VALUE

SYNTAX	Number.MIN_VALUE
ARGUMENTS	No arguments.
DESCRIPTION	This constant represents the smallest non-negative representable double-precision number (based on IEEE-754). This number is approximately 5e-324.
PLAYER	Flash 5

Number.NaN

SYNTAX	Number.NaN
ARGUMENTS	No arguments.
DESCRIPTION	This property represents the IEEE-754 value for Not a Number.
PLAYER	Flash 5

Number.NEGATIVE_INFINITY

SYNTAX	Number.NEGATIVE_INFINITY
ARGUMENTS	No arguments.
DESCRIPTION	This property represents negative infinity. If the result of a calculation returns a result larger than can be represented, that value becomes negative infinity.
PLAYER	Flash 5

Number.POSITIVE_INFINITY

SYNTAX	Number.POSITIVE_INFINITY
ARGUMENTS	No arguments.
DESCRIPTION	This property represents positive infinity. If the result of a calculation returns a result larger than can be represented, that value becomes positive infinity.
PLAYER	Flash 5

Number.toString

SYNTAX	`numName.toString(radix)`
ARGUMENTS	`radix` – Specifies the base to be used (2 to 36) for number-to-string conversion. The default value is 10.
DESCRIPTION	This method returns the string representation of the Number object.
PLAYER	Flash 5

Number.valueOf

SYNTAX	`numName.valueOf()`
ARGUMENTS	No arguments.
DESCRIPTION	This method returns the primitive data type of the Number object. That is, it returns the non-object form of the number.
PLAYER	Flash 5

Object (object)

The Object object is, as you might guess, is the root of all the objects in ActionScript. Movie clips are objects, arrays are objects, and so on. Table B.17 lists the methods for the Object object.

TABLE B.17 Methods for the Object Object

METHOD	DESCRIPTION
`toString`	Returns a string representation of the object.
`valueOf`	Returns the primitive value of the object.

Constructing a Generic Object

SYNTAX	`objectName = new Object([value])`
ARGUMENTS	`value` – A number, Boolean, or string to turn into an object. This argument is optional
DESCRIPTION	This constructor creates a new Object.
PLAYER	Flash 5

(continued)

Constructing a Generic Object (continued)

Uses	It can be useful to create your own objects in order to hold bundles of information that don't fit well into an array. If you're from the Cold Fusion world, use Objects instead of structures.

Object.toString

Syntax	`objectName.toString()`
Arguments	No arguments.
Description	This method converts the object to a string and returns that value.
Player	Flash 5

Object.valueOf

Syntax	`objectName.valueOf()`
Arguments	No arguments.
Description	This method converts the object into its primitive data type, e.g., turns an object that's just a string into a string literal. If the object doesn't have a primitive data type (most objects you create yourself won't), the object itself is returned.
Player	Flash 5

onClipEvent

Syntax	`onClipEvent(event) {`
	        `statements`
	`}`

Arguments	`event` – One of several predefined events that can occur inside a movie clip, either as an action of the Flash player, or the user doing something. Table B.18 lists all the events (remember, these events can only be inside the Object Actions of a movie clip).
Description	This is the event handler for movie clips.
Player	Flash 5

(continued)

onClipEvent (continued)

EXAMPLES	Here's an example from the space game *(chapter3/ space_game_done.fla)*. Check out the actions for the rocket ship. This code looks for a release of the mouse button. When that happens, the code shoots a little yellow energy pellet at the enemy. ```onClipEvent (mouseUp)\n{\n if(!_root.ourHeroShotInAir &&\n!_root.ourHeroDead)\n {\n _root.shot._x = this._x;\n _root.shot._y = this._y - 50;\n _root.shot._visible = true;\n _root.ourHeroShotInAir = true;\n }\n}```
USES	You'll use this event handler a lot—whenever you want the movie to interact with the user and movie clips respond to user actions.

TABLE B.18 Predefined Events for onClipEvent

EVENT	DESCRIPTION
load	Event is triggered when the movie clip finishes loading.
unload	Event is triggered on the first frame after the movie clip is removed from the movie. The actions associated with unload are executed before that first frame's actions (if it has any).
enterFrame	Event is triggered by each time a frame is played.
mouseMove	Event is triggered by the movement of the mouse cursor.
mouseDown	Event is triggered by the pressing down of the mouse button by the user (Windows people: this only tracks the left mouse button).
mouseUp	Event is triggered by the releasing of the mouse button (Windows people: this only tracks the left mouse button).
keyDown	Event is triggered when a key is pressed.
keyUp	Event is triggered when a key is released.
data	Event is triggered when the movie clip completely receives data via loadVariables or loadMovie.

on

SYNTAX	`on(mouseEvent) {`
	`        statements`
	`}`

ARGUMENTS	`mouseEvent` – A `mouseEvent` is an event that is triggered because of something the user did with the mouse. This event handler is used with buttons only—it won't work with movie clips, just as `onClipEvent` won't work with buttons. Table B.19 lists all the different `mouseEvents`.
DESCRIPTION	This is the event handler for buttons.
PLAYER	Flash 2 or later

EXAMPLES	Here's an example from Chapter 2, "Your First ActionScripts" *(chapter2/ buzzkill2.fla)*. If the user releases the mouse button or presses the left arrow, this `gotoAndPlay` is executed.
	`on (release, keyPress "<left>")`
	`{`
	`        gotoAndPlay ("Scene 2", "slide2");`
	`}`

USES	If you want a button to do something, this is how you do it.

TABLE B.19 mouseEvent Used with on

MOUSEEVENT	DESCRIPTION
`press`	The mouse button is pressed while the cursor is over the button.
`release`	The mouse button is released while the cursor is over the button.
`releaseOutside`	The mouse button is released outside of the mouse button after it was pressed while the cursor was inside the button.
`rollOver`	The mouse cursor rolls over the button.
`rollOut`	The mouse cursor rolls off of the button.
`dragOver`	The mouse button is pressed while the cursor is over the button, and then the cursor is moved off of the button with the mouse button still down.
`keyPress("key")`	The user presses the specified key.

_parent

SYNTAX	`_parent.property = value`
ARGUMENTS	`property` – Any property of the parent object of the current object. `value` – The new value of the property.

(continued)

_parent (continued)

DESCRIPTION	This property refers to the parent object of the current object/movie clip.
PLAYER	Flash 4 or later
USES	If you have a small movie consisting solely of actions, you can make it more modular by looking up to whatever movie clip contains it (i.e., its parent object) instead of hard-coding the reference.

parseFloat

SYNTAX	parseFloat(string)
ARGUMENTS	string – Any string
DESCRIPTION	This function converts a string to a floating-point number. If the string doesn't start with a number that can be parsed, a value of NaN or 0 is returned. White space is ignored, as are trailing non-numeric characters.
PLAYER	Flash 5
USES	If you somehow end up with a string that's all numbers that you want to perform some math on, this can be a useful function.

parseInt

SYNTAX	parseInt(expression, radix)
ARGUMENTS	expression – A string, number or expression. radix – The base (2 to 36; default is base 10) of the number to parse.
DESCRIPTION	This function converts a string to an integer. If the string can't be converted, a value of NaN or 0 is returned. Integers beginning with 0 are interpreted as octal numbers. Integers beginning with 0x are interpreted as hexadecimal numbers (see Color.setRGB to see this in action). White space is ignored, as are trailing non-numeric characters.
PLAYER	Flash 4 or later

play

SYNTAX	play()
ARGUMENTS	No arguments.
DESCRIPTION	This action plays the current movie.
PLAYER	Flash 2 or later

prevFrame

SYNTAX	`prevFrame()`
ARGUMENTS	No arguments.
DESCRIPTION	This action moves the playhead to the previous frame and stops the movie.
PLAYER	Flash 2 or later

prevScene

SYNTAX	`prevScene()`
ARGUMENTS	No arguments.
DESCRIPTION	This action sends the playhead to the first frame of the previous scene and stops the playhead.
PLAYER	Flash 2 or later

print

SYNTAX	`print(target, "bmovie"/"bmax"/"bframe")`
ARGUMENTS	`target` – The instance of the movie clip to print. By default, all the frames in the movie are printed. If you want to print only certain frames, attach a #P label to each frame you want to print. `bmovie` – Designates the bounding box of a specific frame in the movie clip as the print area for all printable frames in the movie. Attach a #b frame label to designate the frame you want to use as the bounding box. `bmax` – Designates a composite of all the bounding boxes of all printable frames as the print area. `bframe` – Designates that the bounding box of each printable frame be used as the print area for that frame. This changes the print area for each frame and scales the objects to fit the print area. Use this argument if you have objects of different sizes in each frame and want each object to fill the printed page.
DESCRIPTION	This action prints the specified movie clip. This action results in higher-quality prints than `printAsBitmap`, but it can't print alpha effects or special color effects. Control the print area by using the arguments above.
PLAYER	Flash 5

printAsBitmap

SYNTAX	printAsBitmap(target, "bmovie"/"bmax"/"bframe")
ARGUMENTS	target – The instance of the movie clip to print. By default, all the frames in the movie are printed. If you want to print only certain frames, attach a #P label to each frame you want to print. bmovie – Designates the bounding box of a specific frame in the movie clip as the print area for all printable frames in the movie. Attach a #b frame label to designate the frame you want to use as the bounding box. bmax – Designates a composite of all the bounding boxes of all printable frames as the print area. bframe – Designates that the bounding box of each printable frame be used as the print area for that frame. This changes the print area for each frame and scales the objects to fit the print area. Use this argument if you have objects of different sizes in each frame and want each object to fill the printed page.
DESCRIPTION	This action prints the specified movie clip as a bitmap, at the printer's highest available resolution. This action results in lower-quality prints than print, but this method can print alpha effects or special color effects (so, if your movie doesn't have alpha or special color effects, use print instead). Control the print area by using the arguments above.
PLAYER	Flash 5

_quality

SYNTAX	_quality _quality = value
ARGUMENTS	value – A string that's one of the values listed in Table B.20.
DESCRIPTION	This global property sets or retrieves the rendering quality.
PLAYER	Flash 5

TABLE B.20 String Values for _quality

_QUALITY	DESCRIPTION
LOW	Graphics aren't anti-aliased, and bitmaps are not smoothed.
MEDIUM	Graphics are anti-aliased using a 2x2 grid, but bitmaps are not smoothed.
HIGH	Graphics are anti-aliased using a 4x4 grid, and bitmaps are smoothed if the movie is static. This is Flash's default setting.
BEST	Graphics are anti-aliased using a 4x4 grid, and bitmaps are always smoothed.

removeMovieClip

SYNTAX	removeMovieClip(target)
ARGUMENTS	target – The name of a movie clip created with attachMovie or duplicateMovieClip.
DESCRIPTION	This action deletes a movie clip instance from the movie. Only movie clips created with attachMovie or duplicateMovieClip can be removed in this way.
PLAYER	Flash 4 or later

return

SYNTAX	return [expression]
ARGUMENTS	expression – A number, string, array, object, etc. to be returned as the value of the function that return is inside of.
DESCRIPTION	This action specifies the value returned by a function. Calling this action causes the code in the function to not be executed until the function is called again.
PLAYER	Flash 5

EXAMPLES	`function Dog(slobber,drool)`
	`{`
	`        wetness = slobber * drool;`
	`        return wetness;`
	`}`

_root

SYNTAX	_root.movieClip _root.property
ARGUMENTS	movieClip – The name of the movie clip that's on the main Stage. property – A property of the main movie.
DESCRIPTION	This property refers the top of the Flash movie hierarchy. It's analogous to an absolute URL: you start at the top and specify your way down.
PLAYER	Flash 4 or later

EXAMPLES	`if (romans >= greeks)`
	`{`
	`        _root.romanMovie.stop();`

(continued)

_root (continued)

EXAMPLES (CONT.)	` _root.greekMovie.apollo.play();` `}`
USES	This is useful in order to be sure you're accessing the right movie clip.

_rotation

SYNTAX	`instanceName._rotation` `instanceName._rotation = value`
ARGUMENTS	`instanceName` – The name of a movie clip. `value` – An integer—the amount and direction to rotate the specified movie clip in.
DESCRIPTION	This property specifies the rotation of the movie clip in degrees.
PLAYER	Flash 4 or later

EXAMPLES	This example is from *chapter2/drag_props_done.fla*. It's a little complicated—just check out the last line of code.
	`onClipEvent(enterFrame)`
	`{`
	`    if (_root.rotateDrag)`
	`    {`
	`        xPos = _root._xmouse;`
	`        percentage = ( xPos - _root.rotate-`
	`BarXMin)/(_root.rotateBarXMax - _root.rotate-`
	`BarXMin);`
	`        rotation = (percentage * 720) - 360`
	`        _root.fish._rotation = rotation;`
	`    }`
	`}`

scroll

SYNTAX	`variableName.scroll = value`
ARGUMENTS	`variableName` – The name of a variable associated with a text field. `value` – The line number of the topmost visible line in the text field.
DESCRIPTION	This property controls the display of information in a text field by moving the text field to a specific position.
PLAYER	Flash 4 or later
USES	You can create a scrollable text field using this property, or you can direct users to a certain word or paragraph within the text field.

Selection (object)

The Selection object contains information about text fields: which one the focus is on (that is, which one has the active text cursor in it), and information about the user's selection of text in the text field. Table B.21 lists the methods for the Selection object.

Figure B-3 shows an example of some of these methods—this file can be found at *reference/selection.fla*.

TABLE B.21 Methods for the Selection Object

METHOD	DESCRIPTION
getBeginIndex	Returns the index of the beginning of the selection span. Returns −1 if there is no currently selected field.
getCaretIndex	Returns the index of the current caret (that is, the vertical text cursor) in the currently focused selection.
getEndIndex	Returns the index of the end of the current selection. Returns −1 if there is no selection.
getFocus	Returns the name of the text that has the current focus.
setFocus	Sets the focus on the editable text field associated with the variable in the argument.
setSelection	Sets the beginning and ending index of the selection span.

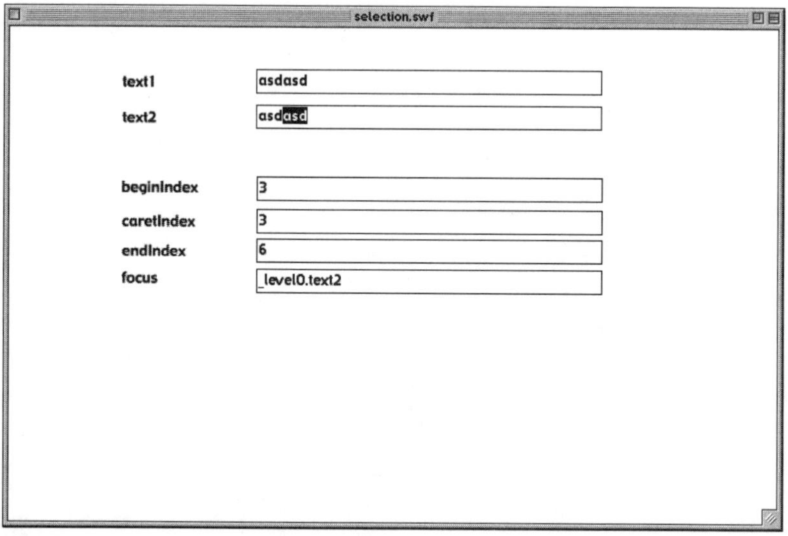

FIGURE B-3 Screenshot of some selection methods at work

Selection.getBeginIndex

SYNTAX	Selection.getBeginIndex()
ARGUMENTS	No arguments.
DESCRIPTION	This method returns the index of the beginning of the selection span. If there is no current selection, this returns −1.
PLAYER	Flash 5
EXAMPLES	Please look at and test *reference/selection.fla*.

Selection.getCaretIndex

SYNTAX	Selection.getCaretIndex()
ARGUMENTS	No arguments.
DESCRIPTION	This method returns the index of the position of the caret, i.e., the text cursor. If there is no current selection, this returns −1.
PLAYER	Flash 5
EXAMPLES	Please look at and test *reference/selection.fla*.

Selection.getEndIndex

SYNTAX	Selection.getEndIndex()
ARGUMENTS	No arguments.
DESCRIPTION	This method returns the index of the end of the selection span. If there is no current selection, this returns −1.
PLAYER	Flash 5
EXAMPLES	Please look at and test *reference/selection.fla*.

Selection.getFocus

SYNTAX	Selection.getFocus()
ARGUMENTS	No arguments.
DESCRIPTION	This method returns the name of the text field that the current focus is on. If no text field currently has focus, null is returned.

(continued)

Selection.getFocus (continued)

PLAYER	Flash 5
EXAMPLES	Please look at and test *reference/selection.fla*.

Selection.setFocus

SYNTAX	`Selection.setFocus(variable)`
ARGUMENTS	`variable` – The name of the variable that is associated with the text field to receive focus.
DESCRIPTION	This method sets the focus on the specified text field.
PLAYER	Flash 5

Selection.setSelection

SYNTAX	`Selection.setSelection(start, end)`
ARGUMENTS	`start` – Index of beginning of selection. `end` – Index of end of selection.
DESCRIPTION	This method sets the selection span of the currently selected text field. If there is no currently selected field, this method has no effect.
PLAYER	Flash 5

set

SYNTAX	`set(variable, expression)`
ARGUMENTS	`variable` – Any valid variable name. `expression` – Any number, string, or expression.
DESCRIPTION	This action assigns a value to a variable. It does the same thing as `variable = expression`, which is what most people are used to.
PLAYER	Flash 4 or later

EXAMPLES	`set("boo"+3,"la la")`
	`trace(boo3);`
	`// displays: "la la"`

USES	Use this method if you need to dynamically create the variable's name, e.g., if the name of the variable has another variable in it.

setProperty

SYNTAX	setProperty(target, property, expression)
ARGUMENTS	target — The name of an object. property — The property to be set. expression — The value to which the property should be set.
DESCRIPTION	This action sets a target's property, just like target.property = expression.
PLAYER	Flash 4 or later

EXAMPLES	Here's some code that will set five movie clips (fish0, fish1, fish2, fish3, fish4) to an alpha setting of 50.
	for(i=0; i<5; i++)
	{
	    setProperty("fish"+i, _alpha, 50);
	}

USES	Use this action if your target name is dynamically created, that is, the name is generated using another variable.

Sound (object)

The Sound object allows you to set and control the sounds of a particular movie clip or the movie as a whole. You have to create a Sound object instance in order to use the Sound object's methods, which are listed in Table B.22.

TABLE B.22 Methods for the Sound Object

METHOD	DESCRIPTION
attachSound	Attaches the specified sound.
getPan	Returns the value of the previous setPan action.
getTransform	Returns the value of the previous setTransform action.
getVolume	Returns the value of the previous setVolume action.
setPan	Sets the right/left balance of the sound.
setTransform	Sets the right/left inputs and speakers for the sound.
setVolume	Sets the volume level.
start	Starts playing a sound from a certain point in the sound. The default is the beginning of the sound.
sound	Stops playing the specified sound, or optionally, all sounds.

Constructing a Sound Object

SYNTAX	`soundName = new Sound([target])`
ARGUMENTS	`target` – The name of the movie clip sound is applied to.
DESCRIPTION	This method creates a new Sound object. If a target is not specified, the Sound object controls all sounds in the movie.
PLAYER	Flash 5

Sound.attachSound

SYNTAX	`soundName.attachSound("idname")`
ARGUMENTS	`idname` – The name for the new instance of the sound. As with movie clips, this name is the Identifier in the Symbol Linkage Properties dialog box.
DESCRIPTION	This method attaches the sound to the specified Sound object.
PLAYER	Flash 5

Sound.getPan

SYNTAX	`soundName.getPan()`
ARGUMENTS	No arguments.
DESCRIPTION	This method returns the pan level set by the last `setPan` call. The returned value is from −100 to 100. The pan setting determines the left/right sound balance for sounds in the movie.
PLAYER	Flash 5

Sound.getTransform

SYNTAX	`soundName.getTransform()`
ARGUMENTS	No arguments.
DESCRIPTION	This method attaches returns the sound transformation information for the specified sound object.
PLAYER	Flash 5

Sound.getVolume

SYNTAX	`soundName.getVolume()`
ARGUMENTS	No arguments.
DESCRIPTION	This method returns the volume level as set by the last `setVolume` call. The returned value is an integer from 0 to 100. The default setting is 100.
PLAYER	Flash 5

Sound.setPan

SYNTAX	`soundName.setPan(pan)`
ARGUMENTS	pan – An integer specifying the left-right balance for a sound. The range is –100 to 100, where –100 is the left channel only, and 100 is the right channel only.
DESCRIPTION	This method determines how much of the sound is played in the right or left channels. For mono sounds, pan affects which speaker the sound plays through. Calling this method overrides any previous `setPan` or `setTransform` settings.
PLAYER	Flash 5

Sound.setTransform

SYNTAX	`soundName.setTransform(transformObject)`
ARGUMENTS	`transformObject` – An object whose properties correspond to the required sound information for an object.
DESCRIPTION	This method sets sound information for a Sound object. Using this method overrides any previous settings made by `setPan` or `setTransform`. Macromedia recommends using 22-Khz, 6-bit mono sounds in order to minimize file size (stereo sounds take up about twice as much memory as mono sounds). Table B.23 lists the parameters for the `transformObject`.
PLAYER	Flash 5

EXAMPLES	`transformObj = new Object();`
	`transformObj.ll = 100;`
	`transformObj.lr = 30;`

(continued)

Sound.setTransform (continued)

EXAMPLES (CONT.)	`transformObj.rr = 40;` `transformObj.rl = -50;` `duckSound.setTransform(transformObj);`

TABLE B.23 Parameters for transformObject

PROPERTY	DESCRIPTION
ll	How much of the left input to play in the left speaker (-100 to 100).
lr	How much of the left input to play in the right speaker (-100 to 100).
rr	How much of the right input to play in the right speaker (-100 to 100).
rl	How much of the right input to play in the left speaker (-100 to 100).

The total right and left outputs are determined by these formulas:

```
leftOutput = ll(left input) + lr(right input)
rightOutput = rl(left input) + rr(right input)
```

Sound.setVolume

SYNTAX	`soundName.setVolume(volume)`
ARGUMENTS	volume – A number from 0 to 100.
DESCRIPTION	This method sets the volume of the specified sound. 100 is full volume and 0 is silent. The default setting is 0.
PLAYER	Flash 5

Sound.start

SYNTAX	`soundName.start([secondOffset,loop])`
ARGUMENTS	secondOffset – The number of seconds into the sound that you want the sound to start playing. That is, if your sound is 10 seconds long and you want to start playing the sound 5 seconds into it, this value is 5. Note that this does not cause a delay, but an immediate playing of the sound that starts in the middle. loop – The number of times the sound should loop.
DESCRIPTION	This method starts playing the Sound object. It plays from the beginning if no argument is provided, or some seconds into the sound.
PLAYER	Flash 5

Sound.stop

SYNTAX	soundName.stop(["idname"])
ARGUMENTS	idname – The name of the sound to stop playing. This is an optional argument. If omitted, all sounds in the Flash movie stop.
DESCRIPTION	This method stops the indicated sound. If no argument is provided, the method stops all sounds.
PLAYER	Flash 5

_soundbuftime

SYNTAX	_soundbuftime = value
ARGUMENTS	value – An integer specifying the number of seconds before the movie starts to stream.
DESCRIPTION	This global property established the number of seconds of streaming sound to prebuffer. The default is 5.
PLAYER	Flash 4 or later

startDrag

SYNTAX	startDrag(target, [lock,[left,right,top,bottom]])
ARGUMENTS	target – The name of and path to the movie clip to drag. lock – Boolean value: if true, the center of the specified movie clip moves to where the mouse cursor is (good for creating custom cursors). If false, the movie clip's motion simply mirrors that of the mouse, regardless of where the two are in relation to each other. This argument is optional. The default is false. left,right,top,bottom – The bounding coordinates of where the movie clip can be dragged. The four values specify a rectangle. These arguments are optional.
DESCRIPTION	This action allows the user to start dragging a specified movie clip. That is, the movie clip starts to move around the screen, following the user's mouse. Only one movie clip is draggable at a time.
PLAYER	Flash 4 or later
EXAMPLES	If you have a movie clip called s1 on the Stage, this code will make it draggable. startDrag(_root.s1, true);
USES	Allows the user to manipulate different images in the movie.

stop

SYNTAX	stop()
ARGUMENTS	No arguments.
DESCRIPTION	This action stops the movie that is currently playing.
PLAYER	Flash 3 or later

stopAllSounds

SYNTAX	stopAllSounds()
ARGUMENTS	No arguments.
DESCRIPTION	Stops all sounds currently playing in the movie. It does not stop the playhead, though.
PLAYER	Flash 3 or later

stopDrag

SYNTAX	stopDrag()
ARGUMENTS	No arguments.
DESCRIPTION	This action causes the current draggable object to no longer be draggable. It doesn't need an argument, because only one object in the movie can be draggable at one time.
PLAYER	Flash 4 or later
EXAMPLES	Here's a clip on code from *chapter2/drag_props_done.fla*. In this movie, the user can only drag objects when the mouse button is pressed down. ```onClipEvent (mouseUp) { stopDrag (); _root.alphaDrag = false; }```

String (function)

SYNTAX	String(expression)
ARGUMENTS	expression – A number, variable, or Boolean to convert to a string.

(continued)

String (function) (continued)

DESCRIPTION	This function returns a string representation of the expression. If the expression is a Boolean, the string is either `true` or `false`. If the expression is a number, the string is simply a string version of the number. If the expression is an object, the return value is dependent on the rules for changing that particular object into a string. If the expression is undefined, the return value is an empty string.
PLAYER	Flash 3 or later

" " (string delimiter)

SYNTAX	`"text"`
ARGUMENTS	`text` – any text
DESCRIPTION	Use quotes to determine the beginning and ending of a string literal.
PLAYER	Flash 4 or later
EXAMPLES	`season = "autumn";`

String (object)

The String object is wrapped over a primitive data type (that is, the data type of strings you're already familiar with). Use of the String object allows you to use the object's methods for manipulating your string.

The good news is that you don't have to create a String object each time you want to use one of the String object's methods. If you have a string literal (e.g., `foo="bar"`), and you call a String object method (e.g., `foo.length`), Flash automatically creates a temporary String object, uses the method on that object, returns the result, then destroys the object (without touching your original string).

Use string literals whenever you can—don't specifically create a String object unless there's a driving need, because String objects can have counterintuitive behavior. The methods for the String object are listed in Table B.24, and its property is listed in Table B.25.

TABLE B.24 Methods for the String Object

METHOD	DESCRIPTION
charAt	Returns the character at a specified position in the string.
charCodeAt	Returns the character at a specified position in the string, but as a 16-bit integer.
concat	Combines the text of two strings together and returns a new string.
fromCharCode	Returns a string taken from a list of character codes in the argument.
indexOf	Returns the position of the value specified in the argument. If the value occurs more than once, the position of the first occurrence is returned. If the value wasn't found, -1 is returned.
lastIndexOf	Returns the last-occurring position of the value specified in the argument. If the value wasn't found, -1 is returned.
slice	Extracts a section from a string and returns a new string.
split	Splits a string into an array of substrings.
substr	Returns a specified number of characters from a string, beginning at a location specified in the argument.
substring	Returns the characters between two indices provided in the argument.
toLowerCase	Converts the string to lowercase characters and returns the result.
toUpperCase	Converts the string to uppercase characters and returns the result.

TABLE B.25 Property for the String Object

METHOD	DESCRIPTION
length	Returns the length of the string.

Constructing a String Object

SYNTAX	stringObject = new String(value)
ARGUMENTS	value – The value of the string object (usually a string).
DESCRIPTION	This constructor creates a new String object. Remember, it's strongly recommended to use string literals instead of String objects.
PLAYER	Flash 5

String.charAt

SYNTAX	`stringName.charAt(index)`
ARGUMENTS	`index` – The position of the character to retrieve. Flash starts counting from 0, so the first position has a value of 0, not 1.
DESCRIPTION	The method returns the character at the position specified in the argument. If the provided index doesn't exist inside the string, an empty string is returned.
PLAYER	Flash 5

EXAMPLES	This and other string-related examples are available on the CD at *reference/string.fla*.
	`forest = "quick brown fox";`
	`forestCharAt = forest.charAt(3);`
	`trace("charAt: " + forestcharAt)`
	`// displays "charAt: c"`

String.charCodeAt

SYNTAX	`stringName.charCodeAt(index)`
ARGUMENTS	`index` – The position at which to retrieve the character's code.
DESCRIPTION	This method returns the character code of the character at the indicated position.
PLAYER	Flash 5

EXAMPLES	This and other string-related examples are available on the CD at *reference/string.fla*.
	`forest = "quick brown fox";`
	`forestCharCodeAt = forest.charCodeAt(3);`
	`trace("charCodeAt: " + forestCharCodeAt)`
	`// displays "charCodeAt: 99"`

String.concat

SYNTAX	`stringName.concat(value1,…,valueN)`
ARGUMENTS	`valueN` – Any number of values to be joined together.
DESCRIPTION	This method combines the specified values and returns a new string. If a value isn't already a string, it is converted into one.
PLAYER	Flash 5

(continued)

String.concat (continued)

EXAMPLES	This and other string-related examples are available on the CD at *reference/string.fla*. `forest1 = "quick ";` `forest2 = "brown ";` `forest3 = "fox";` `forestConcat = forest1.concat(forest2, forest3);` `trace("concat: " + forestConcat)` `// displays "concat: quick brown fox"`

String.fromCharCode

SYNTAX	`stringName = String.fromCharCode(c1,..,cN)`
ARGUMENTS	cN – Character codes
DESCRIPTION	This method returns a string made from the character codes provided in the argument.
PLAYER	Flash 5
EXAMPLES	This and other string-related examples are available on the CD at *reference/string.fla*. `forest = String.fromCharCode(99, 102, 130);` `trace("fromCharCode: " + forest)` `// displays "fromCharCode: cf,"`

String.indexOf

SYNTAX	`stringName.indexOf(substring[,start])`
ARGUMENTS	`substring` – An integer or string—the value to search the string for. `start` – The position in the string to start searching at; 0 is the default.
DESCRIPTION	This method searches the string and if the indicated value is found, returns the start position of where the value is in the string. If the value occurs in the string more than once, the position of the first occurrence is returned. If the value is not found in the string, -1 is returned.
PLAYER	Flash 5
EXAMPLES	This and other string-related examples are available on the CD at *reference/string.fla*. `forest = "quick brown fox";` `forestIndexOf = forest.indexOf("fox");` `trace("indexOf: " + forestIndexOf);` `// displays "indexOf: 12"`

String.lastIndexOf

SYNTAX	myString.lastIndexOf(substring[,start])
ARGUMENTS	substring – An integer or string—the value to search the string for. start – The position in the string to start searching at; 0 is the default.
DESCRIPTION	This method searches the string for the substring and returns the position of the last time the substring appears in the string. If the substring doesn't appear in the string, -1 is returned.
PLAYER	Flash 5

EXAMPLES	This and other string-related examples are available on the CD at *reference/string.fla*.
	`forest = "quick brown fox";`
	`forestLastIndexOf = forest.lastIndexOf("o");`
	`trace("lastIndexOf: " + forestLastIndexOf);`
	`// displays "lastIndexOf: 13"`

String.length

SYNTAX	stringName.length
ARGUMENTS	No arguments.
DESCRIPTION	This property returns the number of characters in the string.
PLAYER	Flash 5

EXAMPLES	This and other string-related examples are available on the CD at *reference/string.fla*.
	`forest = "quick brown fox";`
	`forestLength = forest.length;`
	`trace("length: " + forestLength);`
	`// displays "length: 15"`

String.slice

SYNTAX	myString.slice(start, end)
ARGUMENTS	start – The index of the starting position of the slice. end – The index of the ending position of the slice.
DESCRIPTION	This method copies a section of a string and returns that extract as a new string, without altering the original string. The slice includes the character at the start position and all the characters of the string up to (but not including) the end index.
PLAYER	Flash 5

(continued)

String.slice (continued)

EXAMPLES	This and other string-related examples are available on the CD at *reference/string.fla*.
	`forest = "quick brown fox";`
	`forestSlice = forest.slice(3,10);`
	`trace("slice: " + forestSlice);`
	`// displays "slice: ck brow"`

String.split

SYNTAX	`stringName.split(delimiter)`
ARGUMENTS	`delimiter` – The character used to delimit the string.
DESCRIPTION	This method splits a String object into several substrings, and then places those substrings in an array. If no delimiter is specified, the returned array has only one element, whose value is the entire string. If the delimiter is an empty string, each character in the string becomes a separate element in the resulting array.
PLAYER	Flash 5

EXAMPLES	This and other string-related examples are available on the CD at *reference/string.fla*.
	`forest = "quick brown fox";`
	`forestArray = forest.split(" ");`
	`for(i=0; i<forestArray.length; i++)`
	`{`
	`trace("[" + i + "] " + forestArray[i]);`
	`}`
	`// displays:`
	`// [0] quick`
	`// [1] brown`
	`// [2] fox`

String.substr

SYNTAX	`stringName.substr(start [,length])`
ARGUMENTS	`start` – The beginning position of the substring to be created. `length` – The number of characters in the substring. If this argument is omitted, all the characters to the end of the string are included.
DESCRIPTION	This method returns the characters in the string, starting at the `start` index, and contains `length` number of characters.
PLAYER	Flash 5

(continued)

String.substr (continued)

EXAMPLES	This and other string-related examples are available on the CD at *reference/string.fla*.
	`forest = "quick brown fox";`
	`forestSubstr = forest.substr(3,10);`
	`trace("substr: " + forestSubstr);`
	`//displays "substr: ck brown f"`

String.substring

SYNTAX	`stringName.substring(start, end)`
ARGUMENTS	start – The initial position to start looking at the substring. end –The initial position to start looking at the substring plus 1. Take the index and add 1 to come up with this number.
DESCRIPTION	This method returns a string taken from the original string, consisting of the characters indicated in the arguments.
PLAYER	Flash 5

EXAMPLES	This and other string-related examples are available on the CD at *reference/string.fla*.
	`forest = "quick brown fox";`
	`forestSubstring = forest.substring(3,10);`
	`trace("substring: " + forestSubstring);`
	`// displays "substring: ck brow"`

String.toLowerCase

SYNTAX	`stringName.toLowerCase()`
ARGUMENTS	No arguments.
DESCRIPTION	This method returns a copy of the string object, with all characters in lowercase.
PLAYER	Flash 5

EXAMPLES	This and other string-related examples are available on the CD at *reference/string.fla*.
	`forest = "Quick BrowN Fox";`
	`forestLower = forest.toLowerCase();`
	`trace("toLowerCase: " + forestLower);`
	`// displays "toLowerCase: quick brown fox"`

String.toUpperCase

SYNTAX	`stringName.toUpperCase()`
ARGUMENTS	No arguments.
DESCRIPTION	This method returns a copy of the string object, with all characters in uppercase.
PLAYER	Flash 5

EXAMPLES	This and other string-related examples are available on the CD at *reference/string.fla*.
	`forest = "Quick BrowN Fox";`
	`forestUpper = forest.toUpperCase();`
	`trace("toUpperCase: " + forestUpper);`
	`// displays "toUpperCase: QUICK BROWN FOX"`

_target

SYNTAX	`instanceName._target`
ARGUMENTS	No arguments.
DESCRIPTION	This read-only property returns the target path of the indicated movie clip instance. The path is returned in slash notation. Use `targetPath` to retrieve dot notation.
PLAYER	Flash 4 or later

targetPath

SYNTAX	`targetPath(movieClip)`
ARGUMENTS	`movieClip` – The name of a movie clip instance.
DESCRIPTION	This function returns a string containing the target path to the movie clip for which the path is being retrieved. The target path notation is in dot syntax. Use `_target` to retrieve the notation in slash syntax.
PLAYER	Flash 5

this

SYNTAX	`this`
ARGUMENTS	No arguments.

(continued)

this (continued)

DESCRIPTION	This keyword refers to the current object or instance. For example, in an `onClipEvent`, this refers to the movie clip the script is associated with. Using `this` is rarely necessary, but it increases the readability of the code.
PLAYER	Flash 5

EXAMPLES	Here's a piece of code from the space game on the CD in *chapter3/ space_game_done.fla*. This is some code from the rocket ship objects.
	
	``
	// see if ourHero got nailed
	if ((this.hitTest(_root.mantaShot) ||
	      this.hitTest(_root.spikeShot)) &&
	      !_root.ourHeroDead)
	{
	      _root.ourHeroDead = true;
	      this.gotoAndPlay("pow");
	}
	``

USES	Using `this` can make your code easier to read, even for you as you're writing it. I'm a fan.

toggleHighQuality()

SYNTAX	`toggleHighQuality()`
ARGUMENTS	No arguments.
DESCRIPTION	This action turns anti-aliasing on and off. Calling this action affects all movies in the Flash player.
PLAYER	Flash 2 or later

_totalframes

SYNTAX	`instanceName._totalframes`
ARGUMENTS	No arguments.
DESCRIPTION	This read-only property returns the total number of frames in the specified movie clip.
PLAYER	Flash 4 or later

trace

SYNTAX	`trace(expression)`
ARGUMENTS	`expression` – Any statement to evaluate.
DESCRIPTION	This action evaluates the expression and returns the result to the Output window in Test Movie mode.
PLAYER	Flash 4 or later

EXAMPLES	`if (romans >= greeks)`
	`{`
	`        trace("Toga! Toga!");`
	`}`

USES	Extremely useful in debugging your code by displaying variables at certain times.

typeof

SYNTAX	`typeof(expression)`
ARGUMENTS	`expression` – A string, movie clip, object or function.
DESCRIPTION	This operator returns the data type of the expression: string, movie clip, object, or function.
PLAYER	Flash 5

unescape

SYNTAX	`unescape(value)`
ARGUMENTS	`value` – A URL-encoded string with hexadecimal characters.
DESCRIPTION	This function translates a URL-encoded string into a regular string.
PLAYER	Flash 5

unloadMovie

SYNTAX	`unloadMovie(location)`
ARGUMENTS	`location` – The depth/level from which to unload the movie clip.
DESCRIPTION	This action removes a movie clip instance from the movie. The clip must have been loaded previously, using the `loadMovie` action.

(continued)

unloadMovie (continued)

PLAYER	Flash 4 or later

EXAMPLES	Here's part of the code from *chapter2/duplicate2_done.fla*.
	
	``
	if (_root.counter == 20)
	{
	    loadMovie("whatisthatthing_done.swf", 1);
	}
	else if (_root.counter == 25)
	{
	    unloadMovie(_level1);
	}
	``

updateAfterEvent

SYNTAX	`updateAfterEvent(event)`
ARGUMENTS	event – Any of the events listed in Table B.26.
DESCRIPTION	This action updates the display, independent of the frames-per-second rate of updating the display.
PLAYER	Flash 4 or later

EXAMPLES	This example is from *reference/globalToLocal.fla*.
	
	``
	onClipEvent(mouseMove)
	{
	    punto = new Object();
	    punto.x = _root._xmouse;
	    punto.y = _root._ymouse;
	    this.globalToLocal(punto);
	    _root.out = this._xmouse + " : " + this._ymouse;
	    _root.out2 = _root._xmouse + " : " +
	_root._ymouse;
	    _root.out3 = punto.x + " : " + punto.y
	
	    // causes display to update faster
	    updateAfterEvent();
	}
	``

USES	Good for smoother motion that would otherwise be achieved by the frames-per-second updating.

TABLE B.26 Events for updateAfterEvent

EVENT	DESCRIPTION
mouseMove	Event is triggered by the movement of the mouse cursor.
mouseDown	Event is triggered by the pressing down of the mouse button by the user (Windows people: this only tracks the left mouse button).

(continued)

TABLE B.26 Events for updateAfterEvent (continued)

mouseUp	Event is triggered by the releasing of the mouse button (Windows people: this only tracks the left mouse button).
keyDown	Event is triggered when a key is pressed.
keyUp	Event is triggered when a key is released.

_url

SYNTAX	instanceName._url
ARGUMENTS	No arguments.
DESCRIPTION	This read-only property returns the URL of the SWF that the movie clip was downloaded from.
PLAYER	Flash 4 or later

var

SYNTAX	var variableName = value
ARGUMENTS	variableName – description. value – description.
DESCRIPTION	This action declares local variables. You don't need it to declare variables, but it can help make your code more readable.
PLAYER	Flash 5

_visible

SYNTAX	instanceName._visible = value
ARGUMENTS	value – Boolean value.
DESCRIPTION	This property determines whether a movie clip is visible or not. A button that is not visible cannot be clicked.
PLAYER	Flash 4 or later

void

SYNTAX	void(expression)
ARGUMENTS	expression – Any expression.

(continued)

void (continued)

DESCRIPTION	This operator discards the expression and returns an undefined value.
PLAYER	Flash 5

while

SYNTAX	while(condition)
	{
	    statements
	}

ARGUMENTS	condition – A statement that can be evaluated to true or false. statements – ActionScript statements.
DESCRIPTION	This action acts like a loop: as long as the condition is true, the statements are executed over and over again. If the condition never became false, the loop would never stop. Usually, the condition involves checking if a counter has passed a certain limit.
PLAYER	Flash 4 or later

_width

SYNTAX	instanceName._width = value
ARGUMENTS	value – The width of the movie clip instance in pixels. instanceName – The name of the movie clip instance.
DESCRIPTION	This property is the movie clip's width in pixels.
PLAYER	Flash 4, Flash 5. In Flash 4, this property was read-only.

with

SYNTAX	with(object)
	{
	    statements
	}

ARGUMENTS	object – An instance of an object or movie clip.
DESCRIPTION	This action changes the target path for all the statements. The target path is temporarily set as the same for the object.
PLAYER	Flash 4 or later

(continued)

with (continued)

EXAMPLES	Imagine this section of code is an object action for the movie instance `fish`. We can affect the `shark` instance.
	
	``
	with(_root.shark)
	{
	    _x = 300;
	    _y = 200;
	    gotoAndPlay(10);
	}
	``
	This accomplishes the same thing as:
	``
	_root.shark._x = 300;
	_root.shark._y = 200;
	_root.shark.gotoAndPlay(10);
	``

USES	This can make your code easier to read if you have a lot of actions to do to a different movie clip than the one your script is on.

_X

SYNTAX	`instanceName._x = value`
ARGUMENTS	`value` – The distance from the left edge of the Stage in pixels.
DESCRIPTION	This property returns (or sets) the x-coordinate position of the indicated movie clip.
PLAYER	Flash 4 or later

EXAMPLES	Here's some code from the `manta ship` object in the space game (*chapter3/space_game_done.fla*).
	
	``
	if (_root.enemyDirection == "right")
	{
	    if (this._x < 450)
	    {
	        this._x = this._x + 10;
	    }
	    else
	    {
	        _root.enemyDirection = "left";
	        this._x = this._x - 10;
	    }
	}
	``

XML (object)

Use the methods and properties of the XML object to build, manipulate, read, and send XML documents. You must use the constructor XML() before calling any methods (listed in Table B.27) or properties (listed in Table B.28). Collections for the XML object are listed in Table B.29.

TABLE B.27 Methods for the XML Object

METHOD	DESCRIPTION
appendChild	Attaches a node to the end of an element's child list.
cloneNode	Creates a copy of an element (and optionally, all of that node's children as well). The cloned node has no parent or child (unless the child was cloned).
createElement	Creates a new XML element.
createTextNode	Creates a new XML text node.
hasChildNodes	Returns `true` if the element has children, `false` if it doesn't.
insertBefore	Inserts a node in front of the specified node.
load	Loads a document from a URL.
onLoad	A callback function for `load` and `sendAndLoad`.
parseXML	Parses an XML document into the specified XML object tree.
removeNode	Deletes a specified node from the XML object.
send	Sends the specified XML object to a URL.
sendAndLoad	Sends the specified XML object to a URL and loads the response into another XML object.
toString	Converts the specified node and any children to text.

TABLE B.28 Properties for the XML Object

PROPERTY	DESCRIPTION
docTypeDecl	Sends and returns information about an XML document's DOCTYPE declaration.
firstChild	References the first child in the node's child list.
lastChild	References the last child in the node's child list.
loaded	Checks if the specified XML document is completely loaded.
nextSibling	References the next node at the same level as the indicated node.
nodeName	Returns the tag name of the specified node.
parentNode	References the parent of the specified node.

(continued)

TABLE B.28 Properties for the XML Object (continued)

PROPERTY	DESCRIPTION
previousSibling	References the previous node at the same level as the indicated node.
status	Returns a numeric code indicating success or failure of an XML parsing.
xmlDec	Sets and returns information about an XML object's DOCTYPE declaration.

TABLE B.29 Collections for the XML Object

PROPERTY	DESCRIPTION
attributes	Returns an array containing all of the attributes of the specified node.
childNodes	Returns an array, with each element being an attribute of the node.

Constructing an XML Object

SYNTAX	xmlObject = new XML([source])
ARGUMENTS	source – The XML document to be parsed into an XML object.
DESCRIPTION	This constructor creates an XML object. To create normal and text nodes, you must use the createElement and createTextNode methods.
PLAYER	Flash 5
EXAMPLES	screenplayXML = new XML();

XML.appendChild

SYNTAX	xmlObject.appendChild(childNode)
ARGUMENTS	childNode – The node to be appended as a child to the specified XML object.
DESCRIPTION	This method adds a child node to the specified XML object.
PLAYER	Flash 5

(continued)

XML.appendChild (continued)

EXAMPLES	Here's part of the screenplay example from the CD in *chapter5/xml2.fla*. Two elements are created and then attached to a preexisting element (screenElement).
	`//create first author element`
	`authorElement = screenplayXML.createElement("author");`
	`authorName = screenplayXML.createTextNode("Lorenzo Semple, Jr.")`
	
	`//place first author element`
	`screenElement.appendChild(authorElement);`
	`authorElement.appendChild(authorName);`
	`}`

XML.attributes

SYNTAX	`xmlObject.attributes`
ARGUMENTS	No arguments.
DESCRIPTION	This collection returns an associative array containing all attributes of the indicated XML object.
PLAYER	Flash 5
EXAMPLES	Here's a chunk of code from the screenplay example. We're changing the `"type"` element in the attributes array. The dot syntax may not look like an array, but it is. `charElement2.attributes.type = "major";`

XML.childNodes

SYNTAX	`xmlObject.childNodes`
ARGUMENTS	No arguments.
DESCRIPTION	This read-only property returns an array of the XML object's child nodes. Each element in the array is a reference to a child node of the XML object.
PLAYER	Flash 5

EXAMPLES	`// finding number of child nodes`
	`allTextChildren = allText.childNodes;`
	`numChildren = allTextChildren.length;`

XML.cloneNode

SYNTAX	`xmlObject.cloneNode(recursive)`
ARGUMENTS	`recursive` – Boolean value that sets whether the children of the node are cloned as well.
DESCRIPTION	This method makes a copy of the specified element. You can determine whether all of the node's child elements are cloned as well.
PLAYER	Flash 5
EXAMPLES	`charElement3 = charElement2.cloneNode(true);` `charElement3.firstChild.nodeValue = "Higgins";`

XML.createElement

SYNTAX	`xmlObject.createElement(name)`
ARGUMENTS	name – Name of the new element.
DESCRIPTION	This method creates a new, regular XML element (but not a text node). The new element has no parent and no child—you have to use `appendChild` to attach it to an existing XML object.
PLAYER	Flash 5

EXAMPLES	`authorElement = screenplayXML.createElement("author");`
	`authorName = screenplayXML.createTextNode("Lorenzo`
	`Semple, Jr.")`

XML.createTextNode

SYNTAX	`xmlObject.createTextNode()`
ARGUMENTS	name – Name of the new element.
DESCRIPTION	This method creates a new XML text element. The new element has no parent and no child—you have to use `appendChild` to attach it to an existing XML object.
PLAYER	Flash 5

EXAMPLES	`authorElement = screenplayXML.createElement("author");`
	`authorName = screenplayXML.createTextNode("Lorenzo`
	`Semple, Jr.")`

XML.docTypeDecl

SYNTAX	`xmlObject.docTypeDecl`
ARGUMENTS	No arguments.
DESCRIPTION	This property returns information about the XML DOCTYPE declaration. Note that Flash does not perform XML validation. The DOCTYPE information is stored in this property, but no validation on the DTD is performed. If there is no DOCTYPE, then this property is undefined.
PLAYER	Flash 5

XML.firstChild

SYNTAX	`xmlObject.firstchild`
ARGUMENTS	No arguments.
DESCRIPTION	This read-only property is a reference to the first child node in an XML element's child list. If there is no child node, or if the child node is a text node, this property has an `undefined` value.
PLAYER	Flash 5

EXAMPLES	Here's a chunk of code from the screenplay example in Chapter 5, *chapter5/xml2.fla*.
	`charElement4 = charElement2.cloneNode(true);`
	`charElement4.firstChild.nodeValue = "Jobert";`

XML.hasChildNodes

SYNTAX	`xmlObject.hasChildNodes()`
ARGUMENTS	No arguments.
DESCRIPTION	This method returns `true` if the specified XML object has child nodes; otherwise, `false`.
PLAYER	Flash 5

XML.insertBefore

SYNTAX	`xmlObject.insertBefore(childNode, beforeNode)`
ARGUMENTS	`childNode` – The node to be inserted. `beforeNode` – The node that the new node is inserted before. That is, the node that will be after the `childNode` once the `childNode` is inserted.

(continued)

XML.insertBefore (continued)

DESCRIPTION	This method inserts a node before a specified node in an XML object.
PLAYER	Flash 5

EXAMPLES	This example inserts node3 before node1.
	
	`testXML = new XML();`
	
	`node1 = testXML.createElement("node1");`
	`node2 = testXML.createElement("node2");`
	`node3 = testXML.createElement("node3");`
	`testXML.appendChild(node1);`
	`testXML.appendChild(node2);`
	
	`testXML.insertBefore(node3, node1);`

XML.lastChild

SYNTAX	`xmlObject.lastChild`
ARGUMENTS	No arguments.
DESCRIPTION	This read-only property references the last child node in an XML object. Returns `false` if the object has no children.
PLAYER	Flash 5

XML.load

SYNTAX	`xmlObject.load(URL)`
ARGUMENTS	URL – The URL where the XML document to be loaded is located.
DESCRIPTION	This method loads an XML document from an external source. The load doesn't happen immediately—it's convenient to use `onLoad` to hold some instructions for when the document has finished downloading.
PLAYER	Flash 5

EXAMPLES	Another chunk of code from the screenplay example *(chapter5/ xml1_done.fla)*.
	
	`//create XML object`
	`screenplayXML = new XML();`
	
	`// load external file into XML object`
	`screenplayXML.load("screenplay_space.xml");`

(continued)

XML.load (continued)

| EXAMPLES (CONT.) | ```// when loading is complete, go to a special function
screenplayXML.onLoad = loadedXML;

function loadedXML()
{
    ...
}
``` |
|---|---|

XML.loaded

SYNTAX	`xmlObject.loaded`
ARGUMENTS	No arguments.
DESCRIPTION	This read-only property returns whether a document has been fully loaded or not. If so, it returns `true`.
PLAYER	Flash 5

XML.nextSibling

SYNTAX	`xmlObject.nextSibling`
ARGUMENTS	No arguments.
DESCRIPTION	This read-only property references the next child node in the XML object's child list. If there is no next sibling, this method returns `false`.
PLAYER	Flash 5
EXAMPLES	Here's a modified chunk of code from *chapter5/xml1_done.fla*. We're looping through an element's child nodes, moving from one node to the next, and we're using `nextSibling` to do that. ```screenplayXML.onLoad = loadedXML;

function loadedXML()
{
        // set sub-objects
        allText = screenplayXML.firstChild;
        c = allText.firstChild;

        // finding number of child nodes
        allTextChildren = allText.childNodes;
        numChildren = allTextChildren.length;
``` |

(continued)

XML.nextSibling (continued)

| EXAMPLES (CONT.) | ```
for (i=0; i<numChildren; i++)
{
        .. code ..

        c = c.nextSibling;
}
}
``` |
|---|---|

XML.nodeName

SYNTAX	xmlObject.nodeName
ARGUMENTS	No arguments.
DESCRIPTION	This property sets/returns the name of the node, that is, the tag. If the tag is `<author>`, then the nodeName is author.
PLAYER	Flash 5
| EXAMPLES | Here's a modified chunk of code from *chapter5/xml1_done.fla*. We're seeing if a nodeName is "author", and if so, we're seeing if the text node inside the "author" node has a certain value, and if so, we change it.<br>```
cNodeStr = c.firstChild.nodeValue.toString();

// find number of authors
if (c.nodeName == "author")
{
        if(cNodeStr.indexOf("Lorenzo") != -1)
        {
                c.firstChild.nodeValue = "Clark Kent";
        }
        authorName = c.firstChild;
        trace("author: " + authorName);
}
``` |

XML.nodeType

SYNTAX	xmlObject.nodeType
ARGUMENTS	No arguments.
DESCRIPTION	This read-only property returns a 1 if the node is an XML element, and a 3 if the node is a text node.
PLAYER	Flash 5

(*continued*)

XML.nodeType (continued)

USES	This property can be useful if you're parsing through an XML element whose structure you're not 100% sure of.

XML.nodeValue

SYNTAX	xmlObject.nodeValue
ARGUMENTS	No arguments.
DESCRIPTION	If the specified XML object is a text node, this property returns (and can set) the value of the node. If the specified XML object is an XML element, then this property returns null and is read-only.
PLAYER	Flash 5

EXAMPLES	Here's a modified chunk of code from *chapter5/xml1_done.fla*. We're checking out the value of a node, and if it's a certain value, we're changing it. That is, if the nodeValue has "Lorenzo" in it anywhere, we change the value of the whole node to "Clark Kent". See Chapter 5 for more details.
	
	`cNodeStr = c.firstChild.nodeValue.toString();`
	
	`// find number of authors`
	`if (c.nodeName == "author")`
	`{`
	`    if(cNodeStr.indexOf("Lorenzo") != -1)`
	`    {`
	`        c.firstChild.nodeValue = "Clark Kent";`
	`    }`
	`    authorName = c.firstChild;`
	`    trace("author: " + authorName);`
	`}`

XML.onLoad

SYNTAX	xmlObject.onLoad(success) xmlObject.onLoad = functionName
ARGUMENTS	success – An argument that's set to true if the document loaded successfully, to false if it didn't. functionName – The name of a function to execute when the XML document finishes loading successfully.
DESCRIPTION	This method is invoked when the XML document has been received, or isn't received, or an error occurs.
PLAYER	Flash 5

(continued)

XML.onLoad (continued)

EXAMPLES	Here's another example from Chapter 5.
	```//create XML object```
	```screenplayXML = new XML();```
	
	```// load external file into XML object```
	```screenplayXML.load("screenplay_space.xml");```
	
	```// when loading is complete, go to a special function```
	```screenplayXML.onLoad = loadedXML;```
	```function loadedXML()```
	```{```
	``` … code …```
	```}```

USES	Since an XML document doesn't load instantaneously, this is a useful method to tell Flash what to do when it has finished loading.

XML.parentNode

SYNTAX	```xmlObject.parentNode```
ARGUMENTS	No arguments.
DESCRIPTION	This read-only property references the parent node of the specified XML object. If there is no parent, the property returns ```null```.
PLAYER	Flash 5

XML.parseXML

SYNTAX	```xmlObject.parseXML(source)```
ARGUMENTS	```source``` – The XML text to be converted into an XML object.
DESCRIPTION	This method parses the XML text in the ```source``` and replaces any existing XML in ```xmlObject``` with the resulting XML tree from the source.
PLAYER	Flash 5

XML.previousSibling

SYNTAX	```xmlObject.previousSibling```
ARGUMENTS	No arguments.

(continued)

XML.previousSibling (continued)

DESCRIPTION	This read-only property references the previous sibling of the specified XML object. If there is no previous sibling, the property returns `null`.
PLAYER	Flash 5

XML.removeNode

SYNTAX	`xmlObject.removeNode()`
ARGUMENTS	No arguments.
DESCRIPTION	This method removes the specified node from its parent node.
PLAYER	Flash 5

XML.send

SYNTAX	`xmlObject.send(URL [,window])`
ARGUMENTS	`URL` – The destination for the specified XML object. `window` – The browser window to display data returned by the server.
DESCRIPTION	This method encodes the specified XML object into an XML document and sends that document to the `URL` using the `POST` method.
PLAYER	Flash 5

XML.sendAndLoad

SYNTAX	`xmlObject.sendAndLoad(URL, targetXMLobject)`
ARGUMENTS	`URL` – The destination for the specified XML object. `targetXMLobject` – The XML object that will hold the returned XML document that is expected from the server.
DESCRIPTION	This method, like `send`, encodes the specified XML object and sends it to the specified `URL` via `POST`. Flash then downloads the server's response (we're expecting that response to be in XML format) into an XML object (`targetXMLobject`). The loading happens in the same manner as the `load` method.
PLAYER	Flash 5

XML.status

SYNTAX	xmlObject.status
ARGUMENTS	No arguments.
DESCRIPTION	This property returns a number indicating the status of success of parsing an XML document (all text) into an XML object. Table B.30 lists the codes.
PLAYER	Flash 5

TABLE B.30 Codes for XML.status

CODE	DESCRIPTION
0	No error; parsing completed successfully.
-2	A CDATA section was not properly terminated.
-3	The XML declaration was not properly terminated.
-4	The DOCTYPE declaration was not properly terminated.
-5	A comment was not properly terminated.
-6	An XML element was malformed.
-7	Out of memory.
-8	An attribute value was not properly terminated.
-9	A start-tag was not matched with an end-tag.
-10	An end-tag was not matched with a start-tag.

XML.toString

SYNTAX	xmlObject.toString()
ARGUMENTS	No arguments.
DESCRIPTION	This method evaluates the XML object and converts it into a string. If you're only using trace, it's not always necessary to use toString.
PLAYER	Flash 5

EXAMPLES	Here's an example from *chapter 5: chapter5/xml1_done.fla* on the CD. `cNodeStr = c.firstChild.nodeValue.toString();`
	
	`// find number of authors`
	`if (c.nodeName == "author")`

(continued)

XML.toString (continued)

EXAMPLES (CONT.)	<pre>{
	    if(cNodeStr.indexOf("Lorenzo") != -1)
	    {
	        c.firstChild.nodeValue = "Clark Kent";
	    }
	    authorName = c.firstChild;
	    trace("author: " + authorName);
	}</pre>

XML.xmlDecl

SYNTAX	`xmlObject.xmlDecl`
ARGUMENTS	No arguments.
DESCRIPTION	This property sets and returns the information about the XML object's DOCTYPE declaration. Note that this declaration is treated as a property of an XML object, not as a node of the object.
PLAYER	Flash 5

XMLSocket (object)

This object implements a client socket that allows the Flash player to communicate with a server via an open connection. This allows the server to send messages to the Flash Player without requiring a request from the client.

In order for the XMLSocket object to work, the server must be running a daemon that understands the XMLSocket protocol:

- XML messages are sent over a full-duplex TCP/IP stream socket connection.
- Each XML message is a complete XML document terminated by a zero byte.
- An unlimited number of XML messages can be sent and received over a single XMLSocket connection.

The XMLSocket object can be useful for applications that require constant communication between the Flash Player and the server, like a chat system. Its methods are listed in Table B.31.

As you might imagine, setting up a server to handle XMLSocket objects can be challenging. If you don't need real-time interactivity, stick with loadVariables and sendAndLoad.

TABLE B.31 Methods for the XMLSocket Object

PROPERTY	DESCRIPTION
close	Closes an open socket connection.
connect	Creates a connection to a specified server.
onClose	Callback function that is called when a connection has closed.
onConnect	Callback function that is called when a connection is created.
onXML	Callback function that is created when an XML object arrives from the server.
send	Sends an XML object to the server.

Macromedia has created a few security measures around the XMLSocket object.

- The XMLSocket.connect method can only connect to port numbers greater than or equal to 1024. This is because many common Web services (HTTP, FTP, Telnet) occur below port number 1024.
- The XMLSocket.connect method can only connect to servers in the same subdomain as where the SWF file lives.

Constructing an XMLSocket Object

SYNTAX	new XMLSocket()
ARGUMENTS	No arguments.
DESCRIPTION	This constructor creates a new XMLSocket object, but it doesn't connect to any server yet. The connection has to happen with an XMLSocket.connect call.
PLAYER	Flash 5

XMLSocket.close

SYNTAX	XMLSocketObject.close()
ARGUMENTS	No arguments.
DESCRIPTION	This method closes the connection of specified XMLSocket object.
PLAYER	Flash 5

XMLSocket.connect

SYNTAX	XMLSocketObject.connect(host, port)
ARGUMENTS	host — A full DNS name or an IP address, or null if you want to specify the current server. port — The TCP port to establish a connection to. Must be a number equal to or greater than 1024.
DESCRIPTION	This method creates a connection to the specified server and returns true or false, depending on whether the initial stage of connection was successfully created or not. You have to use XMLSocket.on-Connect to see if the connection was completed or not.
PLAYER	Flash 5

XMLSocket.onClose

SYNTAX	XMLSocketObject.onClose() XMLSocketObject.onClose = functionName
ARGUMENTS	functionName — The name of a function to call when the indicated connection has been closed.
DESCRIPTION	This method is a callback function that calls a function when the specified connection has been closed. The default implementation of this method (i.e., the one without a function name) does nothing.
PLAYER	Flash 5

XMLSocket.onConnect

SYNTAX	XMLSocketObject.onConnect(success) XMLSocketObject.onConnect = functionName
ARGUMENTS	success — An argument to be set to true or false, based on the success of the connection. functionName — The name of a function to call when the indicated connection has been successfully created.
DESCRIPTION	This method is a callback function that calls a function when the specified connection has been created. The default implementation this (i.e., the one without a function name) does nothing.
PLAYER	Flash 5

XMLSocket.onXML

SYNTAX	`XMLSocketObject.onXML(object)` `XMLSocketObject.onXML = functionName`
ARGUMENTS	`object` – An instance of the XML object containing a parsed XML document that was received from the server. `functionName` – The name of a function to call when the indicated XML object has been received.
DESCRIPTION	This method is a callback function that calls a function when the specified XML object has been downloaded from the server. The default implementation of this method (i.e., the one without a function name) does nothing.
PLAYER	Flash 5

XMLSocket.send

SYNTAX	`XMLSocketObject.send(object)`
ARGUMENTS	`object` – An XML object to send to the server.
DESCRIPTION	This methods uses the specified `XMLSocket` object to send an XML object to the server. The XML object is translated into a string, and a zero byte is tacked on to the end. This method does not return a status on whether the XML was properly received or not.
PLAYER	Flash 5

_xmouse

SYNTAX	`instanceName._xmouse`
ARGUMENTS	`instanceName` – The name of a movie clip on the Stage.
DESCRIPTION	This read-only property returns the x-coordinate of the user's mouse in relation to the coordinate space of the instance.
PLAYER	Flash 5

EXAMPLES	This is from the *Make Frank!* example in Chapter 3, "Adding Power to ActionScripts" *(chapter3/frankenstein_done.fla)*. We're seeing if a user clicked inside a certain part of the screen.
	`// see if the user clicked inside the body`
	`if ((_root._xmouse <= bounds.xMax) &&`
	`        (_root._xmouse >= bounds.xMin) &&`
	`        (_root._ymouse <= bounds.yMax) &&`
	`        (_root._ymouse >= bounds.yMin))`
	`{`

(continued)

_xmouse (continued)

| EXAMPLES (CONT.) | ```// tweak legs
if (_root.legsFade)
{
        _root.body.legs._alpha = 100;
        _root.legsFade = false;
}
else
{
        _root.body.legs._alpha = 30;
        _root.legsFade = true;
}
}``` |
|---|---|
| USES | It can be handy to know where the user's mouse is—it helps your movie react appropriately. |

_xscale

SYNTAX	`instanceName._xscale = percentage`
ARGUMENTS	`instanceName` – The name of a movie clip on the Stage. `percentage` – The value determining the percentage width of the indicated movie clip. The default value is 100. You can use negative percentages to horizontally flip the clip.
DESCRIPTION	This property determines the horizontal scale of the indicated movie clip.
PLAYER	Flash 4 or later
EXAMPLES	Here's part of some code in Chapter 2, "Your First ActionScripts" (chapter2/drag_props_done.fla). ```if (_root.widthDrag)
{
    xPos = _root._xmouse;
percentage = 200 * ((xPos - _root.widthBarXMin)/
(_root.widthBarXMax - _root.widthBarXMin));

        _root.fish._xscale = percentage;
}``` |

_y

SYNTAX	`instanceName._y = value`
ARGUMENTS	`instanceName` – The name of a movie clip on the Stage. `value` – The y-coordinate of the movie clip, based on the coordinate space of the parent movie clip.

(continued)

_y (continued)

DESCRIPTION	This property determines the y-position of the movie clip relative to the coordinates of the parent movie clip. The coordinates are based on the movie clip's registration point (the little crosshairs in the middle of the clip that appear when you select it).
PLAYER	Flash 3 or later

EXAMPLES	Here's an example from Chapter 2 *(chapter2/drag_props_done.fla)*. These are the object actions for the fish.
	
	 ```onClipEvent(keyDown)```
	 ```{```
	     ```if (Key.getCode() == Key.LEFT)```
	     ```{```
	         ```this._x = this._x - 3;```
	     ```}```
	     ```else if (Key.getCode() == Key.RIGHT)```
	     ```{```
	         ```this._x = this._x + 3;```
	     ```}```
	     ```else if (Key.getCode() == Key.UP)```
	     ```{```
	         ```this._y = this._y - 3;```
	     ```}```
	     ```else if (Key.getCode() == Key.DOWN)```
	     ```{```
	         ```this._y = this._y + 3;```
	     ```}```
	 ```}```

_ymouse

SYNTAX	```instanceName._ymouse```
ARGUMENTS	```instanceName``` – The name of a movie clip on the Stage.
DESCRIPTION	This read-only property returns the y-coordinate of the user's mouse in relation to the coordinate space of the instance.
PLAYER	Flash 5

EXAMPLES	This is from the *Make Frank!* example in Chapter 3 *(chapter3/frankenstein_done.fla)*. We're seeing if a user clicked inside a certain part of the screen.
	
	 ```// see if the user clicked inside the body```
	 ```if ((_root._xmouse <= bounds.xMax) &&```
	     ```(_root._xmouse >= bounds.xMin) &&```
	     ```(_root._ymouse <= bounds.yMax) &&```
	     ```(_root._ymouse >= bounds.yMin))```

(continued)

_ymouse (continued)

EXAMPLES (CONT.)	<pre>{
	    // tweak legs
	    if (_root.legsFade)
	    {
	        _root.body.legs._alpha = 100;
	        _root.legsFade = false;
	    }
	    else
	    {
	        _root.body.legs._alpha = 30;
	        _root.legsFade = true;
	    }
	}</pre>

USES	It can be handy to know where the user's mouse is—it helps your movie react appropriately.

_yscale

SYNTAX	`instanceName._yscale = percentage`
ARGUMENTS	`instanceName` – The name of a movie clip on the Stage. `percentage` – The value determining the percentage height of the indicated movie clip. The default value is 100. You can use negative percentages to horizontally flip the clip.
DESCRIPTION	This property determines the horizontal scale of the indicated movie clip.
PLAYER	Flash 4 or later

EXAMPLES	Here's part of some code in Chapter 2 *(chapter2/drag_props_done.fla)*.
	<pre>if (_root.heightDrag)
	{
	    xPos = _root._xmouse;
	percentage = 200 * ((xPos - _root.heightBarXMin)/
	(_root.heightBarXMax - _root.heightBarXMin));
	
	    _root.fish._yscale = percentage;
	}</pre>

Index

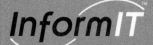

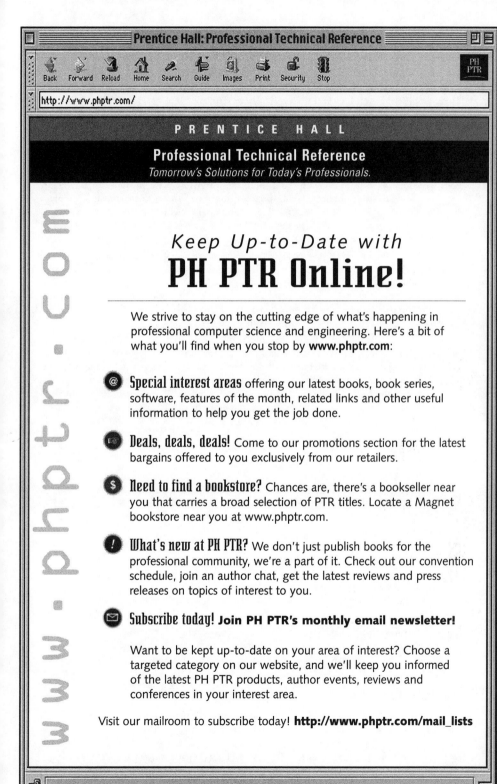

in the Documentation. The Company does not warrant that the SOFTWARE will meet your requirements or that the operation of the SOFTWARE will be uninterrupted or error-free. The Company warrants that the media on which the SOFTWARE is delivered shall be free from defects in materials and workmanship under normal use for a period of thirty (30) days from the date of your purchase. Your only remedy and the Company's only obligation under these limited warranties is, at the Company's option, return of the warranted item for a refund of any amounts paid by you or replacement of the item. Any replacement of SOFTWARE or media under the warranties shall not extend the original warranty period. The limited warranty set forth above shall not apply to any SOFTWARE which the Company determines in good faith has been subject to misuse, neglect, improper installation, repair, alteration, or damage by you. EXCEPT FOR THE EXPRESSED WARRANTIES SET FORTH ABOVE, THE COMPANY DISCLAIMS ALL WARRANTIES, EXPRESS OR IMPLIED, INCLUDING WITHOUT LIMITATION, THE IMPLIED WARRANTIES OF MERCHANTABILITY AND FITNESS FOR A PARTICULAR PURPOSE. EXCEPT FOR THE EXPRESS WARRANTY SET FORTH ABOVE, THE COMPANY DOES NOT WARRANT, GUARANTEE, OR MAKE ANY REPRESENTATION REGARDING THE USE OR THE RESULTS OF THE USE OF THE SOFTWARE IN TERMS OF ITS CORRECTNESS, ACCURACY, RELIABILITY, CURRENTNESS, OR OTHERWISE.

IN NO EVENT, SHALL THE COMPANY OR ITS EMPLOYEES, AGENTS, SUPPLIERS, OR CONTRACTORS BE LIABLE FOR ANY INCIDENTAL, INDIRECT, SPECIAL, OR CONSEQUENTIAL DAMAGES ARISING OUT OF OR IN CONNECTION WITH THE LICENSE GRANTED UNDER THIS AGREEMENT, OR FOR LOSS OF USE, LOSS OF DATA, LOSS OF INCOME OR PROFIT, OR OTHER LOSSES, SUSTAINED AS A RESULT OF INJURY TO ANY PERSON, OR LOSS OF OR DAMAGE TO PROPERTY, OR CLAIMS OF THIRD PARTIES, EVEN IF THE COMPANY OR AN AUTHORIZED REPRESENTATIVE OF THE COMPANY HAS BEEN ADVISED OF THE POSSIBILITY OF SUCH DAMAGES. IN NO EVENT SHALL LIABILITY OF THE COMPANY FOR DAMAGES WITH RESPECT TO THE SOFTWARE EXCEED THE AMOUNTS ACTUALLY PAID BY YOU, IF ANY, FOR THE SOFTWARE.

SOME JURISDICTIONS DO NOT ALLOW THE LIMITATION OF IMPLIED WARRANTIES OR LIABILITY FOR INCIDENTAL, INDIRECT, SPECIAL, OR CONSEQUENTIAL DAMAGES, SO THE ABOVE LIMITATIONS MAY NOT ALWAYS APPLY. THE WARRANTIES IN THIS AGREEMENT GIVE YOU SPECIFIC LEGAL RIGHTS AND YOU MAY ALSO HAVE OTHER RIGHTS WHICH VARY IN ACCORDANCE WITH LOCAL LAW.

ACKNOWLEDGMENT

YOU ACKNOWLEDGE THAT YOU HAVE READ THIS AGREEMENT, UNDERSTAND IT, AND AGREE TO BE BOUND BY ITS TERMS AND CONDITIONS. YOU ALSO AGREE THAT THIS AGREEMENT IS THE COMPLETE AND EXCLUSIVE STATEMENT OF THE AGREEMENT BETWEEN YOU AND THE COMPANY AND SUPERSEDES ALL PROPOSALS OR PRIOR AGREEMENTS, ORAL, OR WRITTEN, AND ANY OTHER COMMUNICATIONS BETWEEN YOU AND THE COMPANY OR ANY REPRESENTATIVE OF THE COMPANY RELATING TO THE SUBJECT MATTER OF THIS AGREEMENT.

Should you have any questions concerning this Agreement or if you wish to contact the Company for any reason, please contact in writing at the address below.

Robin Short
Prentice Hall PTR
One Lake Street
Upper Saddle River, New Jersey 07458

About the CD-ROM

This book comes with a CD-ROM that contains all of the Flash 5 movies that are referenced in the text. These movies will work on computers with Windows 95/98, NT 4 2000 or later, and MacOS 8.5 or later. Any computer with Flash 5 loaded will be able to read these files.

Please note that it's important you *not* try to use the Flash application to open and test *chapter4/quotes1.swf* (note that's the SWF file, not the FLA file). You won't break anything if you do open and test this file in Flash, but you'll cause a JavaScript error in any browser that happens to be open. This happens because quotes1.swf calls for a Java-Script function called showAlert, and if the SWF can't find that function, an error is thrown into any open browser. Thus, the only error-free way to test that file is to open quotes1.html in a browser, a Web page that contains both the quotes1.swf file and the showAlert function.

If you have any trouble, check out the book's companion Web sites at *www.phptr.com/advancedweb* and *www.wire-man.com/flash5*. You can download the movies from these sites, as well as get updates to the book and maybe a few extra bonus movies if you're lucky.

CD Technical Support

Prentice Hall does not offer technical support for this software. However, if there is a problem with the media, you may obtain a replacement CD by sending an email describing your problem to: disc_exchange@prenhall.com.